I0820350

ALSO BY PAUL STAITI

Samuel F. B. Morse

Of Arms and Artists: The American Revolution Through Painters' Eyes

THE KILLING *OF* JANE McCREA

An American Tragedy *ON THE* Revolutionary Frontier

Paul Staiti

WESTHOLME
Yardley

Westholme Publishing, LLC
904 Edgewood Road
Yardley, Pennsylvania 19067
Visit our Web site at www.westholmepublishing.com

ISBN: 978-1-59416-446-0
Also available as an eBook.

Printed in the United States of America.

For Monika

CONTENTS

. ILLUSTRATIONS

I.

FACT AND FABLE

I HAVE BEEN HAUNTED for decades by a painting from 1804 that hangs in a museum in Hartford, Connecticut. When I first encountered it, I was struck by the gruesomeness of the scene: a terrified woman, down on one knee and flanked by two hatchet-wielding assailants, pleads hopelessly for her life at the edge of a dark forest. Few pictures in the history of the fine arts in America ever treated murder in such uncompromising terms. Soon thereafter, I became equally affected by the determinedly stereotypical way the artist depicted those assailants. Make no mistake, Jane McCrea, who is pictured, was indeed butchered at the beginning of the third year of the American Revolution, and that was a tragedy. But I came to realize that the brutality on display, laced as it is with racial tension, existed in order to mobilize public sentiment against these and all other Native Americans populating the continent. The picture was as political as it was personal.

For the sake of argument, let me take John Vanderlyn's painting to be a portal to the past and, for a moment, accept that what we see is accurate and true. If we do, then the story of Jane McCrea's violent death would go something like this:

Fort Edward, New York, July 26, 1777. The British are rapidly advancing into the Champlain and Hudson corridor from Canada in an audacious effort to divide the rebellious colonies and smash the fledgling United States. With an impressive force of their own men, augmented by German troops, local Loyalist units, and about 400 Native Americans, the army formed by Lieutenant-General John Burgoyne is nearing Fort Edward, fifty miles north of Albany, where a few of his Native American auxiliaries encounter a young woman. Rather than flee the British advance like everyone else, twenty-five-year-old Jane McCrea, daughter of a Presbyterian minister, had remained in Fort Edward in anticipation of her imminent marriage to a Loyalist fighting for Burgoyne, Lieutenant David Jones.

In Vanderlyn's reckoning of what happened next, two of the Native warriors in Burgoyne's employ have taken her out of Fort Edward to the edge of a dense forest where they push her to one knee. A barefoot attacker, indifferent to her plight, grips her pale forearm, raises a tomahawk, and targets her forehead. She stares upward into his crazed face, her mouth distorted in horror, a single tear running down her cheek. She is dressed for marriage that day, in a powder-blue wedding gown, now hopelessly misshapen from the struggle, leaving her exposed and debased. Her fiancé, Lieutenant Jones, a tiny figure deep in the far-right distance, runs toward her screams, but will never arrive in time to rescue her.

A second warrior charges from the right in homicidal frenzy. With teeth clenched, he takes hold of her blond hair, yanks it back, and prepares to slice off the scalp. Muscled male bodies overpower soft female forms. Dark-skinned hands squeeze ghost-white flesh. Death and dismemberment are imminent.

If only history were as tidy as works of art. The picture's snapshot brevity and necessary adherence to the dictates of fine art has turned something knotted and complex into the visual equivalent of a sound bite. To be sure, Vanderlyn's searing image is so visceral that it lingers in the mind like no written account possibly can. But if we want to fully recover Jane McCrea's story and restore its true historical significance, we need to look past Vanderlyn to investigate her life, death, and especially her long and strange afterlife, based on all available evidence. Think of that project as an explosion in the night sky, illuminating a historical terrain long since shrouded in misinformation, mired in controversy, and relegated to mythology. Coming into view is a set of persons, cultures, actions, and motives that fatally converged on that hot July morning in 1777, and then scattered into fragments that we can now reassemble.

First on the investigative agenda is Jane McCrea's personal history and the sequence of events that put her in the deadly path of a British war

John Vanderlyn, *The Murder of Jane McCrea.* 1804. Oil on canvas. Hartford, Wadsworth Atheneum Museum of Art; purchased by subscription.

machine intent on delivering a knockout blow against the rebellious Americans.

Second is the murder and the crime scene. As in any cold-case investigation, scraps of documentary material (in this instance gathered from the eighteenth century) will need to be pieced together to reconstruct the homicide and determine the precise when, where, and how of the crime. We will want to know what brought Native warriors into her neighborhood and what caused them to join the British in an intractable white man's war. We will need to ask why they abducted her, ascertain how many were involved, and if McCrea was a British sympathizer and betrothed to a Loyalist officer, hypothesize a plausible motive for why they killed her.

Third and perhaps foremost, we have to assess the far-reaching consequences of her death for each of the three major parties involved in the Northern Campaign of 1777—the Americans, the British, and the Native Americans—and, also, to introduce the two key historical figures connected to her death: British commander of the Northern Expedition, General Burgoyne, and American commander of the Northern Army, Major-General Horatio Gates.

Though the killing might simply be ascribed to random bad luck, and thus dismissed as yet another civilian casualty in a deadly war zone, McCrea's murder emerged for the Americans as a useful partisan tool in a new public relations offensive against the British and their Native American auxiliaries. The violation of a woman in wartime sets off explosions in people's psyches, and in McCrea's case widespread newspaper coverage and a publicity campaign hatched by Gates turned her into the great cause célèbre of the Revolution. She, more than anyone, became the sympathetic American victim who, it was hoped, would expose Britain's core malevolence in its execution of the war. Despite being engaged to a Loyalist officer fighting for the Crown, she came to symbolize the righteousness of the American cause.

For the British, however, her killing became a political and ethical scandal that tarnished the polished surface of the nation's honor and provoked Whig politicians to shout out her name in Parliament as an example of how low Britain had fallen. To the Whigs who vehemently opposed the war, the only ethical thing left for Britain to do in the wake of her murder was to declare an immediate end to hostilities.

For Native peoples, recruited by both the British and the Americans, the consequences were far worse. McCrea's killing was the opening salvo in a vicious chain of bloody retribution that would engulf all three parties in the New York borderlands. The venerable Iroquois Confederacy would rapidly disintegrate and ultimately be obliterated by the Continental Army. After that, the new United States turned its voracious attention to land acquisition, which would seal the tragic fate of Native America over the next century.

After examining her death in 1777, we will delve into McCrea's long afterlife; that is, how her story took on a life of its own for more than a hundred years. Within a decade of the event, legends arose about how the killing of a beautiful and promising young woman had so rejuvenated the Continental Army that she deserved a certain amount of credit for the momentous American victory at Saratoga. As if she were a miracle worker, McCrea—perhaps it would be more accurate to say McCrea's spirit—appeared to project uncanny power over subsequent revolutionary events that led to American independence. Americans would make her into a martyr—dare I say a saint—worthy of a place in the Valhalla of fallen heroes. Tourists journeyed to the site of the crime and shed tears by her grave. Historians quickly folded her story into the American saga. And though neither her life nor her death, of and by themselves, may have been especially important, an army of journalists, novelists, poets, painters, printmakers, songwriters, theater producers, and circus impresarios turned her last moments into riveting spectacles of drama and violence. Vanderlyn, for one, painted his vision of her death in Paris, and in doing so helped make her an international sensation. For more than a century after the killing, just about every American could recognize her name, visualize her grisly death, imagine they felt her trauma, and believe she was a prime actor in the Revolutionary struggle.

The nightmarish image of a young woman slaughtered on the New York frontier endlessly obsessed white Americans who feared Native Americans as irredeemable savages incapable of civil decency.[1] McCrea's murder would become their cautionary tale, an enduring example of what happens when white women are not protected from the barbarity ascribed to all First Peoples. As a result, she emerged as a novel political instrument after the British were gone. She would help justify the subjugation of Native Americans, validate their expulsion from Eastern lands, and open the doors for an expansionary United States that was fully intent on transforming the American continent into its own image.

Surely, had Jane McCrea never existed or not been killed, then some other unlucky woman would have been recruited to play her role in the drama of America's founding. If, in another scenario, the victim that day had been a man, or an elderly widow, or a person of color, the death would have been overlooked. By rights, McCrea herself should have been relegated to the same miserable fate of anonymity that befell all those civilians along the Hudson River who were shot, stabbed, bayonetted, scalped, and burned to death in 1777, their lives registered as "collateral damage," which is history's version of the mass grave. Instead, because of her youth, gender, beauty, and race, Jane McCrea crystallized the desires of a new nation that was busy inventing its foundational stories.

Here was a girl from New Jersey who had somehow moved onto the nation's center stage. And that was in spite of the public knowing little about her, except that she was a young white woman born to a family politically split by the war, living near Fort Edward with her brother, and romantically engaged to a lieutenant in one of Burgoyne's Loyalist units when she died. Few personal documents related to her survive—no letters, family stories, or life portraits.[2] Nothing, that is, that might illuminate her character or appearance, express her thoughts about the Revolution, or tell us whether she had blue or brown eyes, blond or brown or red hair. It is not known precisely how she was killed or exactly by whom, or if she was to be married that fateful day, or merely awaiting her fiancé's arrival.[3] The lack of concrete information meant there would be no limits to embroidering her story, no impediments to elevating her from random victim to national legend. Chroniclers of the Revolution were thus given unimpeded license to make her into whatever they wanted—or needed—her to be. Her life may have been uninteresting, but her death was epic, her afterlife angelic.

With each iteration of her story, decade after decade, "Sweet Jane" became prettier and taller, her flesh whiter, her hair blonder and longer, her killers more cold-blooded and savage, and her love for her fiancé more ardent and tender.[4] The obscurity of her actual death led to endless sensationalizing. Native warriors killed and scalped her outright. Or, friendly American fire killed her and the Natives who found her took her scalp. Warriors might have pulled her from a basement and killed her. Possibly they were escorting her and giving safe passage so that she could meet her fiancé when a feud broke out and a warrior killer her. The "Wyandot Panther" committed the crime, or maybe "Le Loup." The marauding killers might have been Mohawks or Ottawas or Hurons or Wyandots. They acted independently. Or a hundred British soldiers witnessed the killing. Persistently reengineered, the story of her last moments became an ever-fulsome excursion into revolutionary pathos. In death, she came to possess a significance that she never possessed in life.

If we could imagine it possible to interview her in the afterlife, we might discover Jane startled to learn that history regarded her as a pillar of America's history. Her fame, after all, did not evolve from achievement. That was beside the point. What she did was to endow Americans with purpose. She gave Patriots—and even American Loyalists and some British Whigs—a cogent reason to condemn General Burgoyne, Native Americans, British Secretary of State George Germain, Prime Minister Lord North, and King George III for prosecuting war in a despicable way. To them, her death further justified independence from Britain, clarified the wisdom of armed uprising, rationalized retribution against Britain and its Native auxiliaries, and rallied national unity. Her story, perpetually retold like a bloodcurdling folk tale, a venerated saint's life, or a timeless legend, was not only heartrending on its own, it also brought her enshrinement in the American temple of fame.

2.

THE CLAN McCREA

JANE'S ROAD TO DEATH was as luckless as it was tragic. Behind the mythic stories told in paintings and poems was a young woman of the McCrea clan that hailed from Kintail in the Ross-shire part of the Scottish Highlands. This was a family mired in religious controversies and political conflict. As Covenanters, they were Protestants involved in the seventeenth-century Presbyterian movement that fiercely opposed King Charles I's plan to link England and Scotland by foisting Episcopal liturgy onto the Scottish.[1] During the British Civil Wars (1639–1653), about 25,000 Highland Scots, including Jane's great-grandfather, Walter McCrea, felt compelled to move to Donegal in Ulster County, Ireland, where mounting friction and ultimately war developed between Protestants and Catholics, followed by decades of violence, persecution, and resistance.[2]

In a desperate move to escape Ireland, around 15,000 Scots-Irish migrated to North America, beginning in 1718 when the Covenanters' leader, the Reverend William Tennent, arrived in Bucks County, Pennsylvania, and founded a seminary in 1727 on Neshaminy Creek in present-day Warminster. William Archibald McCrea (Walter's son and Jane's grandfather, born in 1668) participated in that move to the mid-Atlantic colonies. He and his wife, Margaret Creighton McCrea, along with their son, James (Jane's father, born in Lifford, Ireland, in 1710), settled first in the port of New Castle, Delaware, which was a magnet for the fleeing Scots-Irish.

Soon, they became members of the new White Clay Presbyterian church. James McCrea studied theology and the classics at the Reverend Tennent's seminary, which detractors dubbed "Log College" because of its rudimentary construction (Log College would evolve into the College of New Jersey, a bastion of the Scots-Irish that was renamed Princeton in 1896).

Log College was an incubator of the Great Awakening, a powerful mid-eighteenth-century evangelical movement meant to counter eighteenth-century Enlightenment rationality by spurring parishioners to accept without qualification the outpourings of the Holy Spirit. Unlike the traditional "Old Side" ministers who graduated from Yale and Harvard, the "New Side" Presbyterian ministers who trained at Log College delivered charismatic sermons meant to rescue sinners from eternity in hell. If parishioners sincerely confessed their sins, sought forgiveness, and accepted God's love, they would eventually arrive at a lasting state of grace.

James McCrea became an avatar of the Great Awakening, serving as a "New Light" minister of Jesus evangelically dramatizing for his flock personal salvation before God.[3] In 1739, he tested for the ministry in the Presbytery of New Brunswick. After an exegesis on Luke 13:5 and Romans 5:19, both of which emphasize the linkage between individual repentance and the salvation of all, the Reverend McCrea was deemed to possess the "Soundness in Principles" and "Piety in Practice" to be licensed to preach. McCrea's circuit sent him on a two-hundred-mile route in the vicinity of Morristown, through "trackless forests and swamps" and across "bridgeless rivers" to hold services "in homes or barns, and not infrequently out under the open sky."[4]

In 1740, he married a Scottish-ancestry parishioner, Mary Graham, and settled into the recently constructed fifty-eight-pew Lamington Presbyterian Church in Bedminster, twenty-five miles north of Princeton, New Jersey, where he preached for twenty-six years, earning an annual salary of £65.[5] In 1766, because of "great bodily indisposition," the Reverend McCrea retired to his fifty-acre Burnt Mills farm, dying in 1769.[6]

The Reverend had twelve children, seven with Mary Graham, who died September 15, 1753 at the age of thirty-one: John, Mary, William, James, Samuel, Jane, and Stephen. Jane, born in 1751 or 1752 on a farm along Black River Road in Bedminster, studied traditional subjects, including the classics, at a school run by the Reverend John Hanna, who was married to Jane's older sister, Mary.[7] After his wife's death, the Reverend McCrea had five more children with Catherine Rosbrugh (1734–1813), a parishioner of English heritage whom he married in 1755: Robert, Philip, Creighton, Gilbert, and Catherine.

The Revolution would badly fracture the family. On the one hand, Reverend McCrea's older sons served on the American side. They followed other Scottish Presbyterians, who commonly voiced their support for America's independence and their willingness to fight for the cause, having long been distrustful of British power and freshly appreciative of religious freedom in the New World. During the Revolution, many New Light Presbyterian ministers, especially the Reverend George Duffield of Philadelphia, preached the twinned principles of individual and national liberty. For them, defending the faith was synonymous with defending American independence.[8]

The Reverend McCrea's older sons quickly bid allegiance to the cause. Samuel, William, and James McCrea joined the 12th Albany Regiment. Stephen began the war in the 2nd Regiment of the Continental Army, operating in Canada. On the recommendation of Dr. Jonathan Potts, director general of the northern hospitals, Horatio Gates made Stephen senior surgeon of the northern fleet, which Major-General Benedict Arnold built in the summer of 1776 in anticipation of engaging the advancing British army, then under the command of Major-General Guy Carleton.[9]

Stationed on the hospital sloop *Enterprise* during the fierce Battle of Valcour Island in October of 1776, Dr. McCrea treated hundreds of the wounded who were ferried to the ship. Jahiel Stewart, a Massachusetts militiaman, tersely noted in his diary the calamities that Stephen and the other surgeons faced: "The Dockters Cut off great many legs and arms and Seven men threw overboard that died with their wounds."[10] In the midst of the dying and the dead, Dr. McCrea wrote to his superior to say that the British were unrelenting at Valcour, having overwhelmed "our ruined navy," thus forcing the Americans to detonate gunpowder stocks on most of the ships. Luckily, Dr. McCrea and the *Enterprise* slipped through to the southern fort at Ticonderoga.[11] Stephen would remain near Ticonderoga after Valcour and was nearby when Jane died in 1777. He was among the first to get tragic word of how it happened.

John McCrea, with whom Jane lived near Fort Edward, was the eldest brother, a graduate of the College of New Jersey. He practiced law in Albany, married into the Beekman family, and then farmed in Northumberland (now the town of Moreau), five miles south of the fort on the Hudson's west bank opposite Moses Creek. Described as "an inefficient intemperate man," he was a member of the Committee of Safety for Saratoga and served as a colonel commanding the 13th Regiment from Saratoga.[12] At the end of the war, he would move away from the Fort Edward area and petition the Continental Congress for money to rebuild the White Clay Creek Church in Delaware that his family had first attended. The building was used by American troops in 1777, but was then occupied and damaged by the British during the war.[13]

On the other hand, the Reverend James McCrea's children with his second wife, who was English, were mostly committed to the Crown. Catherine, the youngest, married the son of a British officer. Creighton fought with the British as an ensign in the 1st Regiment of the Queen's Rangers, the company being led by his brother, Major Robert McCrea, who left his studies at the College of New Jersey when the war broke out. The Queen's Rangers was an aggressive unit commanded by Lieutenant-Colonel J. G. Simcoe. Robert was wounded in the chest at Brooklyn Heights, wounded in the leg at White Plains, had his right arm amputated after the Battle of Brandywine in 1777, and had his properties seized under accusation of treason. Later, living in Britain, he claimed losses of four farms and 1,155 acres. He recalled the "unparalleled misfortunes" his family suffered during the war, and condemned his Patriot half-brothers for "sinking under the sanguinary spirit of vindictive republicanism."[14]

Jane moved into her brother John's house in Albany shortly after her father's death in 1769 when the family's New Jersey farm was sold to Cornelius Lane.[15] In 1773 John acquired the Northumberland property where Jane came to live.[16] A Hudson Valley farmer said Jane was "often seen" thereabouts.[17] Unlike her brothers, she left behind no records of her life, except a citation in her father's will. "Exercised with much weakness and pain of body," Reverend McCrea thanked "Almighty God, my creator and Redeemer," before bequeathing the largest portion of his estate to his wife, Catherine, large amounts to his sons, and smaller amounts to his daughters, including £170 for Jane.[18]

While living with her brother in Northumberland, she became engaged to David Jones, whose family also hailed from Bedminster. Because he was male and part of the military, we know more about David than Jane. He had moved away from Bedminster with his widowed mother, Sarah Dunham Jones, first to Connecticut, and then, on the eve of hostilities, to the west bank of the Hudson, opposite Fort Edward and a few miles upriver from the McCreas, where Mrs. Jones operated "Jones Ferry."[19] Her seven sons ran farms on the east bank; David Jones owned an eighty-acre property.[20]

At the outset of the war, the Upper Hudson was home to many Loyalists who mostly welcomed the imminent arrival of Burgoyne. Among the enthusiasts, the Joneses were notable. David Jones's brother, John, joined the 34th British Regiment in 1777 as a captain, whereupon he recruited locals for the Loyal Rangers.[21] Another brother, Jonathan, served seven years as a captain in the army and led his own company of Loyal Rangers during the Burgoyne expedition. He was said to have been wounded during battle and then carried in a wagon to Lake George and finally into Canada.[22] David's brother Solomon Jones, who was studying medicine in Albany when the war began, became a surgeon's mate in the British army. Another brother, Joseph Jones, was a lieutenant in Major Ebenezer Jessup's King's Loyal Americans. Daniel Jones, a mill-wright who owned a 242-acre farm in Kingsbury, north of Fort Edward and near present-day Hudson Falls, joined Burgoyne at Skenesborough in 1777, serving as a supply officer behind British lines.[23]

While David Jones was still living with his Loyalist family in Connecticut in 1775, chroniclers said he had "suffered much at the hands of the Sons of Liberty," so much that it was suggested he "should draught a narrative of his woes."[24] The Reverend Samuel Peters of Hebron, Connecticut, described a heated encounter when a Patriot "mob" leveled "insults" at Jones and threatened him with bodily harm during "these bad times, when things are growing worse."[25] Jones's political experiences as a Loyalist in a state run by the notable Patriot governor Jonathan Trumbull explains some of the vindictive rage he would brandish against Patriots throughout the Revolution.

Shortly after his family's move to the Upper Hudson, he too joined Jessup's Rangers when the unit was assembling near Crown Point in 1776 on the west bank of Lake Champlain.[26] As was the case with all of the Loyalist units, land was promised as an eventual reward for enlistment and service to the Crown. Glimpses of Jones's wartime actions have surfaced. Jessup's Rangers, a notably irregular group, participated in the failed British effort to take Fort Ticonderoga under General Carleton in 1776, after which David Jones and his unit retreated to Canada. When Burgoyne replaced Carleton as commander, Jones returned to action, at first dropping into the Fort Edward area to persuade more men to join the British.[27] We know that in March of 1777, when "a party of Americans, taken prisoners at Lake George, were brought in," a complaint was lodged that "they were daily insulted by David Jones, Ebenezer Jessup, and others."[28] We also know that during the American evacuation of Fort Ticonderoga in July of 1777,

Jones, by then notable as a Tory hothead, joined the British force chasing the retreating Americans to Hubbardton in Vermont.[29]

During that British campaign of 1777, Burgoyne tasked Loyalist units, including Jessup's full battalion, with protecting his regulars and "keeping the country in awe," and also for performing mundane tasks, such as "searching for cattle, ascertaining the practicability of routes, clearing roads, and guiding detachments or columns upon the march."[30] At the same time, Burgoyne admitted that Loyalist units, or the "Provincial Corps," were "a heavier tax upon time and patience." Their motives were rarely synchronized; one "man's views went to the profit which he was to enjoy"; another's "to the protection of the district in which he resided"; and a third "was wholly intent upon revenge against his personal enemies."[31] No one knows David Jones's sentiment, but he would seem to be a blend of the second and third motivations.

On July 25, 1777, all the advanced corps—Loyalist, Native American, Canadian, and British—were camping on land owned by Jones's Loyalist brother, Daniel, two miles north of Fort Edward in Pitch Pine Plains, a forest of hemlocks, spruces, and white and yellow pines.[32] Some sort of communication must have alerted Jane to David's presence nearby. In anticipation of an imminent reunion with her fiancé, Jane McCrea left her brother John's farm to travel up the western bank of the Hudson to spend the night at Sarah Dunham Jones's house before taking the ferry to the eastern side. Jacob Bitely, a teenager working the trans-Hudson ferry, recalled how she looked that day, June 26, "dressed up in her best suit of clothes," crowned with "her wedding cap," which she had put on "at Mrs. Jones's, that morning."[33] Upon arriving at the ferry dock at Fort Edward, Jane walked to the log house of one Sarah McNeil to await a rendezvous with Jones or his Native representatives. The town was mostly empty, as Patriot families, in fear of Burgoyne's advance, had fled southward toward the American encampment. What happened to Jane between her arrival at McNeil's on the morning of the 26th and her death later that same day remains unclear.

If the plan was to have Native auxiliaries retrieve her in order to wed David Jones, the hasty ceremony likely would have taken place at his brother Daniel's farm, north of town. Afterward, she would either have retraced her steps back to John McCrea's farm, a married Loyalist wife in a Patriot household, while her new husband remained in British camp. Or, she would have stayed at Loyalist Daniel's house.[34] If she were hearty enough, she might have kept close to David by joining the ranks of camp followers, those wives and children who traveled with Burgoyne's army on its southward campaign.

Yet there was actually no need for Jane to be escorted to the British camp under the circumstances. As the Americans had mostly vacated Fort Edward, all she needed to do was wait patiently for the imminent arrival of David Jones and the entire British army. Following that scenario, there never would be abductors with marching orders to rescue her. In the end, Jane was never delivered, never married. Instead, she was found dead on an embankment a half mile north of Fort Edward.

Folklore has a shattered David Jones deserting Burgoyne and moving to Canada immediately after McCrea's death. Yet, war records show Jones in the British camp at Sorel, near the city of Quebec, in 1778 and 1779, working on fortifications along with his fellow Loyalists.[35] Under the reenergized command of General Frederick Haldimand, the new Governor of Quebec, Jessup's unit was renamed the King's Loyal Americans and re-outfitted in green coats with dark red facings. Jones became prominent in British Major Christopher Carleton's ferocious raids on the Upper Hudson in 1780, which retraced many of the routes taken by Burgoyne in 1777, this time with 518 British and German soldiers, 150 Loyalists, and 138 Native Americans.[36] The motivating concept was to "destroy the Country," rather than defeat the Americans. Jones himself led a scorched-earth party back to Fort Edward, site of Jane's murder.

"The Great Burning," as it was called, was revenge against Patriots now occupying houses formerly owned by Loyalists. On "a clear cold night, some time in October," one resident recalled years later, they "fell upon us, and burned every house and barn on the west side of the river. . . . It was an awful night." One of houses torched was Philander Doty's, where David Jones and his family had once lived. As the operation moved farther south, wreaking havoc, Jones's unit burned another house, the one owned by Colonel John McCrea and occupied by his fiancée, Jane.[37]

Jones, still in Jessup's Rangers in 1781, was known to be recruiting in New York when he should have been attending to military matters in Canada. He also participated in two abduction initiatives. One was the attempted kidnapping of Major John McKinstry of the Albany Militia and, more spectacularly, of American Major-General Philip Schuyler, an audacious move that the British hoped would allow Haldimand to annex the Republic of Vermont, which had declared itself independent from New

York in 1777.[38] Haldimand trusted Jones and once described him as "a brave young man and a good woodsman."[39]

In late 1781, after Lord Cornwallis's surrender at Yorktown, Jones, who was listed on documents as "Secret Service and Jessup's," became involved in British preparations for an American and French invasion of Canada, which never happened. In the effort to secure Canada's southern border, Jones was sent toward the blockhouses on the Yamaska River, southwest of Trois-Rivières.[40] That same year, his unit, led by Edward Jessup, took control of Lake George, which, it was hoped by Haldimand, would become the new border between Canada and the United States. By 1783, Jones was operating out of Rivière du Chène, near Montreal, where he made an independent exploration of the lands along the Ottawa River, as far as Chaudière Falls.[41] He filed his report on October 29, 1783.[42]

By the end of the war, two of Jones's brothers had died and one moved to Nova Scotia. Along with his remaining brothers, a sister, and their mother, Jones migrated to Canada, with hopes of reuniting in Montreal or one of the tent camps set up at Sorel and Yamachihe, near the Saint Lawrence River.[43] As United Empire Loyalists qualifying for land grants, they eventually resettled in Augusta, 125 miles southwest of Montreal, on "Royal Township" property along the Saint Lawrence River.[44] David, listed in Canadian records as a "pensioner," applied for and successfully won a modest land compensation, called "soldier's bounty," a practice dating back to the ancient Romans, for his losses in the new United States. The British government officially approved his application in October of 1784.[45]

David, who "like all the Joneses was a large robust man," farmed near his brothers, Daniel, Solomon, and John.[46] Solomon at first struggled like many other American refugees, but eventually became a successful physician. Tradition has David Jones dying of unknown causes in 1785, said to have been the aftereffects of a broken heart, though fragmentary records indicate that in 1793 he "wishes to become a settler."[47] Furthermore, in 1796 he and Solomon filed an application for lands and in July of 1797 he was again listed with two brothers in a request for even more "Crown Lands."[48] Entries in the public records of Ontario for November 1797 and June 1798 suggest that David Jones was deceased.[49]

3.

THE LETTER

BEFORE McCREA was scalped and killed, General John Burgoyne—cavalry officer during the Portuguese campaign, as well as London playwright, Member of Parliament, and dashing man-about-town—was directing a British military juggernaut that had seemed unstoppable in the early summer of 1777, having notched overwhelming victories at Fort Ticonderoga and on Lake Champlain. By contrast, the American forces—first under the command of General Philip Schuyler, a New Yorker of Dutch heritage, and then under Major-General Horatio Gates, a British-born veteran of the French and Indian War—were, charitably speaking, in disarray. The Northern Army, in stumbling retreat from a horribly failed campaign to defeat the British at Quebec, and now ravaged by disease and starvation, was being chased down the Hudson by Burgoyne, into Fort Edward, and ultimately toward Saratoga. The betting odds in June favored a massive American collapse.

The audacious British plan, hatched in London by Burgoyne and George Germain, the British Secretary for the American Department, was to cleave the former colonies in two and thus isolate New England from its sister states. The British wanted to accomplish that by assigning to Burgoyne the task of capturing Albany from Canada. Meanwhile, Commander-in-Chief William Howe was to advance up the Hudson from British headquarters in New York. With the six hundred miles from Montreal to New York under their control, British forces planned to march into New England, savage the countryside, and recapture Boston, which they had evacuated in 1776, while their incomparable navy would menace the coast. If all those pieces were to fall into place, the rebellion would come to a crashing end by 1778.

For all the detail and grandiosity of the plan, it gradually unraveled and finally disintegrated over the course of the summer of 1777, in some measure due to Jane McCrea. July 26 was not an especially important date in the annals of that Northern campaign, and Fort Edward was never a particularly significant military outpost.[1] And yet, the killing of a young woman that day acquired an outsized significance. A cluster of factors put her and kept her in the spotlight, including a letter that General Gates wrote to Burgoyne on September 2, 1777, demanding an answer for her unwarranted slaying. To be sure, five and a half long weeks had elapsed since her murder, but it eventually dawned upon the ever-savvy Gates that he had an untapped tool in the form of McCrea. A scalding rebuke of Burgoyne, he figured, might whip up public opinion against the British if the letter were released to the press, which was always hungry for a story with demagogic potential. In the American war of attrition, which theretofore had involved felling trees onto wilderness roads in order to force the British to use precious time, energy, and supplies to clear the path ahead, Gates had devised another tactic for gaining an advantage: propaganda.

Gates's letter was brilliant. In language calculated to sway a divided public that was torn between loyalty to the Crown and support for the rebellion, he mocked "the famous Lieutenant General Burgoyne," whom most consider a "fine Gentleman." He bluntly accused his adversary of putting a ransom on scalps, and then rebuked him for criminally hiring "the Savages of America to scalp Europeans, and the descendants of Europeans." Gates's most indisputable proof was the "lovely" Miss McCrea. He professed knowledge of the "authenticated details" of the "horrid tale" of her death: she was, "with another Woman, and Children taken out of a House near Fort-Edward, carried into the Woods, and there scalped, and mangled in a most shocking Manner." After pinning onto Burgoyne additional responsibility for the fate of the Allen family, grotesquely massacred in nearby Argyle "while quietly residing in their once happy and peaceful Dwelling," Gates returned to McCrea. She was "A young lady lovely to the sight, of virtuous Character, and amiable Disposition, . . . dressed to receive her promised Husband," but butchered by a "Murderer employed by you."[2] And if that were not incriminating enough, Gates added the final, ironic

James Peale, after Charles Willson Peale, *Horatio Gates*, c. 1782. Oil on canvas. Washington DC, National Portrait Gallery, Smithsonian Institution; partial gift of Mr. Lawrence A. Fleischman.

kicker: Jane McCrea was "engaged to be married to an Officer in your Army." The barbarous British and their savage allies, he charged, could not even protect one of their own.[3]

It was, of course, merely a letter, yet it proved to be a masterstroke. Seventeen American newspapers, from New Hampshire to Georgia, printed it, accompanied by Burgoyne's weak retort, which meant that nearly every American had access to the Patriot version of the atrocity. Though there had been unspeakable violence throughout the region that summer, Gates excerpted McCrea's death and made it special.[4] He easily could have picked one of the countless other slain civilians in New York to showcase. But in choosing—and then broadcasting—the story of an innocent young woman about to be married, he was extracting maximal political gain from her gory death, and assuring, little more than a year after the Declaration of Independence, her eventual status as the first and foremost female martyr of the Revolution. Because of the letter's extraordinary reach across the East Coast and over the Atlantic, we can attribute to Gates, more than anyone else, authorship of McCrea's fame in the annals of the American Revolution.

By rights, McCrea's death should have become a minor footnote to the Northern revolutionary theater, as it was quickly eclipsed that summer by the consequential battles at Bennington, Oriskany, and Fort Stanwix, and the start of the British invasion of Philadelphia. That notwithstanding, Gates avidly flogged the story because it was politically useful, admitting as much in a letter to Jonathan Trumbull, the governor of Connecticut (and father of John Trumbull, who later would paint a colossal picture for the United States Capitol Rotunda of Burgoyne surrendering to Gates). Gates delightedly wrote to Governor Trumbull that the letter he had sent Burgoyne was "a Tickler upon Scalping." That is, a dig or jab meant to rattle Burgoyne, that will eventually "be published by Congress."[5]

Gates had an innate flair for inflammatory rhetoric, aiming letters not only at Burgoyne, but also at George Washington, the commander in chief, then camped in Bucks County, Pennsylvania: "Horrible indeed," he wrote, "has been the Cruelties [that Indians] have wantonly committed upon many of the miserable inhabitants." He hoped "the Bloody Hatchet [that Burgoyne] has so barbarously used should find its way into his Own Head."[6] Gates adeptly groomed John Hancock, president of the Continental Congress. "The Horrid Murders & Scalpings paid for, and encouraged by Lieut. General Burgoyne," he wrote Hancock, "will forever stain the Honour of the British Arms." He recited for Hancock the touching story of the Allen family, also "Cruelly Butchered" by Burgoyne's auxiliaries, and, once more, indicted Burgoyne, "this polite Macaroni," who "paid ten dollars for each of their scalps."[7] Gates's description of the Northern front as a hellscape proved effective, for it persuaded state legislators to send militia to join him at Saratoga and the Continental Congress to restock his depleted army.

Gates did not end his verbal assault there. He warned Burgoyne of his intention to furnish the entire world with the "authenticated Facts" of McCrea's killing, which "shall, in every Gazette, convince Mankind of the Truth of the horrid Tale." In short order, 90 percent of the British press printed transcripts of Gates's letter, turning the deceased young woman into a media sensation there. Britons, largely insulated from the war, were suddenly reading about—and visualizing—all the grisly details, and were further discomforted to learn from Gates that "upwards of one hundred Men, Women, and Children, have perished by the Hands of the Ruffians, to whom you have paid the Price of Blood." Even in his wildest dreams, Gates could not have anticipated the full breadth of his two-page letter's reach or the speed of its proliferation, especially in London where McCrea's story flourished. It was as if he had personally posted broadsides on every wall and fence in the city.

In his September 6 reply to Gates's letter of September 2, written at the occupied mansion of William Duer, south of Fort Edward, "General Swagger," as tart-tongued Horace Walpole once dubbed Burgoyne, found himself on the defensive. He had choices: own up to the wanton behavior of his proxies, diminish the importance of what happened, or outright lie. He blended the three options. While never flatly refuting Gates's accusation, Burgoyne assured his adversary that he never put a price on scalps, only on captured prisoners. "In regard to Miss M'Rae," specifically, "her fall wanted not the tragic display you have labored to give it."[8] Her unfortunate death, he disingenuously declared, was "as sincerely abhorred and lamented by me, as it can possibly be by the tenderest of her Friends."

Burgoyne had framed the killing as a one-off case of bad luck. After all, he had announced to his Native warriors that "aged Men, Women, Children and Prisoners must be held sacred from the knife or hatchet." They did have permission to "take the Scalps of the Dead," but not "from the Wounded or even Dying." Those were his stated ground rules. But the indisputable fact of the matter was that Jane McCrea had been butchered by auxiliaries working for the British.

The fifty-year-old Gates handled Burgoyne with a self-confidence consistent with his powerful position as Commander of the Northern Army. That was in early September 1777. Yet, only five and a half weeks earlier, when McCrea was killed in late July, he was a military subordinate hundreds of miles from the northern theater. His career had begun two decades earlier, during the French and Indian War, while posted along with George Washington to General Edward Braddock's doomed campaign against the French in western Pennsylvania. At the outbreak of the Revolution in 1775, Gates traveled to Mount Vernon to offer his services to Washington, who urged the Continental Congress to appoint him Adjutant General of the Continental Army, in recognition of his administrative skills rather than military prowess. Working under Washington, Gates managed daunting organizational challenges, including the overall welfare of soldiers who were entering combat mostly ill-prepared and ill-equipped. His skills would prove to be invaluable during the Siege of Boston, when Washington had to quickly assemble a functioning army.

In 1776, Congress appointed Gates Commander of the Continental Army in Canada. To his shock, the men he encountered when he assumed the position were "naked, dispirited, ill provided," the grim result of the army's earlier rout in Quebec. Starved and riven with disease, they were chased up the Saint Lawrence River, before retreating along Lake Champlain into Fort Ticonderoga, where Gates ruefully discovered he had lost his command because he had fallen under the jurisdiction of General Schuyler, commander of the Northern Army.[9]

Late in 1776, Washington called Gates and 1,200 men to join him on the banks of the Delaware. Habitually preferring defensive positioning over offensive action, Gates did not cross the river in the famous Christmas night assault on Trenton, instead choosing to meet with Congress, where he lobbied for an independent command of his own. He shamelessly solicited the New England delegates, who fondly recalled his contribution to the expulsion of the British from Boston earlier that year. Falling short of his goal, however, he instead accepted the post of chief officer in charge of Ticonderoga, while continuing to keep one eye on Schuyler's job.

Chronically irked by what he considered disrespect, a miffed Gates returned to Congress on June 17, 1777, to vent his anger at being stuck at Ticonderoga, which led to an even lesser assignment, a penance of sorts in the mid-Atlantic states. At that time, Major-General Arthur St. Clair was presiding over Ticonderoga, which quickly fell to Burgoyne in early July, a debacle that John and Samuel Adams assigned to General Schuyler's incompetence. On July 29, Congress mounted an inquiry into the conduct of St. Clair and Schuyler, and on August 1 Congress relieved Schuyler of his command.

During that upheaval in the Northern Department, McCrea was slaughtered on July 26. At that moment, Gates continued to be marooned at Coryell's Ferry (present-day New Hope, Pennsylvania), sending dispatches to Washington regarding intelligence that the British fleet was carrying General William Howe's army to the mouth of the Delaware River in anticipation of an invasion of Philadelphia.[10] Schuyler's demotion, however, created an opening. Because Gates was politically close to the influential New England delegates, especially John Hancock, Elbridge Gerry, and the Adamses, he thought he might be in consideration to replace Schuyler as Northern commander. He knew that Schuyler had long irritated the New Englanders because he promoted the land claims of New York against those of New Hampshire and Massachusetts. In the end, the New Englanders prevailed in Congress, which voted on August 4 to promote Gates to the position of Commander of the Northern Army. Commission in hand, he immediately began the trek across New Jersey to Peekskill, and up the Hudson to Albany and Van Schaick's Island, north of Albany, where the army was encamped at the confluence of the Hudson and Mohawk rivers, that is, between the British pincers at Fort Ticonderoga in the far north and the city of New York in the far south.

During those early August days, Gates received a detailed and disturbing account of McCrea's killing back in July. Given the twin crises facing the Cause—the Northern Army running from Burgoyne and Washington's army confronting General Howe in Pennsylvania—any incidental news of a civilian casualty might have been treated as insignificant, seemingly not consequential on Gates's or any general's radar. But the political strategist in Gates was intrigued by the possibilities of incoming accounts of her killing. Though history may not consider Gates an especially accomplished military leader or field tactician, it accurately recognizes him as someone who knew a great political opportunity when he met one.

4.

MURDER MOST FOUL, STRANGE, AND UNNATURAL

GENERAL GATES belatedly received news of McCrea's killing from Ivory Hovey, a surgeon in Alexander Scammell's 3rd New Hampshire Regiment, who was writing from Fort Miller, a few miles downriver from Fort Edward, on July 27, the day after the event. The first part of Hovey's letter described the British attack on Ticonderoga and the harrowing American escape into Vermont. That was old news to Gates. However, the second part, about McCrea, piqued Gates's interest. Hovey wrote that McCrea and an "Elderly Lady" were "taken out their House, dragged upon a little Hill, in the woods, but a little distance from a party of our Army and there inhumanly Shott, Tomihawked, and Scalped." Hovey noted that "what is most remarkable in this Instance, is that the before mentioned Persons were high Tories the young woman was Corted by a Tory Capt, in the Regular Service, who was that day to have met her upon that very hill." McCrea's political allegiances notwithstanding, "she was dragd too & Scalped, She plead with the Indians for her life telling them that she was their Friend, and wanted to go with them, but they paid no regard to her Interests."

Hovey's pain-riddled letter went on to describe the terrors he was witnessing inside his surgical tent: "Oh the bitter Groans & lamentations that

I have heard. . . . An Account has Just Come in that the Indians Knocked one Childs Brains out against a Tree—" There are "many women, Crying, Lamenting" over their mutilated husbands. Confessing that "I am Naturally a great Cowerd," he saw no future for himself either, "the Grave may be my bed before I have opportunity of writing you a 2nd letter."

Anticipating a question Gates might ask, Hovey added, "You doubtless would be glad to know how we came by these perticulars." He said that "a Negro wench who hid in the Cellar gives this report."[1] Hovey's account was thus secondhand, but close to the killing in terms of the timeline and physical distance. The "Elderly Lady" was Sarah McNeil, whose servant or slave remained sheltered in the cellar during the abduction, yet must have heard words and screams from the assault. She could have assumed the worst for both women before learning later that McNeil had been separated from McCrea and taken safe yet shaken to the British line.[2]

McCrea was now officially on Gates's political agenda. In his September letter to Burgoyne, he would minimize her engagement to a Loyalist officer and omit some other key details—in particular McNeil and the African American woman—in order to streamline the plot and focus on the most heartbreaking feature, namely McCrea. He tested an early draft of the letter on Major-General Benjamin Lincoln and aide-de-camp Lieutenant-Colonel James Wilkinson. When they weakly questioned the striking ad hominem tone that sarcastically derided "the famous Lieutenant General Burgoyne" for unleashing terror on civilians, Gates proudly crowed "By G-d, I don't believe either of you can 'mend it."[3] Tellingly, Gates did scratch out the final sentence of an earlier draft version before sending it. It read, "The law of retaliation is a just law, and you must expect to feel its force." On reflection, Gates probably thought that was perhaps too vengeful, risking public scorn instead of the outrage he was soliciting.

Gates's motive in writing the letter was apparent to Burgoyne, who instantly spotted a public relations campaign intended to demonize the British by sensationalizing McCrea's gruesome death. One British officer at the time felt that "The Americans took great pains to sully the Character of the Lt. Genl. Burgoyne on the above melancholy Accident."[4] After all, wrote a lieutenant, when McCrea's killing is "put in competition with all the horrors attendant on this unfortunate contest, and which, in all probability, are likely to increase hourly, [it] is but of little moment."[5] When Burgoyne himself looked back at the whole fiasco ten months later, during a Parliamentary investigation, he could retrospectively see how he had been played by Gates. The letter, he knew, was pure propaganda.[6]

Burgoyne himself had first learned of McCrea's death on the day of the killing, when the main force of his army was occupying Fort Anne, twelve miles north of Fort Edward. The British campaign that had seemed unstoppable in the early summer of 1777 was bogged down in July because of the unexpectedly difficult terrain that forced them to build forty bridges over deep ravines, march through thick woods, and slog across swamps. General Schuyler made all of that exponentially worse by felling trees on already muddy roads and scattering the cattle that might have fed British soldiers.

While Burgoyne's main force struggled, the nimbler advanced guard, including David Jones and his fellow rangers, was moving south to Pitch Pine Plains on land owned by the Jones family, halfway between Fort Anne and American-held Fort Edward. Included within that advanced force were Native warriors who continued to sweep through the woods and wreak havoc as they had on previous days. At Fort Edward, 150 of American Major Daniel Whiting's picket guard remained in place while the Continentals, under Colonel John Nixon, retreated to an encampment six miles south at Moses Creek.

On July 26, at "8 at night," Burgoyne informed a captain leading the advanced corps at Pitch Pine Plains of "the news I have just received of the savages having scalped a young lady, their prisoner." The killing, a shaken Burgoyne confessed, "fills me with horror." His genuine animus over the monstrosities committed by his own proxies mingled with his fear that the murder might come to taint his professional career. He confided to Brigadier-General Simon Fraser, "I would rather put my commission in the fire than serve a day if I could suppose Government would blame me for discountenancing by some strong acts such unheard of barbarities."[7] Though the murder of the entire Allen family in nearby Argyle was equally disturbing, McCrea loomed larger in Burgoyne's mind because she was engaged to an officer in one of his Loyalist units.

His response was to go to the Indian camp the next morning, where he expected Major John Campbell, British commander of the Western tribes, to have assembled all warriors, "none absent." Burgoyne interrogated the Indians on the 27th and listened to their version of the killing. It is not known what he heard, but in the storyline he packaged for Gates he wrote, "Two chiefs who had brought her off for the purpose of security, not of violence to her person, disputed which should be her guard; and in a fit of savage passion on one, from whose hands she was snatched, the unhappy woman became the victim." In Burgoyne's telling, there was "no premeditated barbarity," merely a fatal outcome resulting from an irresponsible quarrel.[8] No mention was made in his letter of a scalping, a fiancé, an elderly lady, or an African American. Where Gates had the warriors dragging McCrea involuntarily out of a house, Burgoyne emphasized the desire to rescue her from a war zone. His high-minded scenario reads like an episode from an eighteenth-century etiquette book.

Burgoyne needed to mete out punishment on the 27th, British style, for violating the rules he had laid down on proper military behavior. He thought an "ignominious death" was called for. However, according to an unidentified British soldier claiming to have been at the scene: "the Guilty Savage was given up to him [Burgoyne]; but his life being begged by the Warriors, and from the Character given off by them as a rising Warrior, and the repentance the whole seemed to shew for what had happened, his life was granted him."[9] Burgoyne phrased the adjudication of the crime in a more complex way: "Upon the first intelligence of this event I obliged the Indians to deliver the murderer into my hands." Reflecting for a moment on the oddness of a British general punishing an indigenous man, Burgoyne concluded that it "would have perhaps been unprecedented."

Burgoyne had become "convinced, by circumstances and observation, beyond the possibility of a doubt" that he should pardon instead of execute the killer. But only "under the forms which I prescribed and they accepted," the "they" referring to the entire band of Native auxiliaries, and the "forms" presumably being British supervision in the future and an oral contract never to repeat the offense. As he explained to Gates, a warning would be "more efficacious than an execution to prevent similar mischiefs."[10]

That was *politesse* for the underlying weakness of the British situation. The British were dependent on the Native Americans who understood the difficult wilderness terrain and were skilled at spreading "Alarm," as Burgoyne euphemistically rephrased the word Terror. His Native forces operated in advance of the main army, thus inducing American civilians to flee and the Continental Army to recede downriver, paving the way for the British regulars. If Burgoyne were to execute McCrea's killer, his indispensable Native auxiliaries would simply quit and go home. He was told as much by one of the handlers of the Western Indians from the Great Lakes, La Corne Saint-Luc, an aging yet ferocious Québécois who was present at Burgoyne's confrontation at the Indian camp on the 27th.

If fully punished, the Native auxiliaries might not only walk away from the Northern Campaign, Saint-Luc informed Burgoyne, but also commit greater atrocities on their way back home. In the apocalyptic words of a

Robert Baldwin and Thomas Kitchin, *Part of the counties of Charlotte and Albany, in the Province of New York: being the seat of war between the King's forces under Lieut. Gen. Burgoyne and the rebel army. 1778.* Engraving. [A. Ticonderoga; B. Skenesborough; C. Fort Anne; D. Fort Edward; E. Moses Creek; F. Mohawk River.] Washington DC, Library of Congress, Geography and Map Division.

sergeant under Burgoyne, that would have meant "massacring every body and destroying every thing before them."[11] To prevent that action and persuade them to extend their "services," according to Ensign Thomas Anburey, who was present at the "trial," Burgoyne thought he needed to indulge "all their excesses of blood and rapine."[12] Burgoyne's leniency would prove to be successful in retaining the Native warriors, but only momentarily. Because of the reprimand for McCrea's scalping, a stream of desertions eventually followed, leaving Burgoyne few warriors for the fateful battles at Saratoga.

Another weight pressing on Burgoyne's decision-making at the Indian camp was the need to save face in London by minimizing the seriousness of the murder. If word reached Parliament that he was executing Native Americans because they were killing women and children in the name of Britain, he knew that he and the Tory government would have hell to pay. Perhaps a slap on a wrist would be less attention grabbing than an execution and allow him to avoid professional embarrassment and a public relations nightmare.

Numerous accounts, close in date to the killing and mostly military, add substantially to the Hovey letter and the Gates-Burgoyne exchange, yet they do not perfectly square with them or with each other. Josiah Bartlett of Massachusetts, a surgeon stationed at the American camp in Moses Creek, five miles south of Fort Edward, wrote to his superior on July 26 at 10 P.M. He had alarming news "from Fort Edward, where a party of hell-hounds, in conjunction with their brethren, the British troops" were prowling. "Poor Miss Jenny McCray, . . . and the woman with whom she lived, were taken by the savages, led up the hill to where there was a body of British troops, and then the poor woman was shot to death in cold blood, scalped, and left on the ground, and the other woman not yet found. The alarm came to camp at 2 P.M. I was at dinner."[13] Bartlett's intelligence pinpointed the assault to the morning of the 26th, a Saturday, and put British soldiers nearby. As soon as Bartlett heard of the killing, he immediately "set off to collect all the regular surgeons" to find the bodies, but was unsuccessful.

A second American surgeon, Estes Howe of Belchertown, Massachusetts, kept a concise medical diary during the Saratoga campaign, mostly concerned with treatments for wounds and inoculations for smallpox. On July 26 his tone changed dramatically. "A number of Indians ad[vanced]

Near Fort Edward to a hous. Take Two White Women and a negro Man and woman. One of the White Women they Kill upon a Hill and Skelpt her. The other is yit missing." The next day he added, "This moment hear that the other Woman [McCrea] is found Dead this Morning."[14] Howe's account, like Hovey's, added African Americans to the McCrea party.

James Thacher, a surgeon's mate in the Continental Army, kept a military journal that he eventually published in 1823. In it, he blended diary entries from 1777 with later ruminations on the campaign. For example, in his entry on September 2, thirty-seven days after the killing, he recalled McCrea awaiting her fiancé's arrival "in order to have the marriage consummated." Love, it seemed, conquered politics, leading her to reject her brothers' Patriot passions. Most civilians had evacuated the garrison town of Fort Edward in anticipation of Burgoyne, yet she "had the indiscretion to remain behind, probably with the expectation of meeting her lover." As a result, she was made "their prisoner, and on their return towards Burgoyne's camp, a quarrel arose to decide who should hold possession of their fair prize. During the controversy, one of the monsters struck his tomahawk into her skull, and immediately stripped off her scalp."

The "quarrel" scenario matches Burgoyne's story, though Thacher's account does not confirm Burgoyne's claim that the Native warriors had begun with the purpose of protecting McCrea and guiding her to safety. Thacher did verify Gates's assertion that McCrea had decided to remain in Fort Edward in anticipation of a rendezvous. As expected, Thacher concluded by condemning the use of warriors as a "disgraceful" practice "countenanced and recommended by his Majesty."[15]

Colonel Wilkinson wrote a military memoir of his wartime experiences in 1816. He recalled the day Gates summoned him to the commander's tent while composing the letter to Burgoyne. The twenty-year-old Wilkinson said Gates was eager to direct "particular attention to the fate of a young lady, a Miss M'Crea." In his opinion, upon reviewing Gates's draft of the famous letter, he thought the commander "gave loose to his imagination," not necessarily fictionalizing as much as painting "the tragic scene in such colours, as could but excite the sympathy, and rouse the indignation of the country." In Wilkinson's estimation, Gates was ginning up the crime for political gain, "and on this ground and these motives only, was the murder of the unfortunate girl recorded."[16]

Wilkinson, who clashed regularly with Gates and would challenge the general to a duel in 1778, proceeded to tell his own, unsentimental version of "the melancholy incident" as "it has been represented to me" from an undisclosed source.[17] When "stripped of its high colouring," a deglamorized picture of a young and vulnerable woman emerges: "Miss Jenny M'Crea, a country girl, of an honest family in circumstances of mediocrity, without either beauty or accomplishments" found herself marooned "when the American army retreated from Fort Edward the 23rd of July." She "had the indiscretion to remain behind, and thus voluntarily put herself in the power of the enemy." The "Indians entered immediately after we retired from the place and made her prisoner; and as the party returned towards General Burgoyne's camp . . ., they halted at a spring near the side of the road, where a controversy arose as to the right of property in the person of the captive." Then, "to put an end to the dispute, a monster tomahawked her, and thus she fell a victim to the ferocious brutality of the Indians."

Wilkinson corroborated the quarrel cited by Burgoyne. Gates also must have known of the quarrel since he was privy to the same information as Wilkinson, but cleverly did not acknowledge it in his letter to Burgoyne. Wilkinson added the detail of McCrea dying by a spring, which Gates also omitted, then insisted once more that that there was nothing notable about McCrea, bluntly declaring, "her character was unexceptional." At the same time, Wilkinson noted the precise feature that makes Jane McCrea so exceptional in the annals of the Revolution and that led to a century of poems, paintings, and novels: "A personal attachment induced her to remain behind," when most civilians had fled southward toward Albany. She had, as he put it, "died for love," hoping against death that David Jones would arrive, sweep her to safety, and then marry her. And because of that, "her memory should be honoured and embalmed in the bosom of sensibility."[18]

William Scudder, an officer camped at Moses Creek with the 1st New York Regiment, had been ordered on the 26th to "the heights beyond Fort Edward," a small rise north of town. He heard that Indians "took" Jane McCrea from Sarah McNeil's house to the heights, where they "murdered and scalped" her. They also captured and "stripped poor Van Vechten [Lieutenant Tobias Van Vechten], and after scalping him, stabbed him in several places," before they "fastened a tomahawk in his breast, sharpened a stick and erected him on his feet, by bracing the sharp part of the stick under his chin, and left him."[19] Scudder said he saw the two corpses "side and side in a horse cart!" The next day, he helped carry Van Vechten's body to a grave. "Miss M'Crea was also buried in the same grave with him."[20]

A few other accounts from late July cite the killing in passing, the most poignant from Dr. Jonathan Potts, whose senior surgeon was McCrea's younger brother, Stephen. On July 28, the doctor received a letter with news that Burgoyne had taken Fort Edward, and that Indians "killed 5 men & a young lady, sister of one of my Surgeons, all of whom they scalped & most barbarously butchered."[21] For that, Potts announced, "*Lex Talionis,*" the law of revenge, by which no British or German "officer or soldier shall have mercy from my hands."

Benedict Arnold, writing on July 27 from Snook Hill, three miles south of Fort Edward on the west bank of the Hudson, described the difficult situation in the north for General Washington, who was himself preparing for the British invasion of Philadelphia. "We are dayly insulted by the Indians, who on the 22d Inst. attacked our Picket Guard, killd & scalp'd five Men wounded Nine & took one Prisoner, On the 24th they kill'd & scalpd two Officers between Fort Edward & our Lines. Yesterday Morning our Picket at Fort Edward, where we have one hundred Men Advanced, was attacked by a large Party of Indians & Regulars." Then he turned to Jane McCrea: "the Indians took two women Prisoners from a house near the Fort carried them to the Regular Troops who were paraded near the Fort where they were Shot, scalp'd, strip'd & Butcherd in the most shocking Manner, one of them, a young Lady of Family who has . . . an Officer in the regular Service."[22]

Arnold put British troops near the murder, which was a plausible scenario.[23] British Lieutenant-Colonel Mason Bolton noted the discomfort experienced by the professional soldiers witnessing such acts: "I am really of opinion that to keep the Indians in good Temper (as it is called) has cost Old England much more than all the Posts are worth. . . . As to their scalping Women Children and Prisoners I find it not possible to prevent them; such cruelties must make an Expedition very disagreeable to the Kings Troops when order'd on service with them."[24]

General Schuyler, in his last days as commander of the Northern Army, also wrote Washington, corroborating Arnold's news: "A Body of Indians and regular troops attacked a Picket detached from a body of about 150 which we keep at Fort Edward, killed & scalped a Subaltern, two Serjeants and a private and took four Prisoners." He added, "They also scalped a Woman and carried off another."[25] Colonel Morgan Lewis, Gates's eventual chief of staff, said he saw Jane McCrea early on the morning of her killing. His account came by way of a granddaughter compiling his biography from journals and interviews. As Lewis was retreating southward, his granddaughter said he "passed the house in which she had rested for the night," stopped and "roused the inmates, and informed them that the hostile Indians were not far in his rear." McCrea "came to the window to speak to him." She did not, in Lewis's telling, "altogether justify the epithets of the lovely, the accomplished Miss McCrea." Lewis "begged her to put herself under his protection," but she refused, believing "she had nothing to fear from the allies" of her fiancé. "The result is well known."[26] Lewis was said to have found McCrea's body "near the spring, and stripped naked." He found "nine wounds which appeared to him to have been inflicted by a knife."[27]

On the 28th, Leonard Gansevoort, a member of the New York Provisional Congress, wrote his brother Peter, a colonel holding off the British at Fort Stanwix in central New York, with news that "Lieut. Tob: V. Veghten is killed and scalped at Fort Edward together with one Serjeant & four Men." Most disturbing, he reported, "Miss Jenny McCrea & Mrs. McNeal are carried out of the House and the former cut to pieces her breasts rip'd open and scalped. She was found, Mrs. McNeal is not yet found."[28] In all likelihood, given his location in Albany, fifty miles south of events, and his not being a soldier, the narrative of the death was already in the process of amplification. The belief that they were "cut to pieces in the most inhuman manner" also appears in the July 26 entry of Jeduthan Baldwin, an engineer for the Continental Army, who described the July weather as "Blazing Hot with death."[29]

American newspapers closely followed the macabre slaying of McCrea. The *Pennsylvania Evening Post* published an unattributed dispatch, dated July 27 and published August 12, which detailed the size of Burgoyne's army upon its arrival at Fort Edward: 6,000 regulars, 400 Indians, and 200 Canadians. American officers and soldiers, the paper reported, had been "scalped while yet alive." The *Post* then spotlighted "Jenny M'Crea, of a good family, and some share beauty," who was "taken by the savages" and then "with a barbarity unheard of before, they butchered the poor innocent girl, and scalped her." In a moralizing postscript, the paper intoned that this transpired "in the sight of those very men who are continually preaching up their tender mercies, and the forbearance of their more than Christian King." Surely, the *Post* asked, "is not this sufficient to congeal the heart of humanity with horror, and even oblige a Tory of liberal sentiments to curse the cause which approves of or winks at such worse than hell-like cruelties?" A second dispatch in the same newspaper said she was "shot twice through her body, her clothes torn off her back, and left scalped in the bushes." Four Indians were said to have been there, "under cover of three hundred British regulars, drawn up at a small distance, and in sight of an advanced party of Americans, who could give her no assistance."[30]

Of all the recollections of McCrea's death, the most famous is that of Private Samuel Standish, Jr., a twenty-three-year-old militiaman from Stockbridge, Massachusetts, who testified in his pension claim to the federal government that he saw, firsthand, what happened to McCrea on July 26.[31] In a lengthy affidavit, he would refer to himself in both the third person and first person. That morning, he wrote, he "was with others called on to relieve a guard on the hill north of the Fort." Before long, "he heard an Indian Scream and Instantly was fired upon by them. He ran towards the River and Fort & before he arrived he met three Indians coming from the River between him and the Fort who all fired upon him but missed him, where he was taken prisoner by them taken up the hill again near to a spring, was there striped of his hat coat & handkerchief and pilfered by them."

After a short time, "I saw a party of Indians coming with two women. They came up the hill to a spring and they seemed to be in a quarrel. They shot one of the women and scalped her. The woman I knew to be Jennie McCrea." Standish said, "I had seen her before when the Americans offered to take her down the river she refused to go said she was not afraid to stay."

In a separate interview with Harvard College professor Jared Sparks, Standish added a few more details: Jane's "hair was long & flowing, and the same chief took off the scalp, cutting so as to embrace nearly the whole of that part of the head on which the hair grew. He then springed up, tossed the scalp in the face of a young Indian standing by, brandished it in the air, and uttered a yell of savage exultation." Standish claimed the warriors stripped the body, inflicted knife wounds, and crushed the skull. At that point, the quarrel ceased and the whole party moved off quickly, for the fort had already been alarmed.

Standish's account confirms Burgoyne's: there was an argument, McCrea was shot, and then scalped. However, Standish did not stop there. In Sparks's notes, Standish "understood in camp [presumably British camp where he was prisoner] that the Indian chief, who had murdered her, brought the scalp to Jones, her lover, who had employed the Indians to bring her into camp," adding he "always understood" the intended reward for the rescue was "to be a barrel of rum." A different recollection also mentions the rum reward, in which Jones hired Indians to take "Miss Jennett McCrea" to Fort Anne, promising "the chief who should deliver her to him with a certain quantity of rum."[32]

Standish was seemingly the only eyewitness to the killing, yet his two accounts are degraded by their being narrated more than fifty years after the fact. Though Sparks thought "these particulars Standish related with great confidence, and affirmed that there could be no mistake," the question remains whether Standish's memory had been colored over the decades by scores of Jane McCrea stories, each one vying for graphic authenticity or narrative gaudiness.[33] Furthermore, Standish was seventy-eight years old when he applied for a pension in 1832. The government-appointed interviewer noted his "old age and the consequent loss of memory." We have no way of measuring the accuracy of Standish's recollection of McCrea's killing, but in an aside later in the pension document he said that "he saw Indian Col. [Joseph] Brant" while he was a captive in the British camp. But on that day Brant was in the Mohawk Valley.

Jane McCrea's killing appeared in British and German military accounts, too. William Digby, a senior subaltern in the grenadier company of Captain John Wight, kept a journal during the war and published it with later emendations and reflections. He described in detail the arduous process of moving wagons and artillery down roads the Americans had made impassible, and gave gruesome accounts of encountering unburied dead. Digby recalled one evening when "our Indians brought in two scalps, one of them an officer's which they danced around in their usual manner," the other belonging to "the unfortunate Miss McCrea, which affected the general [Burgoyne] and the whole army with the sincerest regret and concern for her untimely fate." In narrating the killing, Digby substantiated Burgoyne's official letter to Gates, adding one new detail—that the Indians were "detached on scouting parties, both in our front and on our flanks." His description of McCrea was an odd blend of raw facts and hearsay. Though he never set eyes on her or her corpse, Digby said "this young lady was about 18," and "had a pleasing person."[34]

Julius Friedrich Wasmus, a Braunschweig (often called Brunswick) surgeon with the German corps who was later captured at Bennington, noted in his journal, "the savages have scalped a beautiful young woman, Miss McCrea; . . . An English captain, who had made her acquaintance here, wanted to marry her and take her with him; tomorrow they were to be married. This misfortune caused quite an uproar in the army, everyone mourned the fate of this fine young woman. . . . What a cruelty."[35] If Wasmus is to be believed, the plan for Jane was to become an army follower after the wedding ceremony.

Luc de La Corne Saint-Luc, c. 1778. Gouache and watercolor on ivory. Montreal, Musée McCord Stewart.

Who actually killed McCrea? In testimony before a Parliamentary inquest after he returned to England, Burgoyne drew a distinction between the "domiciliated" nations "near Montreal," and the "remote tribes" that were more "warlike."[36] Those were the four hundred new recruits from "northern regions and other places," coming from as far as Green Bay and Mackinac, who were delivered on July 17 to the British army by Saint-Luc and his colleague Charles-Michel de Langlade, a *métis*, or mixed-race, Ottawa/French trader. When the Western Indians got to British lines at Fort Anne on July 21, Burgoyne advertised their ferocity by announcing that he had acquired "Five Hundred Savages from the upper nations."[37] Burgoyne's first plan was "to turn this whole corps to the Connecticut immediately," but upon further consideration he decided to employ them "by their terror," to disrupt the enemy in advance of his main force.[38]

This newly arrived group was markedly unlike the warriors of the Northeast, and so were the reputations of their managers. Langlade was notorious for having captured the Miami chief Memeskia in 1752, then having him killed and publicly cannibalized by his soldiers. He also had a hand in engineering the fatal 1755 ambush of British General Edward Braddock, with whom Horatio Gates had served, and he may have been instrumental in the killing of British General James Wolfe on the Plains of Abraham in 1759. He was now the go-between for the British and the Ottawa, Chippewa, Menominee, Foxes, Winnebago, and other nations from the Great Lakes.[39]

A *chevalier*, Saint-Luc had a monstrous reputation as a vicious mercenary, as well as a con man, thug, and slave trader. American Colonel Samuel Mott thought Saint-Luc "the arch devil incarnate, who has butchered hundreds, men, women and children."[40] Thomas Jefferson considered him "our most bitter enemy . . . the greatest of all scoundrels," whose specialty was brutality.[41] Even one of Burgoyne's own German officers wrote that Saint-Luc "is said to possess a rare treasure of very many English scalps," acquired as booty when he worked for the French during the French and Indian War.[42] He had acquired his reputation in 1757. The British surrendered Fort William Henry on the condition that the lives of the soldiers in garrison be spared. After that was agreed to, Saint-Luc, in Jefferson's words, "had every soul murdered in cold blood," 200 in all.[43]

Saint-Luc, Langlade, and the Western warriors were not about to acquiesce to restrictive British codes of conduct. As *commandant des sauvages*, Saint-Luc advised the British to unleash the Indians "contre les misérable Rebels," which meant "imposer de terreur sur les frontières." To achieve victory, he bluntly stated, "il faut brutaliser les affaires, assurément."[44]

According to German Colonel Johann Friedrich Specht, who assembled notes from a Braunschweig regiment that had grown accustomed to the "domiciliated" Iroquois auxiliaries, Saint-Luc's "Quatoais," or Ottawa, warriors stood apart. Formerly "the sworn enemies" of the English during the French and Indian War, they were now working for the British Crown, and even in an already violent war zone they were notable as "a very formidable and belligerent nation, but also harsh and mean."[45] Thus came into Burgoyne's camp leaders and warriors who would introduce a cold ruthlessness antithetical to British military etiquette. Where Burgoyne had preached civility to the Native warriors, Saint-Luc and Langlade encouraged the opposite.

In his London testimony on the abject failure of the Saratoga campaign, Burgoyne would condemn the Western Indians. Assessing the causes that led the Ottawa and other distant nations to walk away in the midst of the march toward Albany, he cited "Miss Macrea" by name, claiming that her death was the pivot point in British/Native American relations. In his opinion, the defection of the warriors was the direct result of his response to the "murder" and the subsequent "restraints" he had placed on them.

That, in turn, left his army exposed by the time he engaged with Gates's reinvigorated forces at Saratoga in October.[46]

In defending himself and the loss of key auxiliaries, Burgoyne denounced the Western Indians' "depravity," "ferocity," "rapacity," "ill-humour," "mutinous disposition," "evil passions," and "wild honour." That last accusation—"wild honour"—fits the tale of homicide as told by Thacher, Anburey, Wilkinson, Digby, Standish, as well as Burgoyne himself: The rules of Native American warfare regarding credit for the right to McCrea's capture, totally incomprehensible to the British, led to a quarrel and ultimately to her honor killing.

Both the timing of the death a few days after the arrival of the new warriors, and the circumstantial evidence coming from a number of different military accounts, point to the Ottawa, Winnebago, and other Western warriors as the likely murderers of Jane McCrea.[47] Three days after they arrived, regaled in bird feathers and animal skins, Burgoyne himself imagined the "great enormities" that they were capable of.[48] One American soldier grimly noted the consequences of their presence: "The Indians are all around us, they are very bold, they often kill and scalp sentries and others, in sight of the army; they have killed and scalp'd about 60 men, women and children, making no distinction between Whigs or Tories."[49]

Though records often identify the Ottawa as the specific killers, almost all accounts of her death were written by the British, who rarely distinguished warriors of one Western nation from another. Given that, the only conclusion to be reached is that it was a warrior from the Great Lakes who killed McCrea.

Samuel Standish also mentioned the "wild honour" of the Western Indians in his interview with Jared Sparks in 1830. He said, "there were two chiefs in the party . . . one was a winnea & the other a Kahnawake [a Canadian tribe also known as Caughnawaga]. The quarrel was between them." Tehoragwanegen, a mixed-race Caughnawaga/Mohawk chief known as Thomas Williams, corroborated that account. He worked in the Burgoyne camp and had descended from one of the white families captured in Deerfield in 1704. By his account— written decades later by his son, the Reverend Eleazer Williams—David Jones, out of concern for his fiancée's safety, had asked Langlade to employ "Ottawas, Chippeways, Menominies, and Winnebagos . . . to bring Miss McCrea into the camp." Langlade agreed to the plan, but made a mistake by employing "two chiefs of different bands" to carry out the mission, "each ignorant of the object of the other in the enterprise. One of these had succeeded in getting the young lady safely in their hands, when the other party coming up found the object of their pursuit already obtained, and their head warrior demanded of the other party to give her up to him and his friends, as they had been sent by Captain Jones to bring her in." According to Tehoragwanegen, "the former replied, 'We are on a similar errand, and the bird is in our hands.' Upon which a contest ensued between the leaders, and in the affray the lady was murdered."

Tehoragwanegen urged his fellow Iroquois chiefs to ask Burgoyne "to put an end to this inhuman conduct" by the Western Indians, which the general did, but "in such a manner that they were offended, and soon after deserted from the army." According to the same account, on July 24, two days before the killing, David Jones had approached Tehoragwanegen in the British advance camp "for assistance in bringing the young lady within the British lines," but the warrior wisely "declined to undertake so delicate and dangerous an enterprise." Tehoragwanegen said to Jones, "you will have to conquer the country; if you succeed you will have your white squaw," adding "she is now safe, and to attempt to take her by force by our Indians may endanger her life, as there may be a skirmish in so doing."

Tehoragwanegen was in effect telling Jones that the Native warriors deployed toward Fort Edward that day were to terrorize pickets, not rescue maidens. If they truly were being sent out with dual orders—to harass and kill some people and save others—that would be a recipe for disaster. He made a point of exonerating his fellow Mohawk while condemning the Western nations. Years later, his son, then a missionary, was told in Green Bay that, "a Winnebago chief related to him more than once of his having a hand in this murder."[50]

A British noble, Lord Francis Napier, a nineteen-year-old lieutenant in one of Burgoyne's light infantry companies, further corroborated the Tehoragwanegen-Standish-Burgoyne account blaming a Western warrior. In a brief journal entry for July 27, he wrote, "one of the Ottawas the Evening before having scalped a Young Girl."[51] Another British officer whose identity is unknown but whose journal survives, wrote on the 27th of "one of the Ottawan Savages thro' Jealousy and Spite most inhumanly scalped a Young Woman about 17 Years of Age, upon a dispute arising about whose property she was. The woman's Name was McCrea, of an Amicable Character, and was to have been married to a Young Man, an officer belonging to the American Volunteer Corps, in the King's service." No accident, it was "Murder, for Murder I must call it."[52]

After Jane McCrea's killing, the fate of her corpse generated as much speculation as did her murder. A Yale professor, Benjamin Silliman, published a statement from James McCrea, stating that John McCrea, Jane's brother, heard news of their sister's death the evening of the killing. After dispatching his family to the safety of Albany, John "repaired himself to the American camp, where he found his sister's corpse, shockingly mangled. Two of the neighboring women, whom he had brought with him, washed and dressed her remains, and he had her interred with one Lieutenant Van Vechten three miles south of Fort Edward. She was twenty-three years of age."[53]

Standish said that "The bodies of Miss McCrea, & Lieut. Van Vechten were first brought into Fort Edward. They were then buried in the same place about three miles below the fort." William Scudder, an officer, wrote in 1794 that "The next day I was a pall-bearer to assist in conveying my good friend [Van Vechten] to his last retreat, which could not be done with dry eyes; he was buried with the honors of war. Miss M'Crea was also buried in the same grave with him."[54] Private Luther Shaw testified in his pension application that he was there when "Miss McRea, who had been killed by the Indians, was brought in, and the body laid out in an Officer's Marquee." Clearly visible was "the wound of the tomahawk that had been struck into the breast."[55] No mention was made of a gunshot wound.

Epaphras Hoyt, a resident of Deerfield, Massachusetts, interviewed local residents who were part of the Saratoga campaign. One veteran remembered a detachment finding "the slain [pickets] horribly mangled, among whom was an officer." They then spotted McCrea's shoes "upon a twig." Her body emerged when "the brush was cleared away." The detachment removed two bodies from the site, hers and that of the "officer," who was Lieutenant Van Vechten.[56] They were "conveyed down the river and buried with military honors on the east side of the road, north of a small stream then called Sauncher's Creek," now known as Black House Creek. The site was "a small distance north of a house since known by the name of the Black House tavern."[57]

Hoyt's version, from an undisclosed source, is similar to one proposed by William Leete Stone, a nineteenth-century authority on McCrea, in which a detachment took her body and that of a Lieutenant Palmer (most likely Van Vechten) to the same location south of Fort Edward. Stone said that Colonel Morgan Lewis, the man claiming to have seen her the morning of her killing, supervised the burial.[58] James Holden, the official historian of New York State, had evidence that John McCrea came to the burial; adding to that, an anonymous report from the front, published in Philadelphia, claimed that en route to burial, the "maid's corpse was brought to Snook Hill [near the McCrea farm on the west side of the Hudson], last night." Holden added a tidbit about a soldier named Elijah Sweet standing guard "over the remains of Jane the night before burial."[59]

Asa Fitch, a resident of Salem, twenty miles east of Fort Edward, took oral histories of elderly residents who remembered Jane McCrea. His papers proliferate with varying—and usually contradictory—recollections of her being attacked and killed. Only a few of the stories describe her burial. Robert Blake said that the British burned the bodies of most of the deceased Patriots they encountered. However, he believed McCrea "was not buried by the Americans, for they had all fled, but by the tories in the neighborhood. My uncle's folks assisted in her burial, and showed me her grave only a few days after it." If that was the case, she was momentarily laid to rest near where she was killed, slightly north of Fort Edward. Then, "she was taken up, and carried down to the Black House and reburied."[60]

The name of the enslaved woman that Ivory Hovey mentioned in his July 27 letter to Gates was Dinah. Asa Fitch related her story of seeing Jane, dressed in "a light chintz frock" over "a black callamink" (a calamanco, or petticoat, made from worsted wool). Dinah recalled McCrea was found with parts of the dress cut off. The "body was placed on a float in the river, for the purpose of bringing it down to her brother's, near Snook Hill. But Mrs. [John] Mc[Crea] said she did not want it brought there, so they stopped some ways above [near Black House], and buried it on the shore of the river."[61]

Fitch also acquired from Warren Bell gruesome details of the time her remains were disinterred and reburied in the Fort Edward Burying Ground in 1822, a mile north of her original grave near Black House. "The coffin was made with wrought nails 3 inches long. The bones were in a good state of preservation. There was only a little hair about the back part of her head: fine, short, and red, like horsehair." The hair may have reddened over time. Her clothing was "all decayed and gone." The back of the skull "was fractured and driven in; a portion of it, shaped like an inverted 'A' two inches long had its apex driven in two louver angles holding it in its place." Bell said he pushed "the depressed apex out into its natural position, as much as I could, with my fingers, but could not get it perfectly back." As for Van Vechten, Bell had the coffin opened to confirm he was male and that his group had correctly identified McCrea.[62]

Doctor William Norton led the 1822 disinterment team. Fitch's interview with him, however, did not entirely jibe with Bell's story. In Norton's account, the grave was four feet deep, the coffin "made of white pine." The bones "were of a large size," which caused the crew to doubt momentarily they had the right skeleton. The small strands of hair were black, not red. He did confirm blunt force trauma as the cause of death. "There was a fracture of skull, on top of the head, about the middle of the sagittal bone [the front-to-back suture], . . . some 2 or 3 inches long—quite too large to have been made by a bullet." At the time, Norton recalled, this discovery refuted one theory that Americans had accidentally shot her to death. For the reinternment, he summoned a Presbyterian minister to deliver an address and arranged the erection of a "plain tombstone." Too plain, by some accounts. As one citizen remarked, "What an outrage was that which moved her bones to this spot, and then in it niggardly [way], only gave her this paltry tombstone!"[63]

At the 1822 reburial, she was placed next to Sarah McNeil in a brick-lined vault.[64] McNeil had survived and became a raconteur of the July 26 ordeal. The reinternment ceremony was "solemn and impressive," according to Jared Sparks. "A procession of young men and maidens followed the relics" and "wept in silence when the earth was again closed over them."[65] The Reverend Hooper Cumming, journeying from Albany to officiate, read from the Book of Micah, which includes a passage on the sinful misuse of power.

In 1852, her remains were again exhumed and moved to Union Cemetery, where an iron palisade surrounded her plot, creating the sense of an outdoor shrine. At one point in the late nineteenth century, parts of the enclosure and tombstone had to be replaced because of "relic hunters and souvenir fiends" who had "badly scarred" it.[66] In 2003 and 2005, a forensic team spearheaded by archaeologist David Starbuck, dug down to the coffin to discover the two skeletons. When the crew separated McCrea's skeleton from McNeil's and reassembled both on a table, analysis showed she was in her 20s, petite, between 5 feet 2 inches and 5 feet 4 inches tall, with no evidence of any injuries on the bones that were still in the grave. To the team's surprise, her reassembled remains revealed a picked-over skeleton. In addition to not finding her skull, also missing were vertebrae, ribs, and hand and foot bones.[67]

There had been suspicion since 1852—reported in a local newspaper—that a box containing Jane McCrea's bones had been "broken open and nearly all the bones stolen," and "scattered all over the country."[68] One story has the "leading citizens" of Fort Edward taking souvenirs, and a "dr. Sanford of New York" making away with her skull, said to be "kept on a shelf in a cabinet."[69] The forensic team placed her remaining bones in a new coffin, a Presbyterian minister conducted another service, and she was reburied.[70] When the town replaced her cracked tombstone, the dedication ceremony featured the singing of the "Star-Spangled Banner," a recitation of the Pledge of Allegiance, and a reading of the preamble of the United States Constitution.

Bone collecting was popular, often conducted for ethnographic purposes—usually for phrenological study of nonwhites or for medical investigations into the mysteries of the human body.[71] It was also an obsession. In 1676, Pilgrims had hung the remains of Metacomet, the vilified Wampanoag chief known as King Philip, on trees and pikes. The Reverend Cotton Mather admitted to ripping the jaw bone off the skull of the "Blasphemous" Indian.[72] Some of the bones of the Reverend George Whitefield, who was Reverend James McCrea's mentor, were unearthed and stolen in the nineteenth century.[73] Most famously, George Washington's dentist, John Greenwood, extracted the president's last tooth, mounted it in a golden locket as if it were a sacred relic from the body of Saint Anthony of Padua, and then attached the locket to his watch fob.[74]

Collectors fetishized Jane McCrea's bones, the cracked skull being most desirous. They were material conduits to a moment of high drama, touchstones redolent with Revolutionary aura, the holy relics of an American martyr.[75] The Fort Ticonderoga Museum houses one of her ribs, accompanied by a statement from the donor that "Mr. O. O. Hunter, of Fort Edward, who participated in the [burial] work secured one of her ribs, here shown."[76] Another resident, Mrs. Joseph Clark, casually admitted, "my brother had 3 of Jane McCrea's teeth, and gave two of them to Aunt Shiland."[77]

5.

THE NATIVE AMERICAN DILEMMA

FROM THE BRITISH point of view at the beginning of the Revolution, employing Native warriors was a double-edged sword. By their logic, the services of the warriors were critical in a northern wilderness where a conventional army could not apply its traditional forms of linear march and close-order engagement on open ground. From their experiences during the French and Indian War (1754–1763), when the Huron Confederacy sided with the French and the Six Nation Iroquois Confederacy fought with the British, they understood that Native Americans could play a critical military role along the New York frontier. Now, less than two decades later, the British turned again to the attractive Native American skill set: stealth, independence, mobility, scouting, raiding, wood running, surprise, fearlessness, as well as intimate knowledge of the wilderness terrain.[1]

Doubling the allure of the Native Americans' *petite guerre* tactics, the British felt they were "obliged to run a race" against the Americans for Native American services; if they could not cajole them to their side by any means necessary, the Patriots surely would. Trebling their appeal, total British forces were only about half of what Whitehall thought requisite to achieve the extravagant goal of splitting New England from the other rebellious colonies by slicing down from Montreal and up from the city of New York. If dividing, according to military minds, surely led to conquering, then the British army would need help. While the British navy was unsurpassed across the globe, their land forces were insufficient for the task of defeating and occupying the vastness of British North America.

Given such low numbers, the British ministry hoped to deliver a black eye to the rebels, show who rules, and quickly return them to the British fold. Having failed at a fatal jab, the ministry adopted in 1777 an approach that would bludgeon Americans into compliance. The problem with that strategy was the lack of enough ground forces of their own, forcing the government to augment British regulars with Native auxiliaries, Loyalist battalions, and thousands of paid German auxiliaries. Despite the British government's opinion that American rebels were certifiably treasonous and their rebellion damnably criminal, the raw fact on the ground was that Britain did not have the manpower to execute their audacious plan by themselves. To British strategists enamored with *realpolitik*, Native warriors would hold a special office, spreading terror in advance of the regulars, softening local resistance, and thus saving the main force for direct exchange with the Americans.

At the same time, everyone in the British ministries and most members of Parliament knew perfectly well that by involving Native warriors the British generals operating in America would have to tolerate indiscriminate cruelties that were not consistent with accepted military etiquette. Nonetheless, that was going to be the price to be paid if the American rebellion were to be extinguished. Employing Native American warriors and turning a blind eye to the occasional infraction of British rules was unavoidable.

With that in mind, Burgoyne gathered his diverse army on June 20 at Cumberland Point on the northern shore of Lake Champlain, where he delivered a proclamation laying out his agenda. In the coming weeks, he declared, this "unnatural Rebellion" and the "completest system of tyranny" it represents will be addressed by "the power, the justice, and when properly sought the mercy of the King." Burgoyne swore to protect the "temperate" inhabitants who supported the Crown, Jane McCrea being a good example, in theory. At the same time, he declared that his forces were lethal instruments, prepared "to overtake the harden'd Enemies of Great Britain" with crack battalions, along with "the Indian Forces under my direction, and they amount to Thousands." For those civilians who should resist his authority or insult the Crown, he warned, "devastation, famine & every concomitant horror" would await.[2] Knowing full well the challenge of forcing Native warriors to abide by British rules of engagement, Burgoyne projected confidence that everything was under control.

Stinging parodies of his bombastic declaration captured the ominous mood along the Hudson. In one, an anonymous writer composed grotesque rhyming couplets to mock Burgoyne's public manifesto: "Let loose the dogs of Hell/ Ten thousand Indians, who shall yell/ And foam and tear, and grin and roar/ And drench their moccasins in gore." Native allies of Britain, the satire went on, will have free reign "to scalp your heads, and kick your shins/ And rip your [hearts], and flay your skins." These objectives, the writer added wickedly, were the general's "bowels' yearnings."[3]

The British—and Burgoyne, too—deluded themselves that perhaps they could avoid brutalities altogether. As the British Superintendent of Indians Affairs argued, "The terror of their name, without any acts of savage cruelty, will tend much to the speedy termination of the Rebellion."[4] British officials in the political hothouse of Whitehall supposed the rebels would just throw down their arms whenever they spotted fierce-looking Natives. Warriors, the thinking went, might prove to be more of a psychological threat than a physical one. In Burgoyne's words, the plan was "to speak daggers, but use none." "Dread," he projected, would preclude "the commission of severity."[5] Even George III, surrounded by advisors assuring strategic success, embraced the unrealistic vision of Native Americans successfully integrating into the British plan, having stated in a letter to Prime Minister Frederick North, "Indians must be employed, and this measure must be avowedly directed."[6]

As it turned out, George Germain, Secretary of State for the American Department and architect of military planning for North America, would have little leverage over the methods of Native American combat. As he would rudely discover over the summer of 1777, if you order warriors, you get warriors. Joseph Brant, the Mohawk leader of the Wolf Clan, known in Haudenosaunee as Thayendanegea (meaning two sticks bound together), spoke the cold unromantic truth of Native American warfare when he preached independence of mind to those warriors who would join the British: be autonomous, and only fight under Native rules and Native command.[7]

Burgoyne nonetheless walked into the British fool's paradise. In his "Thoughts for Conducting the War from the Side of Canada," he envisioned "a thousand or more Savages" obediently at his side, working under "the strictest discipline" and sufficient in numbers to "alarm" and "awe" the rebels of the Hudson Valley.[8] British war documents, including Burgoyne's, obsessively used the word "savages" to refer to Native peoples, which itself was a contradiction of the expressed goal of intimidation without violence. But in his imagination Burgoyne envisioned "irregulars" adhering to the civilized British script, while in his heart he knew he was grossly misrepresenting the kind of combat that seasoned Native warriors would bring to the field.

Most of the Six Nation Confederacy of Iroquois, or more correctly the Haudenosaunee, meaning People of the Longhouse—Seneca (Onon'dowagah), Mohawk (Kanien'kehá:ka), Oneida (Onyota'a:ká), Tuscarora (Skarù:re), Onondaga (Ononda'gaga'), and Cayuga (Gayogohó:no')—initially hoped to avoid involvement altogether.[9] Chief Little Abraham of the Mohawks quaintly vowed, "not to take part, but as it is a family affair, to sit still and see you fight it out."[10] The Haudenosaunee's hard-fought union, which dated back to the ancient days of Hiawatha, had put them at peace with one another for centuries. They were now a settled, agricultural people, growing crops of beans, squash, corn, and fruit.

That life had been gravely weakened, first by the French and then by the British, who militarized their lands and Christianized their people. The Europeans also brought catastrophic diseases, most lethally measles, influenza, and smallpox, which decimated whole populations. Ambitious white settlers relentlessly encroached on historic Native lands in defiance of the 1763 Royal Proclamation line that divided European and Iroquois territories, which once stretched uninterrupted from Pennsylvania to the Saint Lawrence River.[11] The French and Indian War, mostly fought in Haudenosaunee territory, further altered relations with Europeans. After the British victory, white traders aggressively expanded mutually beneficial networks throughout the frontier, making Haudenosaunee neutrality or a war alliance with the Americans a problematic choice.

The British had the upper hand over the Americans in winning the Haudenosaunee to their side. They had a long history with the tribes and they were in possession of what amounted to seductive treats. In order to recruit, reward, and then arm American and Canadian warriors for battle against American rebels, the British could disgorge a cornucopia of presents and supplies. William Knox, Germain's undersecretary, and John Robinson, Parliament's treasurer, procured and shipped boatloads of linens, blankets, lace, ribbons, combs, sponges, hats, tobacco, pipes, mirrors, gorgets, buckles, earrings, vermillion pigment, "very gaudy feathers," and medals featuring the king's portrait. The gifts arrived in boxes and bales, and as effective

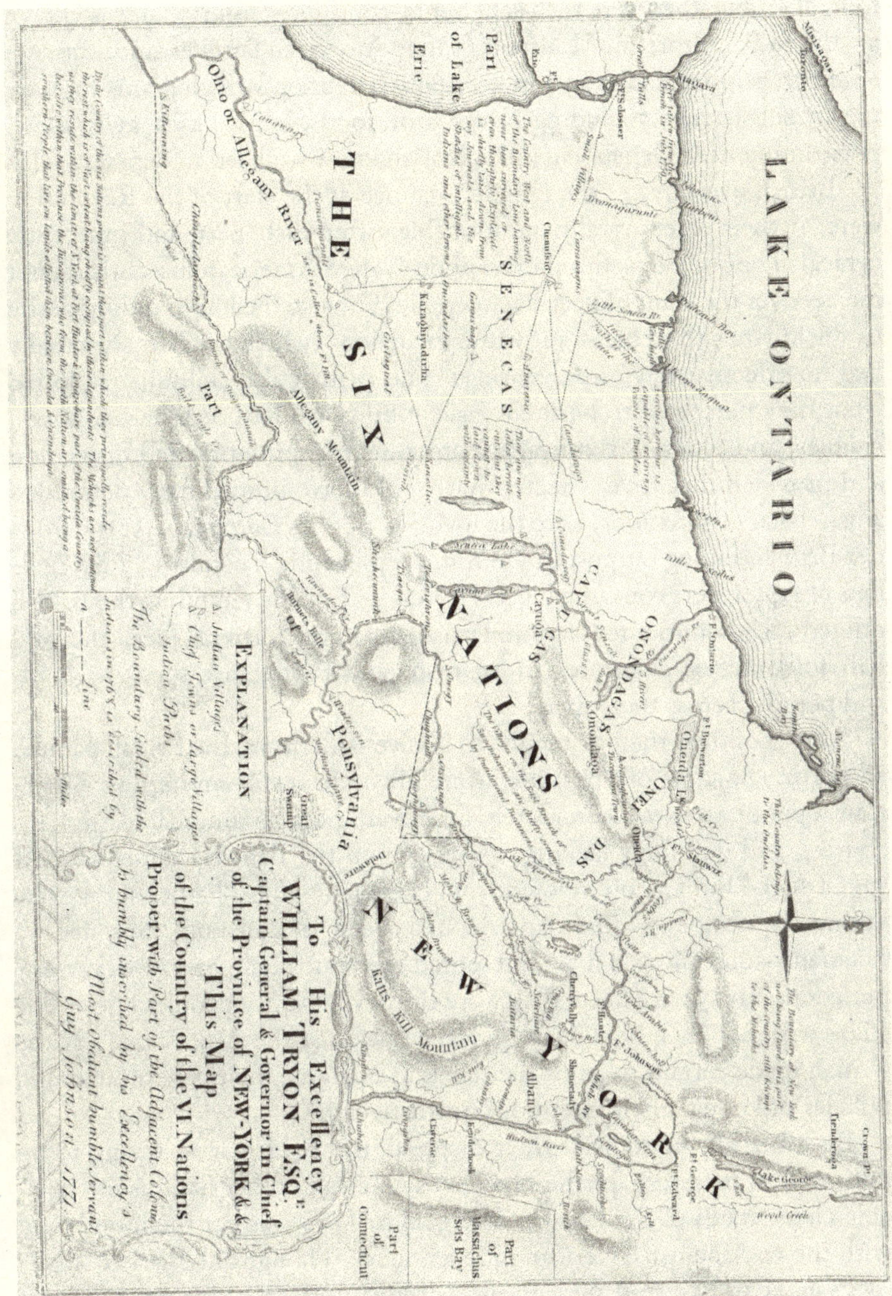

Guy Johnson, 1771, "To his excellency William Tryon Esqr., captain general & governor in chief of the province of New-York & &: This map of the country of the VI. nations proper, with part of the adjacent colonies is humbly inscribed." Engraved in 1851. New York Public Library, Lionel Pincus and Princess Firyal Map Division.

tools of empire they were then sent out by consignees from what was known as "the Indian Store" in Montreal. Native American families since the seventeenth century had grown increasingly reliant on British goods for day-to-day subsistence, including broadcloth, foods, knives, axes, awls, metal pots, and guns.[12] Dependency, the British knew well, led to dependability.

British overtures to the Haudenosaunee at the start of the Revolution were, at their core, morally questionable, often dishonest, and inherently cynical. Their scare tactics preyed upon Native American insecurities, not merely over the want of necessary supplies but also the longstanding desire to shield lands from incessant white incursions (which the British actually had no effective way of preventing). The British also skillfully exploited what they perceived to be their susceptibility to flattery, tobacco, liquor, baubles, and plunder. Extravagant amounts of rum lubricated discussion and provided incentive, a tactic that would have immediately defrauded any normal negotiations, were the involved powers European. At the frontier British trading outpost in Detroit, deep in Indian country, 17,520 gallons of liquor were consumed in 1779 alone.[13] Equally tempting, the British offered cash bounties for captured prisoners in the form of "Joes," the gold half-Johannes coins minted in Spanish- and Portuguese-speaking lands and popular across the Americas.[14]

As part of their rhetorical pitch to Native Americans, the British painted an alarming picture of a possible future life under a still-mysterious American republic that was completely unproven, possibly unreliable, perhaps abusive, and definitely lacking a king, whom the British shamelessly invoked as the Indians' omnipotent yet benevolent white "Father and never-failing Protector."[15] The British had been a constant presence in Haudenosaunee lives. They represented the status quo, and however imperfect that may have been, they were the devils Native peoples knew. The tribes may not have held deep grievances against the Americans, but the British made certain to paint the rebels as upstarts, their government and policies unknown, their intentions untrustworthy.

By using all the tools at their disposal, the British were trying to do nothing less than reshape the Haudenosaunee and other nations into reliable client states of the Crown. The goal in 1775 was get them on board with the war against American independence. Though the British unfailingly spoke to Native Americans in flattering and courteous terms, in private they held them in contempt. They thought them spoiled, childish, pig-headed, ungovernable, and primitive. They wanted Native warriors to join their military missions, but did not intend to integrate chiefs into the chain of command, thus disrespecting them as allies, which in turn prevented the British from ever gaining control over the warriors.

Though they considered scalping barbaric, the British did not think twice about using gifts, supplies, and money as rewards for bringing ferocity to the field, or delivering captured prisoners, or pursuing lethal skirmishes with pickets, patrols, and guards that ended in scalping. Jane McCrea and many other civilians never deserved the brutal ends they experienced at the hands of Native American warriors, and to be sure their deaths were not part of the plan, but the money, goods, and rum that saturated the Native-British relationship led to a moral derangement that turned bodies into expendable commodities.

Britain's multinational strategy for the Northern Expedition, which boldly joined German, Native, and Loyalist forces under one roof, had inherent problems involving sharp differences in culture, race, customs, language, and military tactics. A more perceptive colonizer would have known that the nations and tribes of British North America, stretching from the east coast to the western Great Lakes, represented strikingly divergent cultures. The British were also naïve and arrogant to think that Native warriors—having been imported into an incomprehensible family spat among white Europeans, and truly not angry enough at the "rebels" to kill them—could be persuaded to understand, never mind follow, white-man rules. Warriors were being asked to discern the differences between Loyalist whites and Patriot whites, who were one and the same two years earlier. Look fierce, they were told, but don't behave savagely. Spread terror, but please refrain from scalping unless the victim is an officially approved target. Above all, put aside hundreds of years of inured combat techniques and cultural imperatives in order to proceed under the British doctrine of *jus in bello*. That is, fight in a just, humane way.[16]

"European humanity" was Burgoyne's way of putting it.[17] An entirely foreign concept that Whitehall wanted First Nations to abide by, *jus in bello* established a clear distinction between acceptable and unacceptable behavior in a combat zone. Wounding and killing were permissible when justified. However, excessive brutality against the enemy and all violence against noncombatants, especially women, children, the infirm, and the elderly, was strictly forbidden. These were the rules of warfare Burgoyne had in mind for his Native American allies when he stepped off the *Apollo* on May 6, 1777, at the dock below the ramparts of Quebec.[18] His operational agenda was to uphold the rules, make all the moving parts mesh, execute the strategic plan, and teach his ancient warriors new tricks.

As it turned out, Burgoyne was overmatched by a complex situation not amenable to fiat. *Jus in bello* may have been possible in formalized European wars between clearly defined states, but along New York's borderlands, where Britons, Loyalist Americans, Patriot Americans, and Native Americans each believed they were fighting for their very survival in North America, extreme violence eventually quashed the civilized rules that all parties initially favored. "Existential warfare," as it is termed—that is, doing whatever it takes to avoid extinction—led all parties into unspeakable brutality that by the summer of 1777 was accelerating out of Burgoyne's or anyone's control.[19]

As a group, the Haudenosaunee had learned to negotiate life under British authority, but insurmountable frictions between the tribes naturally arose when they had to debate siding with the British, allying with the Americans, or remaining neutral. Staying neutral during an intra-British civil war was attractive, yet it put the Haudenosaunee at risk of alienating one power or the other, or both. Equally problematic, by remaining passive on the sidelines they would not be fighting for their vital stake within the vast New York and Canadian expanse. If the prospect of turning their backs on the conflict by letting the whites fight it out among themselves was too risky, then they had to pick a winner, hoping their allies would live up to promises to protect their sovereignty, while at the same time praying, in a worst-case scenario, that if they picked incorrectly the winner would refrain from military and economic retribution. The "Imperial Crisis" was not their war. Regardless, all six Haudenosaunee nations found themselves gambling with their lives and the future of their cultures, with full knowledge of the catastrophic repercussions awaiting if they made the wrong choice. As it turned out, all of their three options would have ultimately and inevitably led to their ruination.

The charismatic, erudite, and formidable Mohawk Joseph Brant promoted the British among his fellow Haudenosaunee. He had fought with the British during the French and Indian War, was educated in Moor's Charity School, run by Eleazar Wheelock in Connecticut, was a devoted Anglican, and had command of English and some ability in Greek and Hebrew. At the beginning of the war in 1775, he and Guy Johnson, the new British superintendent for Indian affairs, convened 1,700 Native Americans near Montreal with the goal of pulling their people out of neutrality and into the British camp. Brant's position on which side the Haudenosaunee should align was always calculated: the Americans "began this rebellion to be sole Masters of the Continent."[20] They may seem benign but don't be fooled into thinking they are your friends or that they will respect your lands should they be victorious. Guy Carleton, the governor of Quebec province, posed to the Haudenosaunee the key question during his tour with Brant: "Are you" willing to "suffer them to make horses and oxen of you, to put you into wheelbarrows, and to bring us all into slavery?"[21] In Brant's view, a decision to join Burgoyne in his epic campaign was not driven by love of Britain or hatred of the Americans, but security for themselves and their future, and from the accelerating American expansion into their lands.

The nations that eventually joined the British (Seneca, Mohawk, Cayuga, Onondaga) often did so under duress and overt threat. Carleton made that abundantly clear in his failed recruitment pitch to the outlying Oneida and Tuscarora. After sympathizing with their "melancholy" dilemma (stay neutral or join the rebels or the British), he issued a blunt warning to the Oneida: "To take up Arms against the King is death." He invoked George III as their generous "Father," who, until now, had "spared the shedding of their blood," in "hopes" of restoring the "proper sense of their duty and obedience" to the Crown. If instead they joined the "insolent and wanton" rebels, he promised that Oneida "blood should be spilt in large quantities."[22]

Late in 1775, five months after the Battle of Bunker Hill had escalated the conflict into a war, Brant took his Native-first campaign to London to negotiate the future of North America. He crossed the Atlantic aboard the *Adamant*, along with Guy Johnson, Brook Watson (soon to be the subject of an epic painting by John Singleton Copley), and Ethan Allen (in chains, taken prisoner near Montreal). Sixty-five years earlier, three Mohawk chiefs had come to London on a similar diplomatic mission under the sponsorship of Pieter Schuyler, who was General Philip Schuyler's great-uncle. One of the "wild American chiefs" on the mission was Brant's grandfather, Peter, then considered a representative of "a very rude and uncivilized nation."[23]

Now, however, Joseph Brant was the living model of British hopes for the Europeanization of Native peoples: articulate, refined, diplomatic, and Christian. He dazzled Britons, rekindling fanciful thoughts that Native peoples were noble savages in possession of natural virtue, and thus on track to civilization, according to British standards. Brant took rooms near Guildhall, London's city hall, went to the Newmarket races, joined the Masons, attended a masquerade ball in full warrior regalia, researched Native American portraits at the British Museum, met with George III at St.

James Palace in a bespoke tailored suit, and artfully settled with Foreign Secretary Germain "the grievances of the Six Nations on account of their lands," in exchange for a pledge to support the Crown against the rebellious Americans. The Scottish diarist James Boswell, writing in the *London Magazine*, rhapsodized over Brant's easy meshing with British locutions, manners, speech, and humor.[24]

To the British he embodied a romantic ideal, an understandable supposition since his conduct was impeccable and his aura compelling, especially if George Romney's portrait stands as accurate measure. Painted in London, it shows Brant as a handsome Mohawk gentleman, dignified in expression and refined in pose. He elegantly holds his left hand at his waist, as if he were a Native American Cicero about to address an assembly.[25] Though he actually wore western clothes in London, he dressed traditionally for appearances at public events and during visits to Romney's studio, smartly decked out in red leggings, a silver cuff on the right arm, a feather *kastoweh* on his head, and a green blanket—"gorgeously decorated with a border of red"—draped over one shoulder.[26] Around his neck hangs a silver gorget engraved with the royal coat of arms, a gift from the king. Immense chain earrings, representative of the Covenant Chain linking the Haudenosaunee to Britain, cascade below one shoulder. In his right hand, he good-naturedly holds a tomahawk—the weapon he used to crack open skulls in America—as if it were now an accessory.

Beneath Brant's polite exterior, however, there resided a consummate Mohawk warrior. Upon his return to America in the summer of 1776, he fought with the British during the invasion of New York. Then, disguising himself to sneak through American lines, he arrived in Iroquoia, adorned with official British blessing. Arguing to his brethren for the abandonment of neutrality, he announced the agreement he struck with Whitehall guaranteeing land rights, along with the related assertion that the Americans did not intend to respect them should they prevail over the British. His proof of American ill will was George Washington himself, who intended to acquire 20,000 acres on Ohio's Kanawha River, a land dense with Haudenosaunee and Algonquin peoples.

To his fellow Haudenosaunee, however, Brant seemed too cozy with Whitehall to be fully trusted. Yet, he was undeterred. Surrounded by a hundred Loyalists and Mohawk warriors already committed to him and to the British cause, he barnstormed through Iroquoia to convince the wavering Six Nations to recall their Covenant Chain, renew their devotion to the king, and pledge themselves to stand behind British power and stability.

George Romney, *Thayendanegea (Joseph Brant)*. 1776. Oil on canvas. Ottawa, National Gallery of Canada, Transfer from the Canadian War Memorials, 1921.

Brant's persuasive rhetoric led to a vast conference run by British Major John Butler at Irondequoit on the southern bank of Lake Ontario in mid-1776. Over the course of a week, the Seneca, the most populous of the Iroquois, were flooded with barrels of rum and overwhelmed by mountains of trinkets, from beads to bells, all presented as tokens of the king's love for his children. For the attendees that he had intoxicated with liquor, Butler contrasted enduring British friendship and patronage with devious American intentions to seize their lands and exterminate their race.[27] The rebels were weak, he insisted, and deserving of all the punishment that was their due for gross insubordination. Should Brant's Indian brothers pledge themselves to the British cause, the Crown was prepared to provide warriors with all necessary weaponry and to recommit itself to the protection of Indian sovereignty. Meanwhile, those warriors ready to join the war effort would never have to worry about their loved ones at home, because families, the British promised, would be lavished with "victuals and clothing and every thing that they wanted."[28]

Despite the shamelessness of the British offer, the inclination of the Seneca to remain neutral dissolved into a vow to take up the hatchet for Britain. In time, other nations in New York, the Great Lakes, Canada, and the Ohio Country enlisted in the imperial cause. Three factors tipped the scales toward Britain. First, the Haudenosaunee had sided with Britain in the French and Indian War a decade and a half earlier. Second, they had multiple connections with British officials and had especially revered the former British superintendent, Sir William Johnson, who died in 1774. And third, they feared the existential threat posed by the potent American presence building to the East. In the end, many of the Mohawk and Seneca fought with the British in the Mohawk Valley campaign under the command of Colonel Barry St. Leger, while other nations from the west and Canada joined Burgoyne along the Hudson.

The British ability to win over most Native Americans created consternation in the Continental Congress, which as early as 1775 feared that imported British "arms, ammunition, and clothing," entirely "necessary to their subsistence," would induce "several Nations" to "take up arms against these colonies." Doubling the American predicament was the low status of the Northern Army, which was in desperate need of manpower after suffering a devastating loss at Quebec early in 1776. Generals Schuyler and Gates inherited the remains of that force, accurately described by one officer as "this Retreating, Raged, Starved, lousey, thievish, Pockey Army."[29]

Aware that Britain was mobilizing a sizable Native American force, Congress formed an Indian Committee that included Benjamin Franklin, John Jay, and Richard Henry Lee, and it established a Northern Indian Department officially dedicated to "securing and preserving the friendship of the Indian Nations."[30] Simultaneously, Washington instructed Schuyler and the Northern Army to "use every Method . . . to conciliate their Favour, and to this End, are authorised to promise them [the Haudenosaunee] a punctual Payment, of the Allowance Congress have determined on," for the capture and delivery of "Officers and Privates belonging to the King's

Army."[31] That notwithstanding, Washington conceded the "advantage which the enemy possesses over us, in having the means of making presents much more liberally than we can."[32]

The Marquis de Lafayette, writing in his diary a year later about the British technique for acquiring fealty, discerned that during the Revolution "all the savages were paid and protected by the English party: the Hurons and Iroquois committed their devastations on that whole frontier. Some baubles or a barrel of rum were sufficient to make them seize the tomahawk; they then rushed upon villages, burnt houses, destroyed harvests, massacred all, without regard to age or sex." To illustrate their rage most graphically, Lafayette turned to the example of Jane McCrea, "a young American girl, whom her lover, an English officer, was expecting, that their marriage might take place, was killed by the very savages he had sent to escort her."[33]

Because the Americans had so much less influence over all the Native Americans in the north, General Schuyler urged them to remain neutral in the face of British pressure. "This is a family quarrel between us and Old England," he had told assembled sachems in 1775. "*Brothers and Friends!*" he pleaded, "You Indians are not concerned in it. We don't wish you to take up the hatchet against the king's troops. We desire you to remain at home, and not join on either side, but keep the hatchet buried deep."[34] Though "this island now trembles" and "the wind whistles from almost every quarter," we "ask and desire you to love peace and maintain it, and to love and sympathise with us in our troubles." Be wary, "if application should be made to you by any of the king's unwise and wicked ministers to join on their side, we only advise you to deliberate, with great caution, and in your wisdom look forward to the consequences of a compliance."

While that sounded reasonable, the Americans could be as threatening as the British. One colonel stationed in the Mohawk Valley promised he would "burn all their houses, destroy their Towns & Cast the Mohawks with their Wifes & Children off of the face of the Earth," if they were to join the British.[35] Schuyler would have used all the same tactics of persuasion as the British, if only he could, but fiscal impoverishment restricted Congress to empty promises and real threats. With knowledge that Brant and Johnson were indefatigable in their efforts to win over the same nations, he desperately tried to sustain the Six Nations' commitment to neutrality by organizing his own meetings in Albany and German Flatts. Lasting two weeks in August of 1775, Schuyler's contingent, officially representing the Continental Congress, explained the nature of the dispute with the Crown. The Americans were not fighting for honor, he said, but for the assurance of civil rights and religious freedoms, two platforms that, so far, had only resonated with the Oneida, a nation that, as one Mohawk put it, has already "imbibed the principles of New England."[36] Schuyler implored his "brothers of the Six Nations" that the "twelve United Colonies" want to join them in a "chain of friendship so strong, that nothing but an evil spirit can or will attempt to break it."[37] In the American purview, the Six Nations should belong to them, not Britain.

The proceedings at the conference were protracted and formal, in part because Congress had written the speeches in Philadelphia and sent them northward. One observer said the American delivery was so larded with political theory that they might as well have read a chapter from John Locke's *Second Treatise of Government*. Yet evenings were enlivened by Indian entertainment. The Americans "turned out a Bull for the young Indians to hunt and kill . . . with arrows, knives, and hatchets." On another occasion, Native warriors came to town, "beating their drum, striking sticks together in Exact time and yelling after their Manner. They were almost intirely naked, and after singing some thing in the recitative manner . . . they would strike out into a Dance around the Fires with the most savage Contortions of Body & limb."[38]

The Native warriors were a sideshow, a spectacle for the Westerners. That masked the fact that Congress lacked material incentives, forcing legislators to issue more carrot-and-stick statements from Philadelphia. In one communiqué delivered by Schuyler, Congress argued to the Iroquois, "If we are enslaved, you cannot be free. If [the British] would not spare their own brother, of the same flesh and blood, would they spare you? If they burn our houses and ravage our lands, could yours be secure?" Portraying itself as a band of benign white brothers, Congress admonished the Haudenosaunee to reject the "cruel purposes" of the British, to walk away from the conflict, and to continue to "smoke your pipe in safety and contentment" under "the shade of your trees, and by the side of your streams." Congress hoped they would "look into your hearts, and be attentive," and not be fooled by "a few blankets or a little rum or powder."

Then, having dispatched with the niceties, Congress leveled armed threats. If nations siding with Britain should "hurt any of our people, we shall look upon you as our enemies, and treat you as the worst of enemies."[39] For the Mohawk, Congress promised especially dire consequences, "If you will be our Enemies now, we will never hereafter be your Friends and in a little while there will be no more Mohawks, and as people pass up and down this River they will say there once did live the Mohawks, who whilst they kept Faith were a respectable people: but becoming foolish, and false to their words, they are cast off from the Face of the Earth."[40]

The Oneida initially committed to neutrality. Back in 1775, they told Governor Jonathan Trumbull of Connecticut that "we love you both—old England and new. Should the great King of England apply to us for our aid—we shall deny him—and should the Colonies apply—we shall refuse."[41] However, the Oneida and the tiny band of allied Tuscarora pledged themselves fully to the American cause for a number of reasons: because of their proximity to Albany, a rebel capital, because of the trade, prosperity, and Christianization that came with that, because of the coaxing of Atiatoharóngwen, an African-Abenaki warrior known as Louis Cook, and through the extraordinary influence of the deeply admired Presbyterian minister Reverend Samuel Kirkland, who had been a missionary with them since 1766. As chief Good Peter explained the Oneida's logic, "the love of peace and the love of our land which gave us birth, supported our resolution."[42]

Schuyler, who privately despised the "haughty princes of the Wilderness" and eventually advocated the usurpation of Native lands, thanked them by promising, "I will do my utmost to make you love me as much as I do you."[43] At a liquor-soaked treaty convention to cement the alliance with the Oneida, he observed, "the Consumption of provision and Rum is incredible. It equals that of an army of three thousand Men, although the *Indians* here are not above twelve hundred, including men, women, and children."[44] In that ocean of liquor, Schuyler asked the Oneida "to drink Health, peace and Liberty to your American Brethren and everlasting Friendship." Like the British before, he vouchsafed total protection for swearing allegiance to the American cause: "You will then partake of every Blessing we enjoy, and united with a free people your Liberty and Property will be safe."[45]

By the time of Burgoyne's Northern Expedition of 1777, the British had won the recruitment battle for Haudenosaunee services, with the exception of the Oneida and Tuscarora. In June, additional warriors from the Saint Lawrence River valley began assembling at the British position on the Boquet River on Lake Champlain. This was the first Native American gathering—comprising four of the six Iroquois nations, as well as Abenaki, Oswegatchi, Nipissing, Canasadaga, and Caughnawaga—that Burgoyne grandiloquently addressed. He opened by invoking "the troubles in America." Surely, these sagacious and faithful Indians who are devoted to "The great King" have "observed the violated rights of the parental power they love, and burned to vindicate them." The warriors, he said, have exercised admirable restraint against the contemptible "apostates," but as of now, "Warriors, you are free—Go forth in might of your valour and your cause; strike at the common enemies of Great-Britain and America—disturbers of public order, peace, and happiness—destroyers of commerce, parricides of the state."[46]

At the same time, he added, they must do so under the principles of *jus in bello*: "Regulate your passions when they overbear, to point out where it is nobler to spare than to revenge, to discriminate degrees of guilt, to suspend the up-lifted stroke, chastise and not to destroy." In the past, "in taking the field you held yourselves authorized to destroy wherever you came, because every where you found an enemy." However, "the case is now very different. . . . I positively forbid bloodshed, when you are not opposed in arms. Aged men, women, children, and prisoners, must be held sacred from the knife or hatchet." There will be rewards for prisoners, "but you will be called to account for scalps."

Burgoyne acknowledged "your customs, which have affixed an idea of honour to such badges of victory," and thus scalps may be taken, only on the condition that they are from dead enemy combatants. "On no account, or pretence, or subtlety, or prevarication, are they to be taken from the wounded, or even dying; and still less pardonable, if possible, will it be held to kill men in that condition on purpose." Killing for scalps was forbidden, except in the case of "base lurking assassins, incendiaries, ravagers and plunderers," and even those required his, and only his, specific order.[47] In Burgoyne's blueprint, British officers would enforce the rules, though in reality they had little understanding of Native American customs and no ability to speak native languages. Nonetheless, with his rhetorical mission seemingly accomplished, Burgoyne showered food and rum on the gathering and then plotted how to put, in the words of a lieutenant, the "beastly intoxicated" allies to work.[48]

Burgoyne's naïveté was as impressive as his narcissism. He believed that thirty minutes of rousing rhetoric had fully convinced Native warriors to forego deep-rooted and unshakable practices of warfare, and, in their place, quietly acquiesce to the philosophy of *jus in bello*. He was so taken with his own speech that he assured his military colleagues he had "in a great measure Succeeded" in his effort "to keep up their Terror and avoid their cruelty."

Burgoyne's fatal error was treating Native Americans like actors in one of the London stage productions he had mounted in 1774 at the Drury Lane Theatre.[49] When venturing into the war zone of the American Revolution, he imagined he would write the script, visualize the action, and direct the performers. When the curtain rises over Lake Champlain, the drama would comprise three acts with a cast of thousands: heroic soldiers, intriguing foreigners, hundreds of wild men, and a handsome leading man. Take Fort Ticonderoga, march down the Hudson, and seize Albany, while General William Howe sends a column up the Hudson from New York and another British force cuts across New York from Lake Ontario and down the Mohawk River to join the climactic closing scene.

It was a compelling storyline, one in which Burgoyne perhaps saw himself as Bedford, the soldier/courtier in Shakespeare's *Henry VI*, a man of honor and integrity who fights the good fight to prevent the loss of English lands in France. Alternatively, he was in the role of the king in *Henry IV*, defeating the rebels at Shrewsbury. More likely, and unbeknownst to him, Burgoyne was inadvertently becoming Shakespeare's tormented lead in *Richard III*, as recently played on Drury Lane by his friend David Garrick, doomed to be visited on the battlefield by the ghosts of his victims. Burgoyne did not meet his death as Richard had at Bosworth Field, but his accumulated hubris would reach a final reckoning on the grand stage of Saratoga, encircled by Horatio Gates's Northern Army.

In the earliest stages of the British assault from Canada, in June, when he assembled a total of 9,500 men, Burgoyne's strategy worked well, as Native auxiliaries followed the general's script, hunting down scouting parties, harassing pickets, and projecting terror, all without harming civilians.[50] For capturing prisoners, his Native American auxiliaries received gold, as promised. Though their numbers were relatively small, their presence seemed enormous. One American sergeant reported they were "as thick as mosquitoes."[51] American Major-General Arthur St. Clair concurred, "the Woods are so Full of Indians that it is difficult for Partys to get through."[52] St. Clair wrote this in a letter that was intercepted by Burgoyne's Indians and that wound up in the British admiralty office in London, a measure of just how outmatched the Americans were.

The Indian-British marriage, though always precarious, became further complicated with the thunderous arrival of a few hundred Western Indians from the Great Lakes.[53] Independent powers, still residually influenced by the French and long-time rivals with the Haudenosaunee, they "had been sworn enemies of the English up to this time and had frequently caused them grievous damage during the last war," commented a German colonel working for Burgoyne.[54] Now, taking "up arms for the Crown of England for the first time," and led by Saint-Luc, for whom the British were "unable to hear his name mentioned without terror," they were to become the wild cards that altered the dynamics of the Northern Expedition.

Ironically, Burgoyne had been complaining that the northeastern "savages"—his allied Haudenosaunee—were insufficiently bellicose: "I do all I can to keep up their terror but in many cases I find they are little more than a name."[55] They had come to the war already dubious about warfare, preferring neutrality, and not dedicated enough to the British agenda of crushing the American rebellion. They had freely drunk the liquor that was sold or given to them in camp, making them less fierce, more impetuous, and thus increasingly oblivious to Burgoyne's direction.[56] "They are indulged," complained Burgoyne, "in all the caprices and humours of spoiled children, like them they grow more unreasonable and importunate upon every new favour."[57] Warriors were further unaccustomed to camp life, irritated by their peripheral role, impatient with the slow British pace, and maddened by orders from above. They began to lose interest in the campaign that had once been imagined so vividly for them at the Boquet River.

Burgoyne imported the Western Indians to northern New York because of their reputed ferocity and in order to bring the auxiliary forces closer to the numbers the British thought they needed for the twin campaigns down the Hudson and along the Mohawk. Major Arent DePeyster, scion of a Dutch family in New York and commander of the British fort at Mackinac, an island in the straits between Lakes Huron and Michigan, since 1774 had tried to woo the Western Indians to the British campaign. But because he was ineffective at the "painful task of superintending the western tribes," the British had to swallow their pride and rely heavily on French fixers, especially Charles-Michel de Langlade and Charles Gautier, both fluent in the ways of the Native Americans of the Pays d'en Haut.[58]

The Western nations had some of their own reservations about joining a remote war. Still, warriors gathered at Fort Mackinac, each arriving group accompanied by traders and agents who extracted for their clients and themselves gifts of manufactured British goods and distilled liquors.[59] Greeting them at Mackinac were 2,000 kegs of rum, 23 tons of gunpowder, 30 tons of musket balls, all sent from Montreal on hundreds of *bateaux* as the rewards of recruitment.[60] These warriors then traveled to Montreal in

July 1777, when they were joined by the Ottawa, described by a German colonel as "a very formidable and belligerent nation" from Detroit, and then, all together, they proceeded through the Champlain valley to meet Burgoyne on July 17 at Skenesborough on the southern tip of the lake.[61]

In total, Burgoyne had seventeen nations represented in his auxiliary force. From the west came Ottawa, Menominee, Mississauga, Chippewa, Winnebago, Sauk, Fox, Potawatomi, and Santee Dakota. From the Saint Lawrence valley came members of the Seven Nations: Saint Regis, Caughnawaga, Canasadaga, Algonquin, Akwesasne, Nipissing, Lorette, Oswegatchie, and a few small Abenaki tribes. The British could congratulate themselves for assembling a native army recruited from half of North America, though it was folly to think that all those nations would be harmoniously in lockstep with each other under British command, especially when mixed and matched in small war parties. "There is," Burgoyne confessed to General Howe in New York a week after the McCrea debacle, "infinite difficulty to manage them."[62]

With a fifteen-gun salute discharged from warships on Lake Champlain, the British greeted the brightly painted Western warriors, "highly dressed with feathers" and projecting "natural ferocity." Burgoyne again delivered his speech on why fight, how to fight, and when to use restraint, whereupon each Western nation "separately danced their several war dances."[63] One very impressed German officer described the breathtaking warriors as "heathen, tall, warlike, and enterprising, but wicked as Satan."[64] Because of their characteristics, Burgoyne assigned them to the advanced force, which bulldozed a path for the trailing regulars by ambushing American rear guards and pickets, followed by scalping.

In mid-July, the Western Indians now on board, Burgoyne, strangely anxious, wrote to British Secretary Germain with dread. Foreseeing the potential problem the new Native American auxiliaries posed, he worried that if "left to themselves, enormities too horrid to think of would ensue: guilty and innocent, women and infants would be a common prey."[65] In his heart he had to admit to himself that they were "often barbarous" and "always capricious," yet maybe when "united to a regular army, they would be kept under control, and made subservient to a general system."[66]

Given the absurdity of the mental reasoning Burgoyne performed, it was not surprising that the killing and scalping of a civilian woman was shocking to him. After all, hadn't he made a point of telling his New World warriors they needed to be more British? Even *after* Jane's death and the slaughter of a family nearby, he continued to boast that his warriors "Scalp the Dead only; and spare the Inhabitants."[67] Rosy rhetoric aside, if Burgoyne had been fully honest with himself, he would have had to concede that he knew a tragedy like McCrea's killing was inevitable.

Tomahawking followed by scalping was an age-old practice that came with all the Native warriors of the Northeast and Great Lakes.[68] To be sure, Europeans had their own history of extreme violence; bodies had long been tortured and mutilated, heads decapitated and hoisted on pikes. Yet, Native American methods seemed strange and barbaric to the British. Cadwallader Colden, surveyor general of New York and Britain's colonial representative to the Iroquois Confederacy, published a profile of the Five Nations (which later became six) in 1727. In his account, scalps "are the Trophies of Victory, which all the *Indian Nations* carry home with them, if they have time to flea the Scalp from the Skull of their Enemies, when they have killed them, or otherwise wounding them, but leave them in this miserable Condition with their Skull bare."[69] Scalping certified a warrior's kill, established his martial *bona fides*, and more than that, it was a sacred ritual that released a person's essence into the hands of the scalper, and when returned home, into the community as well.[70]

A French print by Grasset de Saint Sauveur, an eighteenth-century diplomat from Montreal who was also an amateur ethnographer, captured the technique of scalping, in which a victim is first subdued and dropped to the knees, a foot jammed into the upper back or neck. A blow to the head might or might not precede the scalping. A knife is pulled from a sheath attached to a belt or pack, or hung from the neck, or tucked into leggings. Roger Lamb, a soldier in the British 9th Regiment of Foot, explained scalping technique in detail: First "He twists one hand in the hair, and pulls forcibly from the Crown, by which means the skin is somewhat lifted from the skull. He then excoriates as much as covers the top of the head with his scalping knife, which he has always by him."[71] An attacker may yank the scalp away by hand or with his teeth. The scalping "is often performed in a minute, and under certain circumstances is fatal, but not always."[72] James Thacher, an American surgeon who logged Jane McCrea's killing into his journal, said Indians accomplished the feat "with wonderful dexterity."[73]

Later, a warrior took scalps back to camp, announcing the kill with a war-hoop. To avoid "wasting by putrefaction," he "spreads and sews them upon a hoop with ligaments of bark or deer's sinews, painting them red for the sake of shew."[74] Sometimes dressed with jewelry and feathers, the scalps "were suspended on poles at the doors of their *wigwams* or huts," where

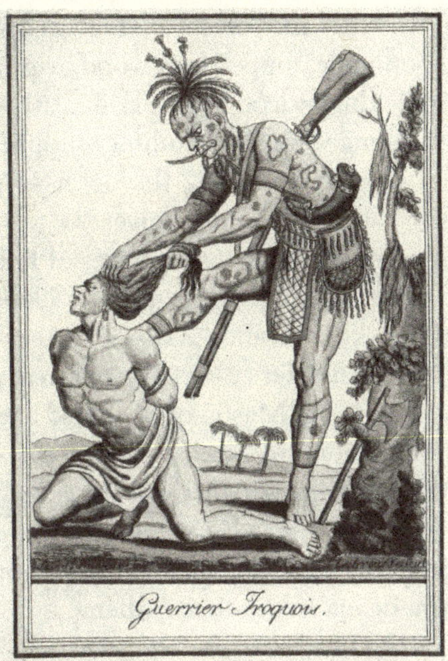

Labrousse, after Jacques Grasset de Saint-Saveur, *Guerrier Iroquois.* 1796. Engraving. Washington DC, Library of Congress Prints and Photographs Division.

they gave "great satisfaction of the whole nation, and carefully preserved in memory of their courage and prowess, in avenging the cause of their country."[75] Thacher added a note on the cataloging of scalps by "showing the number of their victims, and . . . painting on the dried scalp, different figures, and colors, to designate the sex and age of the victim, and also the manner and circumstances of the murder."[76] John Long, a British fur trader, said, "some of the Indians in time of war, when scalps are well paid for, divide one into five or six parts, and carry them to the nearest post, in hopes of receiving a reward proportionate to the number."[77]

George Townshend, a British brigade commander under James Wolfe during the French and Indian War, once tried to send a captured Ottawa warrior to George II as a present.[78] An amateur artist and ethnographer, Townshend painted a unique suite of watercolors in the 1750s, one depicting a war chief walking with a fully dressed and braided scalp in his left hand.[79]

During the Revolution, Americans often could see that scalping knives had been manufactured in Britain for distribution, trade, or sale to Natives.[80] That is, knives with six- or seven-inch narrow blades, slightly curved, sharpened on one side, topped by a wood grip, and held in a sheath richly decorated by individual warriors. The knives arrived in North America in crates and bales, along with other military supplies. One small trans-Atlantic shipment in 1776 included 92 firelocks, 43 powder horns, 250 pounds of musket balls, and 20 scalping knives.[81]

Once on the continent, the British sent boxes of knives to forts for dispersal or to traders for sale. A 1776 shipment to Mackinac included "2 Doz. Split Barrwood scalping knives" and "2 doz. Ditto in camwood." Major DePeyster, the British commander at Fort Detroit, received "132 dozen red hafted scalping knives" in 1779. Mason of Sheffield and Lowcock of London made many of the carbon-steel knives, which carried their stamps on the blade, a marker that inflamed American Patriots when they encountered them. The revulsion increased if the knives were also marked with the initials *G.R.*: Georgius Rex, the man who was, only months earlier, thought to be the Americans' benevolent father.[82]

If we gather the persuasive bits of information written into the military accounts, and at the same time consider the ways in which warriors historically conducted a raid, we can reconstruct the events of July 26 from the Native American perspective, beginning with the dramatic rise in tensions on all sides. The British had been operating in hilly, underpopulated terrain, but the farther they advanced down the Hudson, the greater the number of civilians they encountered. Fort Edward was a hamlet as well as a military base, and though Burgoyne's army quartered remotely at Fort Anne, his advanced guard camped in a pine forest north of town while the American army, having mostly evacuated Fort Edward, regrouped in a makeshift camp a few miles south along Moses Creek.

That meant the armies were, for the first time, within shouting distance of each other, with McCrea, McNeil, and some American pickets marooned in the no-man's-land between them. While some Loyalists, like McCrea and McNeil, might have convinced themselves they were safe, in spite of admonitions from Colonel Lewis to evacuate, most residents had fled south under the protection of Schuyler. The exodus was pitiful: "The roads were filled with fugitives; men leading little children by the hand, women pressing their infant offspring to their bosoms, hurrying forward in utmost consternation, from the scene of danger. Occasionally passed a cavalcade, two and even three mounted on a single steed, panting under its

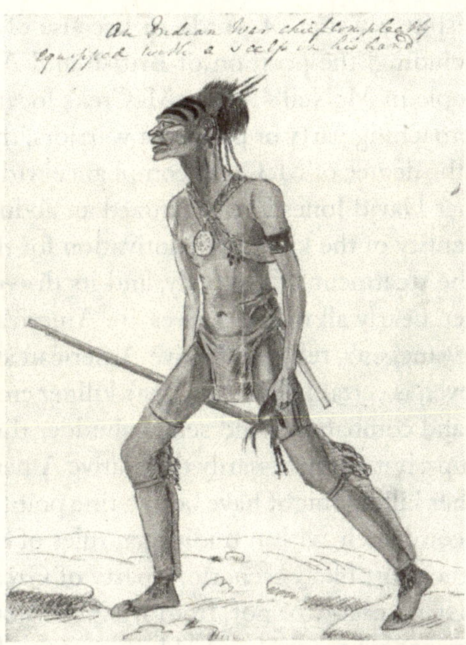

George Townshend, "An Indian War chief completely equipped with a scalp in his hand." 1751–1758. Pen and ink, watercolor. London, National Portrait Gallery. Bequeathed by Robert Wyndham Ketton-Cremer, 1971.

heavy load; sometimes carrying a mother and her child, while the father ran breathless by the horse's side."[83]

The few pickets remaining at mostly evacuated Fort Edward were to provide warning of enemy advance. On the 26th, about twenty were sent to roam the perimeter north of town, where a mixed-nation contingent of Western Indians and Loyalist rangers attacked twenty of them on a hill a mile from the fort. David Jones was active in one of Burgoyne's advance Loyalist units at the time, though it is not known precisely where he was located on the 26th. Five American pickets were killed, including Lieutenant Tobias Van Vechten. The Native warriors chased the surviving pickets southward, toward the fort, and then turned and began to retreat north to British lines, when a few of them entered, either by design or by accident, Sarah McNeil's log house in the near-deserted town.

At that point, the narrative of McCrea's last hours splinters into the endless permutations written into military accounts by Standish, Bartlett, Thacher, Gates, Burgoyne, and many others. We can know almost nothing with certainty. Despite a welter of words, or because of them, most facts remain cloudy, including: the position of British and American soldiers, the number of people in McNeil's house, McCrea's location in the house, the size of the approaching party or parties of warriors, their initial friendliness or hostility, the degree of McCrea's compliance with her removal, the question of whether David Jones had organized an abduction, the precise nationality and identity of the killer, the motivation for the killing, the injuries sustained, the treatment of the body, and its discovery and transfer to burial. Moreover, nearly all the narratives are American or British, and only one, Tehoragwanegen's, tells the Native American story.

One fact, however, is certain. Jane McCrea's killing crossed a sacred line between civilians and combatants, and sent a shudder through the British and American camps, but not necessarily the Native American camp. From their perspective, her killing might have been a fine point of Native American warfare, and completely within traditional rules of engagement, even with civilians. In the most likely scenario, a party of Great Lakes warriors took or escorted her, agreeably or not, from McNeil's house. Traditionally among Native warriors, whoever "lays hold of a captive by the hair of his head, to him he belongs, and none may take him from him," wrote one prisoner of the Western Indians.[84] If there were more than one claimant to the prisoner, the dispute would normally go to a tribal council for resolution. But in a combat zone, that practice changed under two conditions. First, "If any dispute arises between two warriors about a prisoner, he is immediately killed, to put an end to it," wrote an eighteenth-century observer. Second, "If, in spite of all their caution, they are closely pursued, they kill the prisoners, scalp them, and disperse in the woods" in order to escape cleanly.[85] In fact, on the 26th the Continentals and militiamen countered the attack on the Fort Edward pickets, causing the Native auxiliaries to flee toward British lines. If there were also a dispute over possession of Jane McCrea—as Burgoyne and others maintained—and the Americans were in hot pursuit, slaying and scalping her was the time-honored protocol to be followed.[86]

Tehoragwanegen, hailing from the northeastern Caughnawaga and Mohawk tribes, who were long since engaged with British and French cultures, nevertheless thought it criminal. However, when Burgoyne came to the advanced camp, fingered the murderer, and threatened him with death, the Western Indians might have been incredulous. Jane McCrea was of no special consequence to them, and in dispatching a contested captive while being pursued, they were within their normal ways of conducting warfare.

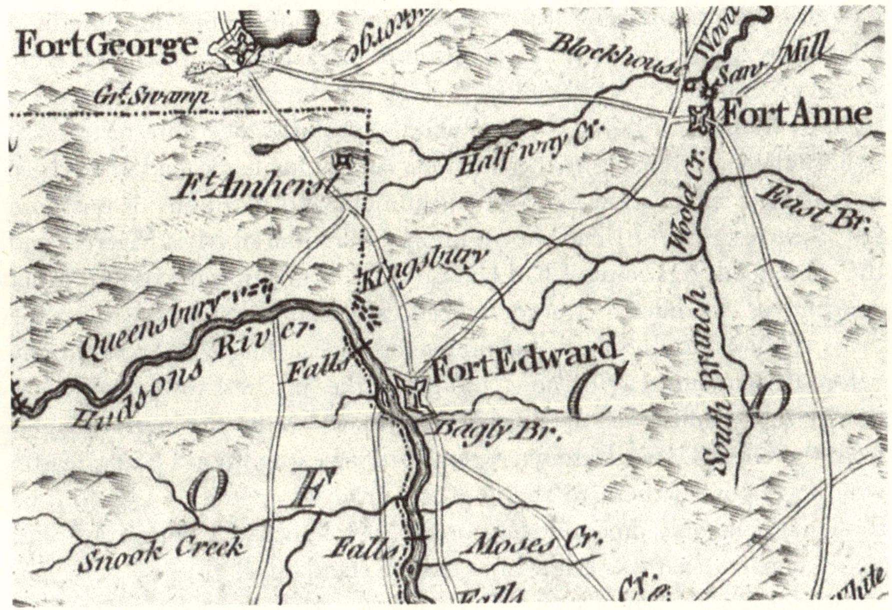

The locations of Fort Anne, Fort Edward, and Moses Creek to the south. Detail from Robert Baldwin and Thomas Kitchin, *Part of the counties of Charlotte and Albany, in the Province of New York*, 1778. Engraving. Washington DC, Library of Congress, Geography and Map Division.

To be sure, the slaying was impulsive and unnecessary, but it was not unprecedented in the annals of Native peoples.

Burgoyne was surprised that his rules of the game had not overridden the hardened cultural norms of the Native auxiliaries. He was commander of all commanders, chief of all chiefs, and death to McCrea's killer was the proper punishment. Nevertheless, his authority was actually reduced when it came to the German and Native auxiliaries, who had their own war captains and military habits. Saint-Luc, aided by his son-in-law Charles-Louis de Lanaudière, correctly suggested Burgoyne should walk away from the intended punishment because the Western Indians had not violated their own rules. If the general did not, they would surely go home, insulted by British words, actions, and philosophy. Burgoyne had asked them to die so that the British army might progress down the Hudson corridor unscathed, which they were willing to do only if there were mutual respect. Instead, they were being held in contempt over a killing that was, for them, of minor consequence.

With execution taken off the table, Burgoyne needed to do something else to assert his authority.[87] In addition to extracting promises that there would never be another killing like McCrea's, he strengthened British oversight of Indian war parties and demanded promises of future restraint, a policy taken as an insult by the warriors. As Burgoyne recalled, his Native warriors started to show signs of "ill humour and mutinous disposition" after "the resentment I had shown upon the murder of Miss Macrea" and the subsequent "restraints I had laid on their disposition to commit other enormities." As much as Burgoyne could no longer trust the Western Indians, the Western Indians could no longer respect Burgoyne. In testimony before Parliament in 1778, he would praise the "progress towards civilization" of the "domiciliated nations near Montréal." As for the "remote tribes" from the Great Lakes, Burgoyne seemed to have forgotten the very reason why he imported them to the conflict. From his perch in London, he thought their "only preeminence consisted in ferocity," a dangerous one-dimensionality that was inimical to British standards.[88]

Colden, Lamb, and Thacher only wrote about scalping by Native Americans, yet whites on the borderlands also scalped, at times turning human flesh into sizable income.[89] Notable examples abounded throughout colonial and revolutionary history. In one instance, a town erected a statue in honor of a white American who scalped Native peoples. Abenakis had captured Hannah Dustin, a Puritan mother of nine, during a raid on Haverhill, Massachusetts, in 1697. In an upside-down version of the McCrea story that Dustin told the Reverend Cotton Mather, she escaped her captivity by killing and scalping ten of the Native family members who were holding her. Taking flight in a canoe, she requested a bounty when she returned home, for which the Massachusetts General Court awarded her 25 pounds sterling. To be sure, she was escaping kidnappers, but she did not stop at killing the adults; she scalped the children as well. For Americans, she was a hero rewarded by an honored place in history, as well as rousing historical paintings and monumental public statuary showing her wielding a hatchet.

During the French and Indian War, scalping was endemic on all sides, yet Americans saw themselves as victims and Native Americans as pitiless predators mutilating the innocent. Scalp bounties were often offered as financial inducement for joining a militia, the amount paid scaled according to rank.[90] Benjamin Franklin injected a dose of realism when he saw Pennsylvanians support the Paxton Boys, a group of white vigilantes who had ravaged a settlement of peaceful Conestogas near Lancaster in 1763. These "poor defenseless Creatures," Franklin lamented, "fell on their Knees, protested their Innocence, declared their Love to the *English*," and then, "in this Posture they all received the Hatchet! —— Men, Women and little Children," and were then "scalped and otherwise horribly mangled."[91]

Much of the Philadelphia population supported the Paxton Boys. When the vigilantes approached the welcoming city in 1764, however, Franklin and a few other leaders intercepted them in Germantown. After miraculously dispersing the "Boys," the appalled Franklin chastised his fellow citizens for justifying the Paxtons' killing of innocent Native peoples: the "only Crime of these poor Wretches seems to have been reddish brown Skin, and black Hair." Franklin heaped more contempt on those who made no effort to differentiate between peaceful Native Americans and dangerous ones. More disturbing, Franklin begged the question of whether white folks had themselves acquired "the Manners of *Barbarians?*" His ugly conclusion was that Anglo-Americans, not Native Americans, were the most brutal and uncivilized people on earth, and that the murdered Conestogas "would have been safe in any Part of the known World, — except in the Neighbourhood of the CHRISTIAN WHITE SAVAGES."[92]

The scalping of Native peoples continued into the Revolutionary period. In 1774, white frontiersmen invited a group of Southern Iroquois into their camp, got them drunk, then killed and scalped them, including the pregnant sister of the chief.[93] In 1780, Joseph Reed, president of the Supreme Executive Council of Pennsylvania, proclaimed cash rewards of $3,000 for "every Indian Prisoner, or Tory acting in Arms with them," and $2,500 "for every *Indian* Scalp." A sickened Onondaga chief, Tioguanda, recalled the Continental Army coming into his village in 1779 and putting "to death all the women and Children, excepting some of the Young Women that they carried away for the use of their Soldiers, and were afterwards put to death in a more shameful and Scandalous manner. Yet these Rebels call themselves Christians."[94]

The financial market for scalps was vast, extending across the eighteenth century and with both white and Native American participants.[95] Macabre collections, taken by whites as well as Native warriors, were sometimes displayed, often at a Native American camp or a British fort, though the town of Salem prominently exhibited the scalps it had redeemed for bounties on the walls of the public courthouse.[96] Henry Hamilton, superintendent of Indian Affairs at Fort Detroit, had as many as 129 scalps in his possession.[97] George Townshend, British officer and artist, not only painted pictures of

Native warriors during the French and Indian War, he also took a Native boy back to England for himself, along with chests of mysterious souvenirs to be opened while entertaining friends. At one dinner party, that boy was "brought to the room to divert his [Townshend's] company." According to one of Townshend's guests, "a box of scalps" was opened, whereupon the Indian boy first grew agitated and then discovered one scalp which "he knew by the hair belong'd to one of his own nation." Exploding "into a sudden fury," the boy grabbed one of the scalping knives in the box and lunged "at his Master with intention to murther him." To defend himself, Townshend opened his shirt, demonstrating he himself had been mauled, and at that point, "the Boy understood."[98]

Given the pervasiveness of scalping practices in the Northeast over at least a hundred years prior to the Revolution, Jane McCrea's slaughter was neither unusual nor unexpected. General Gates was the one who had turned her into a special, almost unique case, yet he knew perfectly well, going back to his own service in the French and Indian War, the grisly history of dismemberment in America. Burgoyne, to his credit, though often pilloried as an accessory to McCrea's killing, was the one person who tried to alter existential warfare in North America by setting humane rules to protect civilians of all races. He ultimately failed in that endeavor, but previously the concept of *jus in bello* was unheard of in Indian country.

6.

CONSEQUENCES

Before July 26, there is scant evidence that Natives were killing and scalping noncombatants. However, on that day, it all changed when the Western Indians not only killed Jane McCrea, but also came upon the family of John Allen in Argyle, a farming district thick with Loyalists. "The Father, Mother & six Children killed and left to be torn by the Hogs," wrote American chaplain Reverend Enos Hitchcock in his diary while camped with the Continentals.[1] The Allens may have been protecting their livestock and goods, just trying to live their lives, when they were approached, figuring that as Loyalists they were safe from predation. By any measure, their slaughter was heinous.

In the aftermath of the slaughter of McCrea and the Allens, British forces continued to forge ahead, seemingly undaunted. They occupied Fort Edward and received needed supplies from Fort George to the north, while the advanced corps continued to press farther south. Native auxiliaries stayed on, supposedly reformed by Burgoyne's reprimand. According to one unverifiable account that had a public relations cast to it, Schawanissie, an Ottawa chief, carried a wounded American officer on his back to a British medical unit.[2]

The new bonhomie abruptly ended when the Western Indians quit a few days later. The stated reason for their departure was the need to be home in time to prepare for the approaching demands of autumn and winter, though underlying that decision were the restrictions Burgoyne had placed on the warriors in the wake of McCrea's killing. From the viewpoint of the Native warriors, they could have stayed another week or two, but Burgoyne's credentials as a leader had shriveled in their estimation. In addition, the Western Indians were right to think the British had exploited them. They were carrying out all the dangerous missions while the British and German regulars were safely encamped far from the fray. Their handler, Saint-Luc, accused Burgoyne of gross ineptitude in his dealings with Natives. He said that Burgoyne's love of "grand maneuvers," his undisguised contempt for the auxiliaries, and his dishonorable abandonment of the wounded and dead had "disgusted" the Native warriors.[3]

If the prospect of the Western Indians abandoning Burgoyne were not problematic enough, many of the warriors from northern New York and southern Canada decided they too had to return home for the approaching harvest. Burgoyne pleaded with all of them to stay. Nonetheless, many departed, leaving Burgoyne with only fifty warriors as he approached an ultimate engagement with the Continentals at Saratoga, the massive October battle that would turn the tide of the Revolution.[4]

The British had expended heaps of money, oratory, and energy in acquiring the 1,000 warriors allied with the campaigns along the Hudson and through the Mohawk Valley, and in short order the entire strategy was on the edge of collapse. Burgoyne knew that his regulars were now left exposed and vulnerable. "My own army was by no means in condition to dispense with [the warriors]." He retrospectively thought the Native warriors "overvalued" and at times a "disgrace of humanity"; nonetheless, they were "necessary" for giving his men "due repose," suggesting an inner squeamishness over the dirty business of guerilla warfare. For him, the British "had been trained to higher purposes; they were destined to lead in the general and decisive combats." In Burgoyne's racial logic, white soldiers "could not be spared, or risked, or harassed."[5] Natives were destined for dangerous perimeter raiding, woodland encounters, and terror, saving the British for the grand moment when armies battle face to face, as if on a stage.

Though Burgoyne had forbidden the killing and scalp-taking of noncombatants, and had only awarded gold for the prisoners taken into camp alive, the shocking wake of Jane McCrea's brutal death now convinced everyone in the countryside, both Patriot and Loyalist, that he had put a bounty on civilian scalps, or worse, that he had instructed the auxiliaries under his command to kill civilians. When McCrea died, the original British concept of Native auxiliaries as effective psychological weapons was instantly exploded. Just the opposite was the new psychology: Natives were not the avatars of terror that Burgoyne thought they would be, they were terror embodied, physical weapons let loose on a civilian population by the British.

As news of McCrea's killing spread, newspaper to newspaper, across America and over to London, Whitehall's strategic design to cut the rebellious provinces in two began to unravel, one setback after another. The depletion of the Native auxiliaries reduced Burgoyne's numbers and diminished the layers of warriors protecting his army. As he continued south, his supply chain grew attenuated, leading to shortages of munitions and food. General William Howe marched into Philadelphia on September 26, when the original plan, never communicated to him by Whitehall, had called for an approach to Albany. Colonel Barry St. Leger, leading the King's 8th Regiment and aided by 400 Native warriors and Loyalists under Joseph Brant, was marching west to east across New York and down the Mohawk River, with the goal of meeting Burgoyne in Albany. When he decided to besiege Fort Stanwix in early August and then engage in a pitched battle at Oriskany, St. Leger created enough time for an American relief column led by Benedict Arnold to force a British retreat to Canada and thus cause the abandonment of the Albany strategy, leaving Burgoyne on his own along the Hudson.

Without Howe and St. Leger, and desperate for supplies, Burgoyne entered his heart of darkness. On August 9, he sent a raiding detachment of Germans, Loyalists, and Native warriors eastward from Fort Edward toward Bennington with the goal of taking horses, cattle, and provisions. To the surprise of the German colonel leading the expedition, 1,500 Patriot militiamen were waiting. After a fierce daylong battle, the raid ended in a catastrophic loss that had two consequences for the British. It reduced Burgoyne's main army by 1,000, and on the American side, it encouraged New Englanders to join the Northern Campaign, now being commanded by Gates, their favorite.[6] By the time of his surrender at Saratoga, Burgoyne's force was reduced to 3,500 men available for fighting.[7]

If Burgoyne's operation leading up to Saratoga was like a scripted drama gone haywire, then the Americans, by contrast, were conducting a mad improvisation as they scrambled to assemble a force up to the task of taking on the depleted but still disciplined British machine. Under Gates, American forces underwent a remarkable rehabilitation from their low in mid-August, 1777, when he could count only 5,888 Continentals and militiamen, all in varying degrees of disrepair.[8] Soon thereafter, Washington, while awaiting Howe's invasion of Philadelphia, instructed two elite combat units of the Continental Army—Brigadier-General John Glover's 1,300 soldiers and Colonel Daniel Morgan's 400 Virginia and Pennsylvania riflemen—to march to the Northern theater. Benedict Arnold arrived with 1,200 soldiers from the Mohawk River. Major Henry Dearborn brought five companies of light infantry. Major-General Benjamin Lincoln and Brigadier-General John Stark delivered 2,000 recruits from northern New England. Militia companies from central Massachusetts began to arrive, while Governor Trumbull raised and sent militia from Connecticut. On the eve of Saratoga, Gates was commanding more than 20,000 infantry, cavalry, artillerymen, militia, and Native warriors, plus hundreds of support staff.[9]

Jane McCrea figured only tangentially into the American military calculus. William Scudder of the New York 1st Regiment said years later that "the death of Miss Jane M'Crea, spread a general alarm, particularly through the New-England states, and I believe drove many to arms, who before seemed to appear in suspense."[10] Other than that, there is scant evidence that the death of a young New York woman betrothed to a Loyalist officer possessed such mobilizing powers.[11] The thousands of new arrivals who left their homes in New England were being motivated by the encouraging victory at Bennington and their corresponding fear that Burgoyne's main force might abandon its southward thrust and march eastward into New England, with sights set on Boston.

That does not mean that the memory of Jane McCrea was not a presence on the Saratoga battlefield. In a speech delivered on the threshold of the most important battle of the Revolution, Gates eloquently inspired his men to fight. Though never mentioning her by name, he exhorted his soldiers by citing her cruel death: "If the murder of aged parents, with their innocent children; if mangling the blooming virgin and inoffensive youth, are inducements to revenge—if the righteous cause of freedom, and the happiness of posterity are motives to stimulate to conquer [our] mercenary and merciless foes, the time is now, when [men are] called on by their country, by their general, and by every thing divine and human, to vanquish the foe."[12] Gates, already savvy enough to have implanted McCrea's killing into the public mind, was now instilling her into the hearts of new recruits and old soldiers.

On September 20, 1777, Gates received a contingent of 112 Oneida and Tuscarora, led by Hanyerry Tewahangarahke and the Caughnawaga Atiatoharóngwen, the latter a veteran of the Battle of Quebec.[13] Gates, who knew how to deliver a good storyline, asked them "to avenge yourselves of those people who have deceived you," and then offered a wampum belt decorated with a hatchet inscribed with the letters "U.S."[14] Gates outfitted them with red caps so that they would not be confused with the warriors working for Burgoyne.

Despite all the setbacks, Burgoyne risked everything on a final push toward Albany. He approached the Americans in mid-September, near Saratoga. Burgoyne won a tactical victory at Freeman's Farm on September 19, while suffering massive casualties, and then mounted a second attack on October 7 that left the British devastated, leading to a halfhearted retreat toward Fort Edward. By this point, the British were weak and far away from the safety of Ticonderoga, incapable of breaking through to Albany, and even if they had done so General Howe's army would not be waiting for them. Surrounded, Burgoyne surrendered on October 17.

Gates and Burgoyne agreed to a convention instead of an unconditional surrender, that is, an agreement with full military honors to turn over all arms, return home, and pledge not to reengage in North America. The captured British and Canadian troops, plus wives, children, and even pets, were marched first to Cambridge under an American detachment, where they billeted for a year. About 1,300 escaped. Because of failed negotiations between Congress and Whitehall and troubles finding sufficient food, the remaining prisoners were then marched six hundred miles in the snowy winter of 1778–1779 to Charlottesville, Virginia, where they had to build crude barracks, which they occupied until 1781. A print appearing in a volume of one British officer's recollections of life in Charlottesville shows the soldiers practicing subsistence farming.[15]

The treatment of convention prisoners was relatively decent compared to the Americans warehoused at the same time aboard the sixteen British prison ships in New York harbor. Conditions were so brutal there that deaths from starvation, disease, poisoning, and physical abuse exceeded kill rates on the battlefield. Henry Laurens, the new president of the Continental Congress, deplored "the cruelties of the English," whose treatment of American "Prisoners is not to be parallel'd in [the] History of Civilized Nations—nor indeed are they exceeded by the practices of the barbarous Indian Allies of our Enemies," who have "scalped and butcher'd and burnt many of our inhabitants." The "English have starved our [incarcerated] People, suffer'd them to lose their limbs by frost and to linger out a miserable life." They have "smother'd them in Prison Ships, killing every night five, six, and more, have kick'd, beat and abused, have loaded Officers with Irons and a thousand other savage Acts they have been guilty of."[16] One escapee from the notorious prison ship *Jersey* described prisoners "eaten up alive. Their sickly countenances, and ghastly looks were truly horrible; some swearing and blaspheming; others crying, praying, and wringing their hands; and stalking about like ghosts; others delirious, raving and storming, — all panting for breath; some dead, and corrupting. The air was so foul that at times a lamp could not be kept burning, by reason of which the bodies were not missed until they had been dead ten days."[17]

In Charlottesville, however, Governor Thomas Jefferson, forced to preside over an unexpected prisoner situation, became friendly with British Brigadier-General William Phillips of the Royal Artillery and Major-General Friedrich Adolf von Riedesel, the German commander of the Brunswick and Hessen-Hanau brigades, as well as his three daughters and charming wife, Frederika, who kept a diary of her American adventures. Soldiers built a camp theater where comedies featured drummers dressed in drag. During musicales at nearby Monticello, Jefferson played duets on the violin with a Hessian captain while his wife accompanied on the piano. Dances followed in the evening. When Phillips and Riedesel were exchanged for General Benjamin Lincoln in 1780, Jefferson hoped he would meet up with Phillips in the future, which he almost did, because in 1781 Phillips led a British force of 4,500 soldiers into Virginia with orders to capture Jefferson. Meanwhile, after hundreds more prisoners escaped, the remaining 2,600 of Burgoyne's soldiers marched to cantonments in Pennsylvania, where they remained until the end of the war when their numbers had been reduced to 470.[18]

Gates, at the summit of his career, exulted in his monumental victory. The French were now eager to join the American bandwagon, and Gates felt optimistic enough to write directly to the British Parliament, urging an end to hostilities: "Instantly withdraw your Fleets & armies; cultivate the Friendship & commerce of America." If Britain wants to save its "Sinking State," then end the "Blood shed in this Fatal contest."[19] Congress honored him by commissioning a commemorative medal that Benjamin

Gilbert Stuart, *Horatio Gates*. c. 1793–94. Oil on canvas. New York, The Metropolitan Museum of Art, Gift of Lucille S. Pfeffer, 1977.

Franklin had minted in Paris. On it, Burgoyne reaches forward to hand his sword to Gates while the British army lays down its arms. Arcing overhead, three words summarize his achievement: "SALUS REGIONUM SEPTENTRIONAL": The Safety of the Northern Region. Gates proudly wears the medal in Gilbert Stuart's majestic retirement portrait of 1794.

Gates's glory was short-lived, however. Though he was brilliant at handling the propaganda war surrounding Jane McCrea, the success of the Northern Army at Saratoga was attributable to the efforts of Daniel Morgan, Enoch Poor, Benjamin Lincoln, and Benedict Arnold. A few months after Saratoga, Washington came to believe that Gates was leading a conspiracy, supported by some congressional representatives and military officers, to relieve him as commander in chief. Gates apologized for the "misunderstanding"; nonetheless, the affair led to an estrangement between the two generals. Congress assigned the chastened Gates to minor posts, first to Fishkill on the Hudson after most of the Northern Army had moved on and the militias had returned home, and then to Boston and Providence to command the mostly inactive Eastern Army.

However, in 1780, with the fall of Charleston and the capture of General Lincoln's Southern Army, Congress put him back on center stage. Gates took command of the remaining Continentals in central North Carolina and marched them to Camden in South Carolina, where a British force led by General Charles Cornwallis completely routed Gates's army. As one of his officers, Ortho Holland Williams, put the defeat, "picture it as bad as you possibly can and it will not be as bad as it really is." Nathanael Greene replaced the humiliated commander, after which Gates retired to his home in rural Virginia. A congressional board of inquiry looked into his conduct but never pursued charges.

1777 is often called the Year of the Hangman because the last three digits resemble gallows. For Burgoyne and the Northern Army, Saratoga signaled the death of the British military's most ambitious strategic plan. At the same time, it reinvigorated Benjamin Franklin's pitch to the French to actively align with the war effort in North America. Through Pierre Beaumarchais, a notable playwright who acted as intermediary, France had already been providing covert aid—firearms, field pieces, bayonets, and blankets—to the American armies, including the majority of the arms used at Saratoga. What the Americans wanted now was France's total involvement.

As lead American envoy to the Versailles court, Franklin received word of Burgoyne's surrender on December 4 at his home in Passy. Instantly, he had acquired another bargaining chip with the French, who were itching to avenge their losses in the Seven Years War, but were understandably dubious about the viability of the new United States. In two days' time, Louis XVI invited Franklin to begin a new round of negotiations with his foreign minister, the Comte de Vergennes. Saratoga had helped legitimize the United States in French eyes and convinced the king and ministry that the war was winnable.

American and French plenipotentiaries signed two treaties on February 6, 1778, less than four months after Saratoga, one of which committed France "to make all the efforts in its Power" to defend the "liberty, Sovereignty, and independence absolute and unlimited of the said United States." On March 20, at a formal ceremony at Versailles, three days after Britain declared war on France, Louis XVI received the treaty's American commissioners and launched an alliance that radically altered the future course of the Revolution.

Throughout his tenure in France, Franklin, who knew of Jane McCrea and other victims, had raged at the extreme violence occurring on the Northern front, including the practice of scalping. He accused the British of "Depravity," for having committed "numberless Barbarities" in their "Prosecution of the War." They were guilty of encouraging "Savages to Massacre the Families of Farmers" and indulging themselves in "publick Rejoicings on Occasion of any News of the Slaughter of an innocent and virtuous People."[20] In 1779, he accepted an unprecedented assignment from Congress to hire a French artist to engrave thirty-five prints to be assembled into a children's schoolbook that would tell the sordid tale of "British Cruelties" over the first four years of the Revolution. The goal, he said to David Hartley, a sympathetic British official, was "to impress the minds of Children and Posterity with a deep sense of your bloody and insatiable Malice and Wickedness."[21]

With the help of Lafayette, who also knew of McCrea's killing, Franklin imagined frightful scenes of violence that were truly for adult eyes only. Towns—Charlestown, Falmouth, and Norfolk—aflame. Captured soldiers butchered after laying down their arms. Prison ships rife with disease and starvation as "British officers Come to laugh at 'em and insult at theyr Miseries." Then he turned to the Burgoyne campaign. Franklin and Lafayette pre-visualized the suite.[22] Engraving number 11: "Savages killing and scalping the frontier Farmers and their Families, Women and Children" while "English Officers . . . giving them Orders & encouraging them." Number 13: the British "Commanding Officer at Niagara" receiving "The Scalps of the Wioming Families." Number 14: "The King of England" being handed "a Schedule intitled *Acct. of Scalps*, which he receives graciously." And number 18: "Prisoners kil'd and Roasted for a great festival" at which "Canadian Indians are eating American flesh," while Loyalist Colonel John Butler is "Setting at table."[23] Not only intended to illustrate a book, Franklin wanted the images pressed onto coins as well.

Though Congress had tasked Franklin and Lafayette with educating children, the two men made the project into propaganda aimed at the adults they wanted to awaken and mobilize against Britain. More potent than words, the pictures of unvarnished brutalities would teach Americans to hate their former masters. Franklin got as far as hiring an engraver, and had a few plates printed. The Reverend Samuel Cooper of Boston thanked Franklin in 1780 for the "Caracatureas" that "afford a striking Picture of Barbarity." Most likely, these were proofs or early drafts, the full run of finished prints never realized for reasons unknown.[24] The idea was audacious. It derived from the tradition of the *Book of Martyrs*, John Foxe's 1563 illustrated compendium of the sufferings of Protestants at the hands of the Catholic Church.[25] Franklin substituted a political and humanitarian rant, making the unrealized suite of prints a precursor to Francisco Goya's eighty-two *Disasters of War*, which graphically tell the tale of atrocities committed by the French during the occupation of Spain early in the nineteenth century.

During the peace negotiations with Britain in 1782, which led to the Treaty of Paris that closed the war, Franklin was still thinking about the toll that scalping took. He had once hoped for some kind of reconciliation with Britain, in addition to the peace itself. To achieve "Goodwill" after so many barbarities, however, would require "some Mark of Concern for what was past, and some Disposition to make Reparation." He "wish'd England would think of offering something to relieve those who had suffer'd by its scalping and Burning Parties."[26]

Because reparations were not on the British agenda, Franklin tried to whip up support by fabricating a fake issue of the *Boston Independent Chronicle* in 1782, which he sent to British newspapers, as well as to John Adams in Amsterdam and John Jay in Madrid, facetiously claiming he had chanced upon it. Dated March 12, 1782, the fake newspaper narrates the experiences of an American militia captain who intercepts letters and packages intended for the British governor of Canada. To his horror, the officer empties the eight packages. Number 1: 43 scalps of soldiers, "stretched on black Hoops, 4 Inches diameter"; also "62 of Farmers, killed in their houses; the Hoops red; the Skin painted brown, and marked with a Hoe; a black Circle all round, to denote their being surprised in the Night; and a black hatchet in the Middle." Number 2: 98 scalps of farmers "killed in their Houses." Number 3: 97 more, "killed in their fields." Number 4: 102 scalps of farmers, some having been "burnt alive, after being scalped, and their Nails pulled out by the roots"; also "a clergyman, his clerical collar attached to the scalp," plus 67 "very grey Heads." Number 5: scalps of 88 women, all mothers, some having "had their Brains beat out."

Franklin's list got more gruesome. Number 6: "193 Boys' Scalps." Number 7: "211 Girls Scalps." Number 8: "29 little infants Scalps," some with "a little black Knife in the middle to shew they were ript out of their Mothers' Bellies." In Franklin's fictional tale, the Seneca Chiefs who proudly assembled the packages of horrors hoped the British governor would "send these Scalps over the Water to the great King, that he may regard them and be refreshed." Perhaps the government could hang them "all up in some dark night on the trees in St. James's Park."[27]

A masterpiece of public propaganda, the fake news attempted to induce reparations for those Americans brutalized by the British via their Native

American proxies, whom Franklin presented as pure bloodthirsty monsters. Though Franklin's demand failed to be written into the Treaty of Paris, it helped the Americans gain overall leverage against the already humbled British in Paris. When the British team insisted upon reparations for dispossessed Loyalists, Franklin produced a long list of British crimes. The next day the British dropped their Loyalists claims.

The British and Americans had courted Native alliances in order to apply extrajudicial terror to the prosecution of the war, but in a grotesque turn, all parties resorted to some of the brutish methods thought to be unconscionable. After the British defeat at Saratoga, inhuman carnage spread across the Northern territory, becoming an unstoppable contagion that consumed every nation involved. The upper Hudson Valley and inland New York became places of unremitting misery, pocked with ethnic marauders intent on violence and vendetta. The brutal logic of the wilderness, where cruelties and cycles of revenge were the true rules of engagement, quickly extinguished the enlightenment dream of warfare conducted humanely. The New York frontier became "Dangerland," as one historian put it, a "world of irregular combat and terror," where "fighting was hard to control and could easily lead to excess."[28] This was the frightening "netherworld of dirty deeds," in which the boundaries between civility and savagery broke down, leading all parties to abandon *jus in bello*.

For the Haudenosaunee of New York, the American Revolution was nothing less than a catastrophe. All along, there had been fissures within their confederacy, papered over by intermarriage, trade, and the rewards of peace, but those divisions enlarged when two nations joined the Americans and four allied with the British. The breaking point occurred in August of 1777 during the British campaign to cut across Iroquoia from Lake Ontario in order to meet Burgoyne at Albany. At the Battle of Oriskany in central New York, when eight hundred Seneca, Cayuga, Onondaga, and Mohawk fought beside the British in pitched battle against the Oneida, Tuscarora, and Americans, the rupture in the Haudenosaunee Confederation became irreparable. The Great Tree of Peace, the symbol of union among the Haudenosaunee, was shattered as if struck by a lightning bolt. Oriskany was a "shocking Slaughter." The respected Seneca warrior Theywonyas (known first as Chainbreaker, and later as Blacksnake), described it as "the most Dead Bodies . . . I never Did see, and never will again." Blood was "a Stream Running Down on the Descending ground."[29] In an afternoon, The Great

Law that had bound the Six Nations dissolved into a civil war among the Haudenosaunee.

If the New York campaigns indicated anything, it was that civilization was marching backward. Orgies of violence swept through the Northeast.[30] In 1778 alone, Brant led an Iroquois attack on Cobleskill, New York, that left a wake of burned bodies, mutilated corpses, and scalped skulls. Soon thereafter, Major Butler's British regiment of Loyalists and Native warriors devastated a frontier settlement in the Wyoming Valley of Pennsylvania, burning 1,000 buildings and taking 227 scalps. Visitors to the site described a mass grave, "a place of sculls" that "may with propriety be called Golgotha." In response, Continental officers swore "civilization or death to all Savages."[31] A militia responded by burning to the ground Onoquaga, Brant's home village, killing the livestock, and murdering Mohawk children "by running them through with bayonets and holding them up to see how they would twist and turn."[32]

And on it went until November of 1778, when Seneca, Mohawk, Loyalists, and British regulars descended on Cherry Valley, New York, a frontier town sixty miles west of Albany. In what amounted to an indiscriminate murder rampage, Seneca warriors devastated the town, abducted seventy civilians, and killed another thirty. One Mohawk leader explained the rationale to an American officer: "You Burned our Houses, which makes us and our Brothers, the Seneca Indians angrey, so that we destroyed, men, women and Children."[33]

After Brant led a 1779 attack on the town of Minisink on the New York border with Pennsylvania, which ended with four townsfolk killed and scalped, Washington tried to bring an end to the remorseless violence on the New York borderlands by sending an army, led by Major-General John Sullivan, into the heart of Iroquoia. Writing from his headquarters in Middle Brook, New Jersey, Washington laid out a fearsome mandate: "the total destruction and devastation of their settlements and the capture of as many prisoners of every age and sex as possible. It will be essential to ruin their crops now in the ground and prevent their planting more. . . . You will not by any means listen to any overture of peace before the total ruin of their settlements is effected. . . . Our future security will be in their inability to injure us [and in] the terror with which the severity of the chastisement they receive will inspire them."[34]

Operating on the theory that ending violence requires the greatest violence, Sullivan's 4,000 troops were a blunt force, able to operate freely with the British now vanquished from upper New York. His army ruthlessly razed forty villages and upward of seven hundred dwellings, displaced 5,000 Haudenosaunee, robbed graves, destroyed 160,000 bushels of subsistence corn, as well as thousands of fruit trees and livestock. One of Sullivan's lieutenants remarked on "the country which, a month previous, appeared like a beautiful and flourishing garden, now presented to the eye little else than a dreary waste, or a smoking heap of ruins."[35] After it was over, Washington boasted he had "completed the entire destruction of the whole country of the Six Nations, except so much of it as is inhabited by the Oneidas, who have always lived in amity with us."[36]

Such scorched-earth devastation, the likes of which was not to be seen again until General Sherman's 1864 annihilation of Atlanta, earned Washington the Seneca name "Town-Destroyer."[37] Cornplanter would inform the "great Councillor of the thirteen fires" that whenever Washington's name is heard, "our women look behind them and turn pale, and our children cling close to the necks of their mothers."[38] Yet, even Sullivan's expedition could not end the unbroken chain of cruel and violent actions against civilians, both white and Native. Even into the early 1780s, British-allied Native American war parties continued to raid white settlements on the New York border, while the Seneca flattened Oneida towns.

When the Treaty of Paris ended the war, the British would make no effort to protect or reward those nations that fought with them. As they had always feared and expected, the Seneca, Mohawk, and others were abandoned by their father, George III. Their lands were not British lands, yet that did not prevent the British from giving them away to the "*thirteen fires*," as Cornplanter put it. The Americans immediately started to encircle Haudenosaunee territory, insult sovereignty, and create inland islands of vanquished refugees, dispossessed from most of their territories and dependent on state annuities.[39] "You are a subdued people," they were told. "You have been overcome in a war which you entered into with us, not only without provocation, but in violation of most sacred obligations."[40] For them, there would never be a just peace.

Even the Oneida, loyal to the American cause, convinced by the highest principles of self-determination, and promised—promised repeatedly—that the new United States would protect them, were betrayed. In the immediate wake of Burgoyne's defeat, Congress verbally reaffirmed its gratitude to them: "We have experienced your love, strong as the oak, and your fidelity, unchangeable as truth. You have kept fast to the ancient covenant chain, and preserved it free from rust and decay, and bright as silver. Like brave men, for glory you despised danger: you stood forth, in the cause of your friends, and ventured your lives in our battles." Congress went so far as to guarantee their future: "While the sun and moon continue to give light to the world, we shall love and respect you. As our trusty friends, we shall protect you; and shall at all times consider your welfare as our own."[41]

That idealistic rhetoric quickly evaporated. For all that they contributed, in the aftermath of the war all Native Americans were reviled and all white settlers were patriots. By 1780, the Oneida people were destitute, their villages mostly destroyed, forcing them to live in huts near Schenectady, where, in addition to starving, they contracted smallpox and suffered from persistent assault from the American soldiers garrisoned at the nearby fort.[42] The federal government completely ignored their plight, fulfilling Brant's warning that the Americans would turn on the Iroquois. The Oneida would not be able to return to their ancestral homelands until 1784, and by then nearly everything had been destroyed.

As much as the Revolution was a war for independence, it was also a war of white expansion that fulfilled a particular vision of a country clear of Indians. In 1775, one New England minister imagined a world where the earth will be "adorned with a beautiful variety of fields, meadows, orchards, and pastures" that are "clothed with flocks, the valleys also are covered over with corn; they shout for joy, they also sing." Ironically, the Haudenosaunee landscape was exactly that. The reverend nonetheless persisted in hopes of vanquishing "Satan's seat," where the "uncultivated wilderness" is rife with "smoky huts and wigwams of naked, swarthy barbarians."[43]

The Oneida futilely petitioned Congress for their losses by invoking their dedication to the making of the nation, but legal machinations, outright lies, conniving land speculators, fraudulent deals, and shameless greed conspired against them.[44] One group of Indians loyal to the Americans lamented in 1787: "The late unhappy wars have Stript us almost Naked of every thing, . . . our Numbers vastly diminished, by being warmly engaged in favour of the United States. . . . We are truly like the man that fell among Thieves, that was Stript, wounded and left for dead in the high way."[45] More graphic was a chief commenting on the ugly turn away from a noble fight for independence and toward a greedy white grab for land: "It had become a proverb among the white people to say, 'as dirty as an Indian,' 'as lazy as an Indian,' 'As drunk as an Indian,' 'lie like Indians.' And we Indians can only say 'Cheat like white man.' And poor Indians must bear it."[46]

From the Native perspective, the American Revolution merely replaced Parliamentary authority with congressional control. The nadir came in

1788, when six million acres of Haudenosaunee lands were legally declared to be the possession of the State of New York, allowing thousands of white settlers to seize a profitable opening that the Oneida were too depleted to resist. Two million of the six million acres became a military tract, divided up into rectangular plots allotted to American soldiers as bounties for their service, and then given town names like Cato, Cicero, Manlius, Marcellus, Pompey, Virgil, and twenty-two others drawn from antiquity, the rhetorical goal being the erasure of Indian history. The 1794 Treaty of Canandaigua, which affirmed Native land rights, looked promising, but the federal government dishonored it.[47] In 1821, the Ogden Land Company took most of the Oneida lands, and two years later many Oneida were removed to Wisconsin. At best, Native peoples would be tolerated aliens within the new United States, not invited to participate in the republic as citizens until 1924.

The Burgoyne campaign, which only lasted a few months in 1777, was not, by itself, a decisive factor in the crushing of Native America, yet the campaign had everlasting repercussions. The killing of Jane McCrea would feed a propaganda machine for decades, convincing Americans that Indian savagery eternally threatened white women and white ways, and that white expansion into the frontier was a justifiable response to that fear.

For the Loyalists, the Saratoga campaign bore little resemblance to what they had imagined it would be. Many of them were so guilty of violent excess that it led Joseph Brant to say he was "very sorry to say that I have those [Loyalists] engaged with me in service, whom are more savage than the savages themselves."[48] They numbered a mere 83 in early July; by September they amounted to 680.[49] They fought at Freeman's Farm, the first battle of Saratoga, but Burgoyne allowed them to separate from the army before the Battle of Bemis Heights because he thought their punishments if captured would be more extreme than those facing the regulars.[50] Jessups's unit, which included David Jones, continued with the British until Burgoyne released them the day before the October 17 surrender, with the idea that they would slip through American lines and follow "Indian paths" in an attempt to reach Ticonderoga or the other British positions on Lakes George and Champlain, with the goal of eventually regrouping in Montreal.[51] The Jessup brothers, however, disregarded Burgoyne's offer and surrendered with the regulars. As it turned out, Burgoyne negotiated terms that immediately freed Jessup's Loyalists to leave, whereupon they made their way to Lake George and then Ticonderoga.

En route north, some escapees from Saratoga encountered American militia units north of Fort Edward, approximately where Jane McCrea died, whereupon they were recaptured. They had to be sequestered under heavy guard because some militiamen wanted them killed in revenge for civilian deaths, such as McCrea's three months earlier.[52] The Native warriors with Burgoyne were moved to Albany, then settled in the devastated Mohawk Valley before kinsmen escorted them to Canada, where poverty forced them into beggary, the sad consequence of their defense of Britain and the Crown.[53]

As for Burgoyne, the Americans paroled him to England, though not before lunch in Gates's marquee and some days with, of all people, General Schuyler in his country house in nearby Stillwater, where the British officers ate and drank everything in sight. On October 27, Burgoyne was taken to Boston, where he rejoined his minimally confined Convention Army, as it was called, toured the sights, and organized formal dances with the ladies of Cambridge. Instantly, Burgoyne, though sick and nearly immobile, became a celebrity. "So great was the curiosity of the citizens of both sexes, and of all ages and description, to get a peep at Gen. Burgoyne, that the streets were filled, the doors, windows, the tops of the houses and fences crowded."[54]

Mercy Otis Warren, however, thought his "idle and dissipated army" had "corrupted the students of Harvard College, and the youth of the capital and its environs, who were allured to enter into their gambling parties and other scenes of licentiousness."[55] Horrified, Hannah Fayerweather Winthrop cast a critical eye on the German captives, "such a sordid set of creatures . . . poor, dirty emaciated men," accompanied by "great numbers of women, who seemed to be the beasts of burden, . . . barefooted, clothed in dirty rags," plus "children, . . . some very young infants, who were born on the road."[56]

Burgoyne also became embroiled in a month-long court-martial against American Colonel David Henley, who was in charge of the 1,200 men guarding Burgoyne's army. Burgoyne claimed Henley, whom he described as "heinously criminal," had not only stabbed two unarmed soldiers, but was also accused of being an accessory to two other assaults.[57] Animosities between the American guards and British prisoners had turned violent in December. The quick-tempered Colonel Henley was disciplining a British corporal for insulting an American militia officer when words turned to mutual threats. Unable to silence the corporal, Henley ordered a guard to run him through with a bayonet, and when he froze, Henley dismounted his horse and did it himself. Other bayonet stabbings followed, leading Burgoyne to file charges against Henley for his "most indecent, violent, vindictive severity against unarmed men, and of intentional murder."[58] In the subsequent court-martial, Burgoyne took it upon himself to lead the prosecution, which began on January 20, 1778.[59] In one of the most bizarre twists in the history of military justice, a prisoner was to prosecute one of his captors.

The American Judge-Advocate for the defense, Lieutenant-Colonel William Tudor, a protégé of John Adams, defended the attempted murder charge against Henley, as well as the felony charge claiming Henley was an accessory to attacks against other British soldiers. Tudor quickly got Henley acquitted of the attempted murder charges. Tudor's tactic for exonerating Henley for being an accomplice in crimes committed by his subordinates, however, was both novel and astonishing: he brought up the example of Jane McCrea as precedent. If Henley was guilty of inciting his soldiers to crime, then "by the same logic" Burgoyne himself, Tudor argued, ought to face charges because of "the Savages who accompanied and disgraced his army last summer." Did the Natives not do Burgoyne's bidding? Surely, the general was "pleased at the butchery of the nerveless old man, defenseless female, and infant prattler." Thus, was not Burgoyne criminally liable for his Indians' predations against civilians? Reaching for his trump card, Tudor turned to face Burgoyne. After all, "because he hated rebels, he therefore influences the Indians to massacre that young unfortunate, the inoffending and wretched Miss McCrea!"[60]

Thanks to Tudor's defense, the court cleared Colonel Henley of all wrongdoing. Out of frustration, Burgoyne, dramatic to the end, challenged him to a duel that never took place. After consigning £100,000 as punitive payment for all the damage he had done, Burgoyne was moved under guard to Rhode Island, boarded the British frigate *Juno*, and set sail for England on April 15, 1778, landing in Plymouth in mid-May, leaving behind the Northern Expedition, Saratoga, defeat, surrender, and even his army. But not humiliation. Jane McCrea haunted John Burgoyne in England; she would be the phantom Shakespearean ghost visiting the defeated general to the end of his life.

7.

A GREAT NOISE IN BRITAIN AND AMERICA

THE AMERICAN PRESS during the Revolutionary War would prove to be an accelerant on an already burning fire.[1] For example, civilian fear of Native Americans had been rampant long before Jane McCrea's killing. As a case in point, in 1775, General Schuyler had written to Congress to outline the intimidating British plan to recruit Native tribes to their side. Schuyler requested his letter be kept confidential. Yet Congress, acting without Schuyler's permission and wanting to whip up public sentiment against the British in advance, forced the *Pennsylvania Evening Post* to print the general's letter and emphasize, in all caps, that the British were inviting Natives to "FEAST ON A BOSTONIAN AND DRINK HIS BLOOD." In turn, seventeen other papers reprinted Schuyler's original.[2]

After Schuyler's letter was published, a chain of hysteria ensued. Samuel Adams alerted his cousin John that cannibalism was on Britain's strategic agenda.[3] For his part, John Adams was already primed to believe the worst, having written James Warren that he will dread the day that Indians "take up the Hatchet" for Whitehall. "To let loose these blood Hounds to scalp

Men, and to butcher Women and Children is horrid." Natives, he averred, "conduct their Wars, So entirely without Faith and Humanity, that it would bring eternal Infamy on the Ministry." During the French and Indian War, he noted, "The French disgraced themselves . . . by employing them."[4] How low, Adams asked, would the British go during the Revolution?

Adams answered that question in a letter to Abigail in 1776, in which he listed the proxies he predicted the British would be unleashing against the rebellious Americans: "Tories, Landjobbers, Trimmers, Bigots, Canadians." Plus, "Negroes, Hanoverians, Hessians, Russians, Irish Roman Catholicks, Scotch Renegadoes." And, most alarming of all in his estimation and in the American mind, "Indians."[5] Even Thomas Jefferson addressed the issue in the Declaration of Independence: The king is guilty of having "endeavoured to bring on the inhabitants of our frontiers, the merciless Indian Savages, whose known rule of warfare, is an undistinguished destruction of all ages, sexes and conditions."

Print media was a powerful force during the Revolution, especially after the killing of Jane McCrea. Newspapers triggered a frenzy of public fright by casting Native Americans as an existential threat inordinately greater than every other potential menace, including the British army and navy. Accurate or not, the coverage was successful in shaping public opinion of what one New York congressional representative called "treacherous Savages."[6] Stories, some true and many inflated, ricocheted through a jittery population, leading one panicked columnist to a plea directed at the king: "Oh George, what tools art thou obliged to make use of!"[7] When press reports of her death reached Philadelphia, legislators seemed as disturbed as the ordinary citizens in Burgoyne's path. Henry Laurens of South Carolina, incoming president of Congress, wrote portentously about "the British Savages" who have "murdered & scalped some men & many women & Children." He could visualize all the "innocent young girls [who] have been taken as they were amusing themselves in the fields & inhumanely Butchered."[8] Congressional delegate Richard Henry Lee decried the crimes of "Indians" who "scalp and murder all before them, neither age, sex, nor political character makes any difference. Men, women, children, whig, Tory, and Protectiontaker, all promiscuously feel the keen scalping knife and the murdering Tomahawk."[9]

As one might expect, newspapers pounced on McCrea's killing like a prophecy come true. She was gold, both to the press and to the Patriot propagandists wishing to feed anxieties, spur action, and sell papers. A young, innocent, pretty white woman, about to be married, then captured, killed, and scalped by Native warriors in British service was an irresistibly sensational subject. In an instant, as one citizen living along the Mohawk River recalled, "stories of the tragical fate of Jane McCrea" had "spread throughout the continent with the rapidity of lightning; every bosom was thrilled as by an electric shock, and beat in unison."[10]

The panic over McCrea's death, and what it could mean for all civilians, began in the New York newspapers, beginning on July 31, five days after her killing. Within a fortnight, news of the "shocking tale" of a "murdered sweet heart" spread southward to Pennsylvania, Maryland, Virginia, and South Carolina, her death becoming one of the most lurid and talked about storylines of the Revolution.[11] Almost overnight, the news reports of the death of an unfortunate but otherwise unremarkable civilian living in northern New York intensified into a tabloid exposé of Britain's morally depraved war machine and a fierce condemnation of the murderous excesses of the Native auxiliaries working for the Crown.[12]

The *New-York Packet*, reported that "Lieut. Van Veghten was most inhumanely butchered and scalped. . . . Two Serjeants and two Privates were likewise killed and scalped, one of the latter had both his hands cut off." Warriors then "took a young woman, Janey M'Crea by name, out of a house at Fort Edward, carried her about half a mile into the bushes, and there killed and scalped her in cold blood."[13]

As was the custom then, dozens of newspapers across the Northeast and down the coast, from Boston to Charleston, reprinted the *Packet* piece, sometimes embellishing it with eye-catching lines—such as "This brutal scene," or, "Scalped and Mangled"—that set readers on edge. With each iteration of the story, the crimes against humanity multiplied. "The Indians daily scalp men, women and children," claimed a writer for the *Pennsylvania Packet*, "and by what I can learn there is very little difference between the Regulars and Indians, for when Miss M'Crea was butchered and scalped, a large number of Regulars were at a little distance, spectators of the horrid act."[14] Seven papers claimed three hundred British regulars stood nearby. "A young lady of the name of miss Jenny M'Crea, of a good family, and some share of beauty," the *Pennsylvania Packet* wrote, "was taken by the savages. . . . They butchered the poor innocent girl, and scalped her in the sight of those very men who are continually preaching up their tender mercies, and the forbearance of their more than Christian king. Is not this sufficient to congeal the heart of humanity with horror!"[15]

By mid-August, there were said to be four hundred British regulars and Native warriors at McCrea's killing. "They took an officer [Van Vechten], stripped him and wounded him in ten places, with knives and tomahawks then scalped him." The Boston *Independent Chronicle* added, in rising prose, they "dragged an old woman and girl out of the house, killed and scalped the old woman, fired two brace of balls through the body of the girl, and then scalped her."[16]

Newspapers never failed to say she was a "sweet-heart," that her killers were "Devils . . . disposed to murder, merely for the sake of murdering." They told readers that "the harmless, helpless female, by nature, too feeble to make defense, falls a sacrifice to their thirst for blood."[17] Her killing inspired the *Connecticut Courant* and three other newspapers to feature an impassioned plea written by "an officer of distinction": "Hear, Oh Heavens! And give ear, Oh America! And be aroused, as a strong lion, at the infernal ferocity of our enemies, who, devil like, delight in the most barbarous acts of cruelty, sport themselves in inflicting the most excruciating miseries on their fellow-creatures, and have an insatiable thirst for human blood without discrimination for friend or foe."[18]

With the possible exception of independence and the battles of Lexington and Concord, no other war story received such blanket coverage as Jane McCrea's murder. Hers was the inescapable story of the summer of 1777. So was the sidebar story of Burgoyne's inability to punish the perpetrators of her killing, or to reform the practices of his warriors. The *New-York Journal* and ten other newspapers pointed accusatory fingers at "Burgoyne, the chief and director of the King of Great-Britain's band of thieves, robbers, cut-throats, scalpers, and murderers of every denomination, now infesting the northern and western frontiers." Reports in the *Journal* charged that after McCrea's death the general discontinued cash rewards for scalps "from the murdered, and half murdered inhabitants" by his band of "Savage Tories, Indians, Britons, Hessians, Brunswickers, Waldeckers, and other profligate scum of the human race, now in his service."[19] Never mind that Burgoyne never paid for scalps, the claims that he did nonetheless spread like a runaway virus.[20]

Adding to the verbal demolition of Burgoyne, William Livingston, the governor of New Jersey, published in the *Pennsylvania Packet*—as well as newspapers in New York, Boston, and Norwich—a withering parody of the general's threat of brutality against resisters. "I, the great knight of de la Mancha/ Without 'Squire Carleton my Sancha/ Will tear you limb from limb asunder/ With cannon blunderbuss and thunder." To 10,000 Indians,

"I'll give full scope and play, to scalp, rip and flay," and if no one heeds my warning, "I swear by George, and by St. Paul/ I will exterminate you all."[21]

The capstone of coverage came in early September, when Gates released his finely crafted letter to Burgoyne in order to "inflame the populace and blacken the royal cause."[22] Because every active American newspaper carried Gates's letter, as well as Burgoyne's weak reply, eager readers gained front-row access to a vicious dispute at the highest levels of the British and American militaries.

When taken together, from the first reports of her slaying to Gates's public relations masterstroke, Jane McCrea was one of the most universally recognized names in the United States.[23] William Tudor, the defense attorney in Burgoyne's suit against Colonel Henley in Cambridge, knew that. When he invoked McCrea's death in an effort to point an accusatory finger at Burgoyne, he assumed everyone in the courtroom would immediately recognize her and her tragic story because she was the best-known victim of the Revolution, with the exception of Major-General Richard Montgomery and Major-General Joseph Warren, who fell at Quebec and Bunker Hill, respectively, in 1775.

The press coverage offered all the raw evidence needed to convince readers of the ruthlessness of the British war effort and the barbarity of the Native Americans working for Britain. Her killing aroused comradeship among Patriots and nurtured devotion to the cause, as readers from New Hampshire to Georgia collectively lamented her violent death and condemned the evil powers that brought it about. At the same time, McCrea was a potent wedge issue for Loyalists, challenging them to question continuing support for the British, their motives, tactics, and ethics. Even fence-sitters who preferred nonalignment had to ask themselves if they should continue to remain in a state of "passive inaction," as one of McCrea's early chroniclers put it, or decide to embrace "the dangers of a manly resistance."[24]

In Britain, McCrea's murder magnified the rifts that already existed over the war. There, the press, more vigorous, aggressive, and far more vituperative than its American counterpart, had been making a spectacle of Native Americans in British service ever since shocking news arrived in London of savagery during the French and Indian War over a decade before.[25] With the outbreak of the Revolution in 1775, public and political debates over the Native warriors working for the empire were rekindled. Unlike the Tories in Whitehall and Parliament, who justified the use of Native Americans by citing their ability to provoke "dread" among American civilians and soldiers, the opposition Whigs consistently condemned the use of military proxies.[26] How could "savages"—as Native Americans were mostly called—be justified in "butchering our fellow-subjects," wrote an opposition columnist in the popular *Gentleman's Magazine*.[27] Whigs said the hidden goal of government in using Native American proxies was not just "to subdue," but also to "exterminate, a people whom they affected to consider and pretended to reclaim as subjects." Such a strategy will surely backfire, one writer predicted, because the "terror excited by these savage auxiliaries" will force inhabitants to abandon their houses and then take up arms. "Every man saw the necessity of becoming a temporary soldier, not only for his own security, but for the protection and defense of those connections, which are dearer than life itself."[28]

British newspapers dutifully published Burgoyne's June proclamation promising to unleash hell on the Crown's enemies, while at the same time certifying that his proxies were adhering to the principles of *jus in bello*. Soon thereafter, however, front-page dispatches from America told lurid tales of crimes committed near Ticonderoga. One "provincial officer," the London *Gazette* breathlessly reported, was taken prisoner "by a party of savages in the service of Gen. Burgoyne," who "took out his heart, then cut it to pieces reeking from his body, and ate it."[29]

Jane McCrea's killing was the last straw in Britain's growing intolerance of Native auxiliaries capable of committing crimes outside British rules of warfare. Though her death in July was not initially reported in the British press, the letters between Gates and Burgoyne early in September were printed in full, often with editorialized titles, such as "Indian Barbarity."[30] By the end of 1777, her name had appeared in 90 percent of London's newspapers, and as a result, she—and Britain's Native forces in America—were topics for heated debates held in coffee houses, over dinners, and within Parliament. As one British officer remarked on the surprising geographic reach of the Gates-Burgoyne exchange, "That the letters should attain circulation and credence . . . is truly astonishing."[31]

Londoners, like their American cousins, were also privy to the spat between two leading generals. There, in graphic black and white, was Gates shaming Burgoyne for hiring "the savages of America to scalp Europeans, and the descendants of Europeans," and further blaming him for the killing of "Miss McCrea," a betrothed Loyalist girl who was "carried into the woods, and there scalped and mangled in the most shocking manner." Burgoyne's reply, for all Britons to see, looked defensive compared to Gates's bold rebuke. If that exchange were not damning enough, British newspapers managed to acquire and print a note Gates had sent to Congress, in which he ridiculed Burgoyne's evasive reply to McCrea as "so extravagant a performance."[32]

In addition to the reports of her killing and the exchange between the generals, which were compelling reading, Whig newspapers and journals mined the McCrea fiasco to editorialize their large-scale political case against the entire idea of an American war. John Almon, a renowned Whig pamphleteer writing in the *Public Advertiser*, summarized Burgoyne's disgrace in blunt terms: "All generals are accountable for their allies."[33] Another Whig journalist lamented the betrayal of a woman devoted to Britain, albeit with some mistaken information: "The young lady is represented to have been in all the innocence of youth, and bloom of beauty." Her father had been loyal to the Crown, "and to wind up the catastrophe of this odious tragedy she was to have been married to a British officer on the very day that she was massacred."[34]

Those Native allies, Whig newspapers imagined, possessed a hardwired bloodlust: "I shall kill; I shall exterminate; I shall burn my enemies; I shall bring away slaves; I shall devour their heart, dry their flesh, drink their blood; I shall tear off their scalps, and make cups of their skulls."[35] No newspaper would ever make an effort to investigate the actual practices of Native Americans, or to explain the dire situation that had forced them to join the war effort on either the American or the British side. For most readers, Native warriors were by nature inhuman killing machines.

The *St. James Chronicle* turned to sarcasm to mock the Northern campaign in the form of listing fake books for sale: "The Conquest of America, A Fable," nicely summarized the significance of Burgoyne's defeat. More stinging was "Saratoga, An Historical Tragedy by General Gates"; and most pertinent to McCrea, "An Essay on the Origins of Tomahawks and Scalping Knives by General B________."[36]

Quickly, the satirical circus turned visual. As soon as the Gates-Burgoyne letters reached London, detailing McCrea's death, John Williams etched a scathing multi-paneled print entitled *The Closet*. On the upper right, the king presides in his "Closet," a reference to a conference room at St. James Palace where George met with a coterie of advisors, composed of friendly ministers and members of Parliament and teeming with political intrigue.[37] Standing behind the counselors in the left corner the Devil encourages the secret body to persuade the king to pursue the war aggressively.

The Closet. 1778. Etching and aquatint. New York, The Metropolitan Museum of Art, Gift of William H. Huntington, 1883.

On the left side of the print, Williams stacked four panels, each with a devilish episode resulting from the king's meeting. The top left panel depicts a scalping riot with Jane McCrea at the center. To be perfectly clear to whom Williams referred, he etched in her name, "McRae," and in a wicked satirical touch, added a speech balloon that voices her shock on that particular day: "Oh horrid! Is this the Marriage Ceremony?"[38] The town burning in the distance is Esopus, the original Dutch name for Kingston, New York, where John Vanderlyn was born in 1775.

John Almon published a devastating political cartoon that specifically indicted George III for Indian atrocities. Sprawled on the ground, the king cradles a human skull in his left hand while chomping on a femur offered by an obliging Indian. Two other Indians drain blood from the mutilated torso of a child, whose dismembered head, hand, and leg litter the foreground.

On the right, Archbishop William Markham, a toady to the Crown who gave sermons supporting military campaigns in America, walks forward, crozier in hand, preaching, "That thy Ways may be known upon Earth." Following him, a sailor carries boxes of scalping knives, crucifixes, and tomahawks, all marked "Presents to Indians," and declares, "we are hellish good

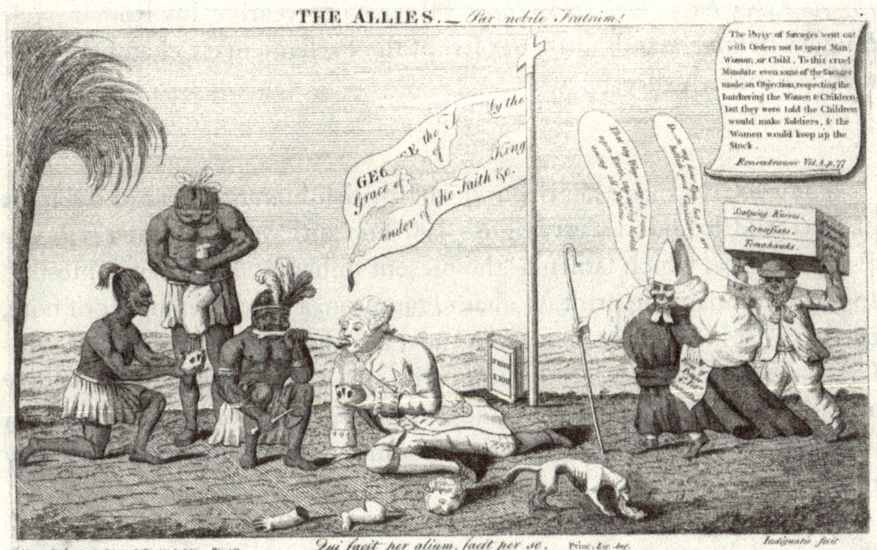

The Allies—Par nobile Fratrum! 1780. Etching. Washington DC, Library of Congress Prints and Photographs Division.

Christians." Hanging from a flagpole topped by a cross, a shredded banner reads, "George . . . [def]ender of the Faith etc." The Holy Bible stands upside-down on the ground.

At the top of the print, the screed continues in the title: *THE ALLIES.-Par nobile Fratrum!*. A quotation from Horace's *Satires*, "A Noble Pair of Brothers," it refers to the unholy alliance struck between Britain and Native Americans. Below, the print is signed "*Indignatio.*" To the left of the signature is a damning caption, again in Latin: *Qui facit per alium, facit per se*, or, "he who acts through another commits the act himself." George III, however distant he may have been geographically, was nonetheless liable for every civilian death during the Revolution; the blood of Jane McCrea was, in effect, on his hands.

London prints naturally raked Burgoyne over the coals. In *The Political Raree-Show or a Picture of Parties and Politics during and at the Close of the Last Session of Parliament, June 1779*, an older man has invited a boy to a peepshow of the British government, a twelve-part spectacle of incompetence. In one panel, "*The Generals in America doing nothing, or worse than nothing*," General Howe takes a break by his marquee while in the background Burgoyne kneels to Gates at Saratoga. In the adjacent panel, "*Prov-*

ing that they have done every thing," Burgoyne, wearing his Roman-style military helmet, stands at the far left of the Parliamentary chamber to demand "Justice: Justice."

Jane McCrea made her debut in the British literary world in the form of Reverend Edmund Cartwright's 190-line anti-war poem of 1779, *The Prince of Peace*, which laments "the present unhappy American contest."[39] In the accompanying print, William Hamilton, a British engraver of note, tried to imagine the woodland scene near Fort Edward seconds before McCrea's death. With access to minimal information, other than the widely accessible letters between Gates and Burgoyne, Hamilton relied on his own imagination to picture the lovers' moonlit rendezvous, interrupted by tragedy.

McCrea and Lieutenant Jones have romantically met by a tree, whereupon two Indians accost them. She drops to one knee and seeks shelter in Jones's arms, but the lead Indian, tomahawk in hand, already clutches her hair above the forehead. Jones ineffectually pushes back, while a second Indian brandishes a scalping knife, intent on taking his reward. More fictional than factual, the print attempts to illustrate Cartwright's poem, which pits Natives, "furious" and "insensible of compassion," against "the inchanting power of female beauty." This is the imaginary moment during the "veil of night," in a "moonlight glade," when McCrea has traveled to "yon sequester'd bower" to "listen to her lover's voice/ In thought anticipate the golden hour/ When holy rites shall sanctify her choice/ Vows of long love she breathes, with fondest breath!" But "Soon to cancel all those vows in death!" In a moment, her "waving ringlets" will turn "stiff with clotted gore!" as the "gnashing unrelenting fangs" of the knife rip off her scalp. Ultimately, McCrea's death served as touching evidence for Cartwright's larger cautionary tale about all those who employ mercenaries and proxies. "BRITONS," he concluded, once "fam'd for gentle Hearts!" have fallen into "shame" and "infamy."

Even more ambitious, the Scottish minister James Murray published a sixty-four-page satire on Saratoga based on information that was readily available in newspapers, including Gates's letter detailing McCrea's death. Murray titled his mock play *The New Maid of the Oaks: A Tragedy, as Lately Acted Near Saratoga, by a Company of Tragedians*, a reference to Burgoyne's 1774 stage play *Maid of the Oaks*.[40] Writing under the *nom de plume* Ahab Salem, Murray caricatured Burgoyne in the character of Tullius Furius, a

William Hamilton, for Edmund Cartwright, *The Prince of Peace*. London, 1779. Etching. Amherst College Archives.

brash general who has foolishly made an alliance with "an Indian Sachem" inauspiciously named Bloody Bear.

Tullius compliments Bloody Bear for his "*scale of talents*," which include the "hatchet, tomahawk, and scalping knife." Rather than return the nicety, Bloody Bear quickly sizes up Tullius as "an empty, frothy, vain, young man; . . . I hate your kind. . . . How many filthy lies have your vile race impos'd upon our tribes?" Nonetheless, he asks what Tullius wants: "Kill! Kill all," was the reply, "man, woman, wife and child, in every hamlet, village, town, or hut, from Saratoga, all the country round; For every scalp two dollars—will that do?" Bloody Bear accepts the offer.

In act I, scene II, by a grove of oaks, we encounter Captain Manley and his bride-to-be, Celia, the stand-ins for David Jones and Jane McCrea. Celia is shaking in fear, having heard Tullius's promise to ravage the local citizenry, but Manley, all bravado, swears he will protect her; "none without first killing me shall hurt one comely ringlet of thy auburn locks." In act II, Celia, her fears not allayed, dresses for her wedding, yet knows "that some unseen disaster's not far off." That proves prescient as Bloody Bear confronts her by "a neighboring wood." Celia begs, "Can a maiden's tears, a bride's entreaty, not touch your cruel heart? . . . What harm have women done you?" Bloody Bear scoffs at her entreaty; it might weaken the sun, the moon, and the rocks on earth, but not this warrior: "Were all the brides and virgins, throughout this country, present here just now, I'd kill and scalp them all." The situation hopeless, Celia resigns to her fate, "Heav'n! thy will be done, my soul submits." Bloody Bear then "Kills and scalps her."

In scene III, Laertius, Celia's brother, arrives in the American camp to tell Horatius—that is to say Horatio Gates—who is "General of the Troops of Columbiana"—the appalling news of a young woman:

Drest in her wedding robes, with bended knees,
And hands stretch'd forth to heav'n, she prayed
"O spare me, Bloody Bear! O spare by life!
What has a harmless virgin done to merit
Such vengeance from thy hand? Oh heaven
Have mercy on my soul, a bloody marriage day . . .
Farewell Manley, world and all!"
Her peerless lips had scarcely spoke these words,
And sent her last request to heaven; when
Soon the fatal blow pierc'd through her skull,
And laid her lifeless, prostrate on the ground.
While reeking in her gore, the savage brute
Detach'd her scalp, went off, and left her dead.

In tragic response, Horatius "stands in silence; the tears dropping from his eyes."

Meanwhile, Tullius Furius staggers toward military ruin, and also moral defeat for having submitted to Bloody Bear, who has "stain'd your honour" by slaughtering innocent civilians. In act IV, during Tullius's surrender to Horatius, Manley confronts Tullius directly, "*holding the Scalp of* Celia *in his Hand.*" The thinly disguised David Jones insists that Celia's "blood calls loud for vengeance, and won't cease to cry, till justice have its course on that vile wretch who shed it." Pushing Celia's bloody scalp up to Tullius in a climactic moment inspired by Shakespeare's *Richard III*, Manley wails: "Thou paid the price for *that*, and hundreds more, whose ghosts will haunt thee till the day of doom, then tear thy soul with scorpions for ever. . . . Thou'rt a murderer, an arrant coward."

The real-life David Jones may or may not have ever set his eyes on Jane McCrea's scalp, yet James Murray took full poetic license to engineer this face-to-face confrontation between Manley and Tullius—Burgoyne's double—in the final scene. Then, in a remarkable twist on the historical record, the playwright walks Manley across military lines and toward the fictional Horatio Gates. "Noble Horatius; will you accept my service, as volunteer in Freedom's worthy cause? I flee from the base country, and those men that murder women. I'll join your line, permit me." Horatius refuses, after all, Manley is a prisoner of war. Left with nothing, the bereft Manley is so tormented that he can no longer live. Without hope he runs toward the Hudson; "Upon the banks he paus'd a while, and stood as in suspense, then plung'd into the flood."

It is not known whether Murray's play was performed on stage—most likely it was for the entertainment of Burgoyne's critics. *The New Maid of the Oaks* was published in 1778, at the height of the controversy over the Northern Expedition, when Whigs were attacking government, Burgoyne was defending his record, Tories were trying to squirm out of responsibility, and Jane McCrea's death was haunting everyone.

Across Britain, the common criticism of the Northern Campaign centered on the misguided decision to use Native Americans, and to a lesser extent Germans, to augment an understaffed British army tasked with an awesome, if not impossible agenda. Inevitably, every blunder made by Britain's allies would become Britain's blunder. In the modern intelligence world, "proxy blowback" is the term used to describe the unintended military or political costs that are paid for auxiliaries who deviate from a sponsor's preferences.[41] To the British, the strategic allure of proxies was obvious: let Native Americans take on the riskiest operations and spare the main force. Yet, there were intrinsic dangers, too. If unregulated, operations can overspill the boundaries set for the proxies. At the end of the day, the proxies themselves are likely to suffer the brunt of countermeasures, both military and political, against the practice. And so too will the original employers, who have to take responsibility for the unauthorized actions of their proxies.

In McCrea's case, a crime committed by Native American proxies in rural northern New York climbed to the level of international scandal, not only reaching the British public, but also entering the halls of Parliament. To be sure, the homicide was an indictment of Britain's Native auxiliaries. But an instant later, it boomeranged back to Burgoyne and Britain for their handling of the proxies and, indeed, the war itself. This crime against humanity, magnified in the media, was threatening to derail the core mission of holding America within the empire.

Foreseeing the inevitable criticisms roused by spreading stories of unauthorized warrior conduct, the British manager of the war, Secretary George Germain, proposed censoring news of atrocities committed by Native Americans.[42] That would have been a futile errand because British newspapers were independent and typically carried an endless number of war dispatches—some inflated for effect. Given that censorship was impossible, recriminations over war policy flourished. The *London Evening Post* expressed a nation's painful regrets. The government, noted the *Post*, had sworn that the point of war was to guarantee our "dear brethren" in America would always be part and parcel of Britain. Yet, upon closer examination, the frightful events that transpired in the first years of warfare made it clear that British policy was indisputably "unjust." "[We] set their cities on fire; we scalped their women and children; and we butchered whole legions of their husbands and fathers for not submitting to this impious claim. This was more unjust still."[43]

Because McCrea was the central figure in the political blowback for the Northern Expedition, she became a lightning rod for the Whig opposition. In the House of Lords, William Pitt, the 1st Earl of Chatham and a former prime minister, called for the cessation of hostilities in a heated speech of November 18, 1777. The "conquest of English America is an impossibility," he opened. Attempts to win were only bringing "ruin" to Britain's door, the result of employing proxies who only stiffened American resolve and brought "indelible stain on the national honour." Who, the aged Pitt rhetorically asked, "has dared to authorize and associate to our arms the tomahawk and scalping knife of the savage . . . to call into civil alliance the wild and inhuman savage of the woods, to delegate to the merciless Indians the defence of disputed rights, and to wage the horrors of his barbarous war against our brethren?"[44] The audience knew the unspoken answer to his question: The king and the Tory government of Lord North.

Upon learning of Burgoyne's surrender on December 3, the renowned Pitt doubled the invective in a spectacular speech. The Indian "scalping-knife and tomahawk," he condemned, had left "a stigma which all the water of the rivers Delaware and Hudson would never wash away; it would rankle in the breast of America, and sink so deep into it, that [Americans] would never forget nor forgive the horrid injury." Pitt unleashed a torrent of words: "infidel savage," "cannibal savage," "satanic," "butchers," "murderers and plunderers," "massacres," "mangled victims," "torturing, murdering, roasting, and eating," and "thirsting for the blood of man, woman, and child." That was the "carnage" being inflicted on "your Protestant brethren." Pitt again begged the question: "Who were the authors and advisers of letting loose those blood-hounds and hell-hounds, the savages of America, upon our brethren?"[45] When taken to a vote, the Tory majority roundly rejected Pitt's impassioned motion to end hostilities.

The Whig opposition, which was small in size yet loud in voice, sought to prove their case with whatever information they could get their hands on, whether it be true, slanted, incomplete, or false. The Tory government, for its part, labored to quell the political panic by pointing to the crimes committed by the rebels and noting the efforts of Americans to recruit the same Native Americans. To Whitehall's way of thinking, using Native proxies was unavoidable.

In response, Pitt's Whig allies in the House of Lords—the Duke of Richmond and the Earl of Shelburne—just ramped up the rhetoric. They spoke of the "inhuman wolves" who slaughtered "the unfortunate Miss McRea" and asked whether the British were really any better. "Was the Indian knife a more dreadful weapon than an Englishman's bayonet?"[46] Relying on Gates's now ubiquitous letter and the agitated reports emanating from American newspapers, the Whigs painted a picture of the Northern Expedition as a giant killing field rife with proxies who carried "desolation and destruction amongst our American cousins." Even though Native Americans were fighting for their own lands and were, in fact, minor players when compared to the German and British armies, they were the epitome of evil in Parliament.[47]

The less genteel House of Commons, meeting in the cramped confines of Saint Stephen's Chapel in Westminster Palace, mirrored and multiplied the attacks in the House of Lords. In December of 1777, Charles Fox harangued the government's "scalping tomahawk measures." If, according to Whitehall's logic, Americans "deprived of their ancient rights are grown tumultuous, bleed them; if they are attacked by a spirit of insurrection,—bleed them! if their fever should rise into rebellion,—bleed them!; . . . more blood! more blood! still more blood!"[48] George Gordon, from Wiltshire, invoked Jane McCrea by name: "And that most horrible massacre of Miss Mac Ray's, will remain an indelible stain on the religion and humanity of Great Britain in after ages." Even when "queen Mary's massacre of the Protestants in England, and the persecutions of the Presbyterians in Scotland by king Charles . . . shall be done away and forgotten," the specter of Jane's McCrea's murder would continue to haunt the nation.[49]

John Wilkes, the most radical of the Whigs—that is, the one most eager to tear down the Tory government and grant independence to the United States—called for an end of "this unnatural, unjust, and barbarous war to our utter destruction." To the ministries in Whitehall, Wilkes was a monster. A pro-Tory engraving in *Westminster Magazine*, titled *The Parricide*, shows a demonic Wilkes instructing an allegorical figure of America to assault a half-naked female figure of Britannia, who is held down and surrounded by Wilkes's fellow Whigs. Wilkes might have been, in the words of one historian, "a demagogue, an adulterer, and even perhaps a perverted infidel," yet all agreed that he was a brilliant political operative who stopped at nothing in his quest for "a full and equal representation of the people."[50] For Patriot Americans he shined as their champion and acted as their cudgel.

To Wilkes, the war had inevitable results: "torrents of blood," the "waste of national treasure," and "no probability of a near and final" end.[51] Especially egregious, he said in a November 1777 speech, were the "circumstances of cruelty, which fill the mind with horror." Turning to the Northern Expedition, he asked, "are the *scalping*-knife and tomahawk necessary *calamities of war?*"[52] Quoting from Burgoyne's promise to unleash Native forces on all who resist, Wilkes remarked, "Merciful heaven! . . . Has the feeble old man, the helpless infant, the defenceless female, ever experienced the tender mercies of an *Indian savage,*" who "drinks the blood of his enemy?"[53] Worse, Wilkes speculated that Burgoyne himself was guilty of "drinking human blood out of the skulls of enemies," as well as consenting "to the mangling of the dead."[54]

According to Wilkes, the stain spreading over Britain could not be hidden because "General Gates's Letters have informed the World with what savage Ferocity and Cruelty the *Indians* carried on a War, to which they were so *strongly* invited. . . . Every Gazette of Europe and America has published . . . the charges of frequent murders and massacres of the defenceless inhabitants."[55] In a May 1778 speech, Wilkes actually read Gates's letter aloud, including the passages about McCrea.[56] Then, in an astonishing turn, he asked the House, "Is not that murder yet *unexpiated?* The fate of the unfortunate Miss McRea is almost the American *sacrifice of Iphigenia.*"[57]

Wilkes, whose speeches were regularly published whole in newspapers, saw in McCrea the outlines of a New World classical tragedy. Agamemnon intends to kill his daughter, Iphigenia, who is betrothed to Achilles, so that the gods, thus appeased, would let the Greek fleet sail to Troy. Wilkes recited—in French—a famous passage from the playwright Racine's

Iphigénie, a tragedy of 1674, wherein Iphigenia's mother, Clytemnestra, "harrows the soul with terror" when she says:[58]

A priest surrounded by a cruel mob,
Will lay a criminal hand upon my daughter?
Tear open her breast, and, with a curious eye,
In her beating heart consult the will of the gods?

In some accounts of the story, Clytemnestra later expiates Iphigenia's death by killing Agamemnon, who was Wilkes's rhetorical substitute for America's father, George III.

With that potent image still lingering, Wilkes read, verbatim, Gates's address to his troops on the eve of the Saratoga battles, complete with phrases like "murder of aged parents," "innocent children," and "mangling the blooming virgin."[59] Then, lurching toward hyperbole, Wilkes questioned the British command, "Is this just and Christian warfare?" How can a government justify "promiscuous carnage" in a campaign in which "scarcely fewer women and children, in some Parts where the War raged with the greatest fury, expired under the torture of the tomahawk and *scalping-knife,* than were killed by the Sword and Bayonet."[60]

Both Wilkes and Gordon were effective, but the political spotlight belonged to Edmund Burke, the greatest orator of the age. In a two-hour speech in November 1777, he questioned how a king, "famed for his humanity, benevolence, and sanctity of manner," could justify hiring "miscreants," known for "brutality, murder, and destruction." In February 1778, in support of a motion to mount an official inquiry into unauthorized warrior predations, including McCrea's killing, Burke delivered a three-hour evening speech before an "entranced assembly"—a speech acknowledged as the most commanding of his career. In it, he was said to have "traversed the whole scale of oratorical emotion" in order to draw outrage over Britain's decision to recruit initially reluctant Native Americans to wage war against Anglo-Americans by doling out hard liquor, false promises, veiled threats, and ample gifts—including crates of scalping knives. "Whole nations of savages," he charged, were "bribed to take up the hatchet."[61]

Burke had long made American affairs his specialty. He had co-authored in 1757 a two-volume *Account of the European Settlements in America*, in which he wrote apocalyptically about Indians, and astutely connected Britain's prosperity to the immoral seizure of Native lands and the exploitation of black slaves.[62] In the 1760s, Burke had closely studied the French and Indian War and argued for the repeal of the Stamp Act. He had opposed the Coercive Acts of 1774, warned Britons not to employ "savage" auxiliaries, served as colonial agent for the assembly of New York until 1775, and in his famous *Letter to the Sheriffs of Bristol* of 1777 passionately insisted that an independent America was preferable to the quagmire of a mutually destructive war. Naturally, he set his rhetorical sights on condemning Burgoyne, who had introduced atrocities by unapologetically assigning Native Americans the task of doing whatever was necessary to, as he put it, "overtake the harden'd Enemies of Great Britain and America."[63]

To be sure, Burke allowed that Burgoyne's proclamation, despite all its "bombast absurdity," had tried to set high-minded rules to prevent unnecessary killing and scalping. That aside, in Burke's estimation the entire Northern Expedition, from Whitehall's strategy to Burgoyne's leadership, was deeply flawed—tactically, ethically, and morally. The tragic proof, Burke asserted before his fellow MPs, was striking. "The horrid story of Miss MacRay, murdered by the savages on the day of Her marriage with an officer of the King's troops," exemplified, to Burke, the sad truth that "savages did, in effect, indiscriminately murder men, women, and children, friends and foes," including the "slaughter" of a young woman who was, ironically, "affected to the King's government."[64]

Burke, whose "enunciation was vehement, rapid, and never checked by any embarrassment," argued before Parliament in his heavy Irish brogue that the ultimate blame for "cruelties too horrible and too full of turpitude for Christian mouths to utter or ears to hear" did not exclusively rest in the hearts and hands of Natives, but also on the British themselves. As government searched for scapegoats, Burke suggested Britons hold up a mirror. Reveling in his I-told-you-so moment, he alleged that civilian deaths like McCrea's were "done at our instigation"; for "*all intents and purposed, as if done by ourselves.*"[65]

Thanks to the British press that had published and republished Gates's scorching letter to Burgoyne, everyone in Parliament, including the Whitehall ministers in attendance, already knew who "Miss MacRay" was. Burke later acknowledged that in England Gates was "not wanting" as a prominent figure. He may have been thousands of miles away, yet he was able, according to Burke, "to aggravate and inflame the picture of these excesses; and with no small effect."[66]

As he continued his speech, an anguished Burke magnified the crime against McCrea by painting for Parliament a horrific tableau of "a Virgin of an honourable place," who "had grown up in the delight and comfort of

Studio of Joshua Reynolds, *Edmund Burke*, c. 1769 or after. Oil on canvas. London, National Portrait Gallery.

a family," and was about to enter a "moment of blessing that God . . . has made the highest point of human felicity and is indeed a part of pleasure and innocence which Angels might look down on and Envy." However, on the appointed day of her marriage, "This poor creature, who for her beauty was the pride and boast of this rude Country," came to meet her lover, "dressed up in those pretty little ornaments [of] ingenious poverty," her "hair dressed for other purposes that morning." Instead, she heard "war whoops that would have appalled the stoutest heart," and in an instant her scalp was "torn from her head to decorate the infernal habitation of cruelty and barbarism and there left naked," her "body a mangled ghastly spectacle of blood and horror, crying through a hundred mouths to that whose image was defaced for Vengeance."[67] Pinning the blame squarely on Burgoyne, Germain, and the Tory government, Burke added, "Those who have ordered have done it."

Any fool, Burke masterfully added, should have known that warriors were not to be contained by "the King's standard" for military etiquette.[68] To capture the magnitude of Burgoyne's—and Britain's—blunder, Burke requested that his legislative colleagues imagine for a moment employing wild animals to quell a riot. Speaking with arch sarcasm, he asked what one might say to the beasts: "gentle lions, my humane bears, my sentimental wolves, my tender-hearted hyenas, go forth"; pretend you are "Christians and members of a civilized society," and by the way, be sure to "take care not to hurt man, woman or children."[69]

Horace Walpole wrote of this extraordinary moment in his diary: Burke "drew such a pathetic picture of the cruelties of the King's army, particularly in the alleged case of a young woman on whose ransom, not beauty, they quarreled, and murdered her,—*that he drew iron tears*" from the eyes of the most hardened men in Parliament.[70] The *Public Advertiser* said Burke had described "shocking cruelties" with a "Pathos which melted the Auditory almost to tears and filled them with the utmost Horror." Burke's "metaphors were Bold, his Expressions nervous," his style "eloquent, and sublime."[71] Remarked George Johnstone, sitting on the floor of Parliament that day, if visitors had been allowed into the Commons gallery, as they were usually, Burke's speech "would have excited them to tear the Ministers to pieces as they went out of the House."[72] Most British newspapers printed summaries of Burke's speeches, which Walpole accurately described as "painted orations," but the "*iron tears*" speech was so extraordinary that the Whig MP Isaac Barré openly wept and suggested it be printed on broadsides and posted on the doors of Britain's churches.[73]

For Burke, who possessed a special ability to visualize tragedy, McCrea was more than an object of pity and outrage; she was the perfect exemplar of the sharp political point he wished to make about the waywardness of entanglements with Indians in the American war, which, he argued, was leading Britain to national disgrace. Merely dropping her name was enough to evoke both sympathy and guilt, but Burke went further by vividly recreating her death in tones so melodramatic that it seemed he was grooming her for immortalization.

Burke was uniquely qualified to imagine McCrea's horror because he was the author of *A Philosophical Enquiry into the Origin of our Ideas of the Sublime and Beautiful*, a well-known treatise that investigated extreme emotional states, in particular how we respond to beauty and terror. Passages from the 1757 treatise come strikingly close to the sublime agony McCrea experienced in 1777. Burke had written of the kind of terror that "naturally arises from a force which nothing can withstand." It generates an uncontrollable "apprehension of pain or death," which in turn produces mental and bodily manifestations "in proportion to the nearness of the cause, and the weakness of the subject." The "weaker subjects," alas, are the ones "most liable to the severest impression of pain and fear." And when we encounter a woman who is attractive and vulnerable, a most peculiar phenomenon occurs, according to Burke's formulation: the magnitude of sublime demise is proportional to the depth of the victim's beauty.

Because Burke's treatise pitted raw power against feminine innocence in a situation of extreme danger, McCrea's defilement was his philosophical treatise come true. Burke even adapted some words and phrases from his 1757 *Treatise* to his "iron tears" speech that featured McCrea. Where he had previously identified "wolves" as "objects of terror," he now substituted "Savages," and for "affecting beauty" in "distress," he held up "Miss MacRay," a "poor creature" and a "Virgin," who lived her last moments in the sublime "universe of Death."

Unlike his colleagues Wilkes, Chatham, and Gordon, Burke made a small effort to avoid racial denigration of Native peoples, as he argued that, "the fault of employing them did not consist in their being of one colour or another; in their using one kind of weapon or another." Otherwise, it was a faint attempt to achieve equanimity. Burke never set foot in America and held long-standing negative predispositions about "Indian character." In his 1757 book on European settlement in America, he devoted an entire chapter to "Indian savagery," yet neglected every other aspect of Native American life. "The Ancients," as he called them, were marked by "horrid appearance," "hideous howlings," and "brutal fury." When they kill, they "satiate their savage fury with the most shocking insults and barbarities to the dead, biting their flesh, tearing the scalp from their heads, and wallowing in their blood like wild beasts."[74]

In front of Parliament in 1778, he said the criminality of the warriors continued to be "their way of making war, which was so horrible that it shocked not only the manner of all civilized people, but far exceeded the ferocity of all barbarians mentioned in history." The "glory of procuring the greatest number of scalps, hung up in their huts as trophies of victory," had led them to unspeakable atrocities. And now, during the American war for independence, "no possible means could prevail on them to alter it," despite the admonitions Burgoyne had given to behave in accord with the law of nations.[75]

Parliamentary speeches typically overstated the size of Native forces. Burgoyne may have ended up with just 400 as part of an 8,000-man force, yet legislators in London visualized hordes of wild men massing for the kill. That may have once been close to the truth during the French and Indian War when "innumerable nations" dominated North America, but in 1777 "no trace remains—great Empires—now shrunk to nothing."[76] Native

Americans "were so reduced in number, that there was no necessity of any connexion with them as nations."[77] This was especially true for the northeastern tribes, which were weak and vulnerable, and mostly wished to be left alone to eke out a living, instead of fighting a white man's war.

All of Burke's efforts to ratchet down what he considered a dirty war would fail in Parliament, yet, undaunted, he attempted on March 26, 1778, to kill funding for Indian expenses in America. The occasion was a bill in the House of Commons aimed at providing an extra £1,406,923 for British land forces. Burke targeted the £160,000 specifically earmarked for Native Americans. In characteristically fierce language, he called upon colleagues to consider what that money was going to do. He hoped "an English House of Commons would never consent to pay this sum," which would be designated to "purchase hatchets, tomahawks, scalping-knives, razors, spurs, etc." that, in turn, would be doled out to "the savages of America to butcher, torture, scalp, and massacre old men, women, children, and infants at the breast."[78] The House rejected that motion, too.

On February 6, 1778, the same day Burke delivered the "iron tears" speech that told the "horrid story" of Jane McCrea, France allied with the United States, pledging to take whatever measures were necessary to defend America "against the enterprises of their common enemy." That meant unleashing France's potent navy and army, opening the doors to its vast depot of matériel, and tapping into its bottomless loathing of Britain. As a consequence of a watershed treaty that would suddenly stack the war in America's favor, Britain faced a global war of epic proportions, instead of what was once a civil war against fellow Britons. Forced to change its tactics, strategies, and prospects for keeping the empire intact, Britain withdrew its troops from occupied Philadelphia and attempted to sue for peace by sending a delegation to the Continental Congress.

Into that political firestorm, John Burgoyne arrived in Britain on May 13, 1778, on parole from the United States, took his seat in the House of Commons, and spent the next two years defending his sullied reputation and ridiculing the British ministry for sending him on a fool's errand.

8.

THE SCAPEGOAT

JOSHUA REYNOLDS painted a swashbuckling portrait of a young John Burgoyne in 1766, when he was a colonel of the 16th Light Dragoons, a cavalry unit he had raised during the Seven Years War a few years earlier. He served in Portugal with foresight and courage at Valencia de Alcantara, a battle visible in the distance. If Reynolds's portrait is any indication, Burgoyne was a sight to behold. Every aspect of his bearing projects personal confidence and professional destiny: head brightly lit against the black smoke of battle, face and eyes angled off-stage, left arm flared akimbo, body set against a low horizon, and right hand clasped onto the pommel of a silver-mounted field sword. Pushed close to us, we are squarely in Burgoyne's aura. His scarlet coat, faced in black with buttons in sets of three and bound in silver embroidery, swings open to reveal a silver-trimmed double-breasted waistcoat and a black sword belt, both trimmed in silver lace. The skirts of the black-lined waistcoat are folded back—like theater curtains—in order to frame his crotch. In his right hand he casually holds his regimental black-japanned copper helmet, topped by a red horsehair crest emblazoned on the front with the Royal Crown and the cypher "GR"—Georgius Rex. Surmounting the helmet, a silver ribbon bears the first half of the regiment's motto, "*Aut Cursu, aut Cominus Armes*"—Either in the Charge, or in Hand-to-Hand Combat.[1]

Reynolds's portrait expertly personifies the two connected sides of Burgoyne's life and career, on the one hand an innovative and often brilliant professional officer, and on the other a semi-professional dramatist and playwright. Burgoyne literally takes the stage as the heroic soldier, posing with a flair for the theatrical that was an essential part of his personality. He, better than anyone else in Georgian England, understood that self-dramatization mattered, and that actions on the battlefield were interchangeable with performances on the stage.[2]

Before he had ever heard of Jane McCrea, Burgoyne was one of London's most colorful characters: avid gambler, urban dandy, fashion setter, aspiring notable, genial designer of *fêtes champêtres*, and devoted Tory Member of Parliament.[3] A regular at White's Club, Brooks' Club, the Thursday Night Club, and the Star and Garter, he was a member of The Ton, a frequent guest at the glittery home of the Duchess of Devonshire, and the improbable upstart who had eloped with Charlotte, the fifteen-year-old daughter of the Earl of Derby. Critics dubbed him The Old Gamester, General Swagger, Julius Caesar Burgonius, and Pomposo Hurlothrumbo.[4] Horace Walpole thought he possessed "more sail than ballast." When he purchased a house in tony Mayfair, he hired Britain's most distinguished architect, the Scotsman Robert Adam, to redesign it. Proof that ordering soldiers was never far removed from directing dancers and actors, he also wrote an extravagant musical comedy in 1774, *Maid of the Oaks*, which was performed at an aristocratic wedding that cost half a million guineas, and that was briefly produced at the Drury Lane Theatre, featuring Fanny Abington as Lady Bab Lardoon.[5]

In 1775, Whitehall assigned Burgoyne to the British garrison in Boston, along with major-generals William Howe and Henry Clinton. He had long favored a strong British hand in America, having voted against repeal of the Stamp Act and in favor of the punitive Coercive Acts, confidently announcing, "I look upon America to be our child, which I think we have already spoiled by too much indulgence."[6] In April—the fateful month marked by Lexington and Concord—the three generals sailed the Atlantic on a ship appropriately named *Cerberus*, the three-headed hound that guarded Hades. Catchy doggerel quickly ensued: "Behold the *Cerberus*, the Atlantic plough, / Her precious cargo, Burgoyne, Clinton, Howe, / Bow, wow, wow!"

Boston had become Britain's troubled archipelago in America, an occupied city on a peninsula, surrounded by 10,000 rebel militia—the British

Joshua Reynolds, *General John Burgoyne*, c. 1766. Oil on canvas. New York, The Frick Collection, purchased 1943.

would say fanatics—itching to engage them. The American *rage militaire* ignited into the first savage battle of the Revolution on June 17, when the British launched a devastating attack on an American militia position on Breed's Hill, across the harbor in Charlestown. Burgoyne, in command of the battery that included massive 24-pounders on Copps Hill in the North End of Boston, unleashed a torrent of incendiary shells—grimly known as carcasses—that burned Charlestown to the ground. He wrote his father-in-law of the resulting apocalypse as if he were painting a picture or designing a stage set: "A large and noble town in one great blaze. The church steeples, being of timber, were great pyramids of fire. . . . The roar of cannon, mortars, and musketry, the crash of churches, ships upon the stocks, and whole streets falling together in ruins." In all, it was "a complication of horror and importance, beyond anything it ever came to my lot to be a witness to."[7]

Burgoyne leavened his jolting introduction to Boston with theatrical productions. To improve troop morale, he wrote and produced *The Blockade of Boston*, a satire performed in Faneuil Hall and acted by soldiers playing Fanfan, Doodle, and Heartwright, the last a caricature of Washington as a bumbling man wearing an oversized wig. One attending British captain confirmed the affinity between the theater and the British military by breathlessly writing home from Boston to announce, "We are to have plays this winter . . . in Faneuil Hall. . . . I am enrolled as an actor. . . . General Burgoyne is our Garrick."[8]

To the Americans in occupied Boston, however, Burgoyne was contemptible. Abigail Adams wrote her husband John, then in Philadelphia, of "the Horrible wickedness of the Man." She thought Burgoyne stood out among the "Virmin and Locusts which infest" the town. Living in an occupied home, he crudely butchered his meats on the owner's "Mahogona Tables." He imposed martial law on Massachusetts. He had the interior of Old South Church stripped, library holdings burned, and the east gallery turned into a tavern. He even had tons of gravel dumped onto the church floor to convert it into a stable for defecating British horses, the insult intended.[9]

For all his showy haughtiness, the ever-astute Abigail detected the flaw behind the polished exterior, "an Abandoned Infamous Gambler of Broke fortune and the Worst Most detestable of the Bedford Gang [nickname for the politicians who advised George III and the Tory government]." He was "wholly bent on Blood, tyranny and Spoil."[10] Arthur Lee, the American diplomat, confirmed Abigail's condemnation: for him Burgoyne was "a man of dark designs, deep dissimulations, desperate fortunes, & abandoned of principles."[11]

In December of 1775, Burgoyne returned to London when a serious illness befell his adored wife, Charlotte. While there, he took the opportunity to propose moving the war from Boston to New York and the Hudson Valley, producing for George Germain, the minister in charge of the war, a strategic plan titled "Reflections on the War in America" for how a New York campaign might unfold. One army would advance up the Hudson from New York, another down from Montreal, meeting in Albany. Burgoyne would become commander of the northern arm of assault. Paradoxically, he was the author of the British strategy that would eventually destroy his reputation.

Burgoyne sailed back to North America in March of 1776, to Quebec, which had been under months-long siege by an expeditionary force of the Continental Army, led by generals Benedict Arnold, Anthony Wayne, and John Sullivan. When Burgoyne arrived, the Americans were being pushed back, having been devastated by a harsh winter, a smallpox epidemic, widespread dysentery and measles, and the shocking death of their commander, Major-General Richard Montgomery. Such a conspiracy of afflictions led John Adams to lament, "Our misfortunes in Canada are enough to melt a heart of stone."[12] Ironically, that broken-down Northern Army would retreat through the Champlain and Hudson corridor to Saratoga, rehabilitate under Horatio Gates, and defeat Burgoyne eighteen months later.

Burgoyne participated in the rout of the Americans from Canada, then took leave in November of 1776, upon receiving news that Charlotte had died and been buried in Westminster Abbey. In London he again met with ministers, had an audience with George III, and formulated further plans for defeating the American rebels. In February of 1777 he offered a new strategic proposal, "Thoughts for Conducting the War from the Side of Canada," that reiterated his "Reflections," but called for a third British column that would sweep in from the west, through the Mohawk Valley, in anticipation of what he imagined would be a perfectly timed reunion of all British forces in Albany.

His final marching orders from the ministry, however, uncoupled the timing of the intended union of armies in Albany. Otherwise, Burgoyne proceeded to enact the plan, received blessings from the king, and, fortified with an ego brimming with self-confidence, he began to assemble an international force. On April 2, 1777, he boarded the aptly named *Apollo*, sailed with a well-stocked fleet from Plymouth, and commenced a fateful journey that would culminate in his massive defeat at Saratoga.

After his arrival in Quebec, the process of assembling an army began. There were seven British Foot regiments, each regiment outfitted with 477 men at full strength, plus Grenadier and Light companies, militia, and one battalion of Royal Artillery. The German troops included five infantry regiments and one regiment of mounted Dragoons. The one artillery regiment had the daunting logistical problem of conveyance in the American backwoods; at their disposal were 52 cannons, plus howitzers and mortars. The small detachment of Loyalists included David Jones, McCrea's fiancé.

The totals as of early July were 3,724 British rank and file, 3,016 Germans, 245 artillery-men, 78 German artillery-men, 250 Canadians and Provincials, and 400 Native Americans who were raised on site. That was far below the 10,000 Burgoyne had originally estimated would be necessary to get to Albany. He also had 1,400 horses, 500 wagons plus wagon drivers, hundreds of 36-foot-long *bateaux*, and thousands of gallons of rum.[13] Arrangements would have to be made for mountains of food to be channeled to men and animals as they progressed southward. As was the custom, families and civilian staff traveled with the army, though Burgoyne's contingent was extraordinary, numbering hundreds of noncombatants, including medical personnel, ax-men, water-men, interpreters, sutlers, and engineers, plus hundreds of children and wives of the soldiers.[14] Overall, his military train was miles long.[15] Despite the low number of combatants, Burgoyne was so confident of victory that he wagered money against Charles Fox, the opposition leader in the House of Commons, that he would return to London victorious by Christmas.

A year later, however, Burgoyne was a broken man, defeated and sick, crossing back over the Atlantic on the *Juno*, on parole granted by Gates, and fully aware that a firestorm awaited him in London for defeat at Saratoga and for the abject failure of Britain's Northern Expedition. In anticipation of his return while rehearsing for his pending self-defense, he wrote to his nieces from Saratoga a letter drenched in self-pity: "I have been surrounded with enemies, ill-treated by pretended friends . . . with my army within the jaws of famine, shot through my hat and waistcoat, my nearest friends killed round me." And after all those "misfortunes and escape, I imagine I am reserved to stand a war with ministers who will always lay the blame upon the employed who miscarries."[16]

Even before Burgoyne arrived in England in May of 1778, an outraged Whig opposition was demanding answers from the government for multiple British catastrophes in America, including Jane McCrea's killing. Burke, Wilkes, and others had already spent months assailing the ministry's Northern Expedition, particularly the disastrous deployment of Native Americans. Now they were seeking sworn testimony, boards of inquiry, and rafts of official papers and letters. In turn, the Tory ministry, in particular Secretary Germain who had so poorly managed the campaign, took advantage of Burgoyne's captivity in Boston to blame him totally for Saratoga and everything that led up to it; but not General Howe who invaded Philadelphia instead of attacking Albany, not the inadequate size of British forces, not all the unanticipated turns of events, and certainly not Germain himself. According to Nathanial Wraxall, a gadabout and observer of the times, Burgoyne was informed while en route from Plymouth to London "that the Ministers would not support him; that Lord George Germain must accuse him, in order to exculpate himself; [and] that the King had imbibed very strong prejudices against him."[17]

To make Burgoyne the scapegoat it was necessary to withhold key documents that might muddy the picture being fashioned of him as an incompetent. "The once favoured general soon discovered . . . that he was no longer the object of court favour, or of ministerial countenance."[18] Hell-bent on saving himself and hiding his blunders, Germain moved to prevent Burgoyne from ever testifying in open Parliament because that might contradict government's narrative of what had happened along the Hudson. At most, the ministry would allow *in camera* questioning that would foil Burgoyne's drive to have his account reach the public.

However, soon after Burgoyne arrived in England, he decided to resume his seat in the House of Commons, representing Preston in Lancashire, thus allowing him a public voice that Germain could not squelch. With Burgoyne now able to speak for himself, the Whig opposition that previously despised him thought he could provide incriminating information against its archenemies, namely Secretary Germain and Prime Minister Lord North. An MP from Lincoln, Robert Vyner, motioned on May 16, 1778, for the creation of a Parliamentary committee of the whole to investigate the Northern Expedition. It was seconded by Wilkes, with the stipulation that it address "the charges of frequent murders and massacres of the defenseless inhabitants," a reference to the now renowned Jane McCrea.[19] Charles Fox, the Whig leader, supported the motion, as did Isaac Barré, a champion of the American cause.

Because Burgoyne was a part of the "whole" of Parliament, he was himself empaneled on the committee investigating what he himself said was "the disaster at Saratoga."[20] He admitted that it was more typical to have one's allies, colleagues, and friends do the bidding for him because that would avoid accusations of "vanity," "egotism," and "self-love" during the proceedings, but claiming the need for "justice" he conducted the interrogation "in my own name."[21] As expected, he jumped at the opportunity to counter the calumnies that the ministry had hurled at his reputation while he was absent, and in the process give the Whigs more ammunition in their campaign against the government. What the Tories had originally hoped would be a closeted inquiry ballooned into an acrimonious floor debate that riveted the British public. Most London and provincial newspapers carried transcripts or summaries of remarks, and Burgoyne himself took the unusual step of having all of it published by John Almon, the most pro-American imprint in London. There was so much public interest in the issues raised that Burgoyne's self-defense pamphlet, *The Substance of General Burgoyne's Speeches*, went through four editions in 1778 alone.

Always voluble, Burgoyne had a lot to say. At the outset, he explained his innate reluctance to use Native Americans. They were a "necessary evil," a requirement imposed upon him by ministers who "had adopted the reasoning that 'partial severity was general mercy.'" "Finishing the war," in Burgoyne's summation of Whitehall's policy, required "carrying terrors," by which he meant Native auxiliaries.[22] He maintained he had no choice other than to follow orders. Though he acknowledged as indisputable that Britain had suffered an incalculable loss, one that historians argue turned the Revolution in America's favor, Burgoyne took a moment in Parliament to congratulate himself for having been "very popular with the Indians," and, in his account, for success in controlling warriors so masterfully that, were his testimony heard today, he might expect to be nominated for a peace prize.

Burgoyne's shameless self-exoneration could not, however, entirely normalize the killing of Jane McCrea, an incident with which every Member of Parliament was already familiar. He tried to minimize her death by claiming he had otherwise instilled kindness in his Native auxiliaries: "I could produce many more instances to show that every possible exertion of humanity was used" during the march down the Hudson, adding, as an afterthought, "the case of miss Macree excepted, which was an accident, not premeditated cruelty." All the overheated stories told about Burgoyne, the Native warriors, and McCrea, he assured his audience, "were merely those fabricated by committees, and propagated in news-papers, for temporary purposes."

After absolving himself, Burgoyne proceeded to indict La Corne Saint-Luc, not only for unharnessing the Indians under his command, but also for having visited the ministry the previous December with the goal of exculpating himself and slandering Burgoyne, whom the *Québécois* called "an unfashionable general." In his retort, Burgoyne painted a picture of Saint-Luc as so "artful, ambitious, and a courtier, and, withal, owing him a grudge for controlling him in the use of the hatchet and scalping-knife," that he was now taking credit for how bravely the Indians had performed until Burgoyne misused, misjudged, and mishandled them, the McCrea fiasco being the primary example.[23] To defend himself, Burgoyne tried to deflect accountability by accusing Saint-Luc of lying to the ministry, spreading falsehoods, and smearing his reputation. If Parliament genuinely wanted to get to the truth, in Burgoyne's opinion, it needed to question Germain harshly. That would reveal "what this man [Saint-Luc] has presumed to say of my conduct with the Indians."[24] That interrogation never happened.

When published in the widely read *Gentleman's Magazine* and other outlets, Burgoyne's Parliamentary speeches ran to thirty-three printed pages, in which there emerged an overblown image of a "persecuted man . . . a marked victim to bear the sins that do not belong to me," one who faithfully executed orders, gave everything he had, and was now worthy of everyone's pity.[25] Instead of the tarnished general who, arguably, helped lose America, Burgoyne cast himself as a tragic hero, a man of honor and feeling who was done in by his auxiliaries, his own government, and fate. His tone was borderline desperate, as he pleaded with his audience to be understood. Eventually, all the British generals in America—Thomas Gage, William Howe, Lord Cornwallis, Henry Clinton, and especially Burgoyne—came back from the war criticizing the ministry for sending them on an impossible mission, for underestimating the strength of the Patriot cause, for overestimating the size of Loyalist support, for understaffing the army, and for ignoring the geographic territory that needed to be won over.

Burgoyne's self-defense did nothing to slow the ministry's dogged efforts to silence him. Germain came up with schemes to expel him from Parliament, and, outrageously, to send him back to prison in America. Instead, Burgoyne, ceaseless in his desire to acquit himself, teamed with his newfound friend Edmund Burke, of all people, to thwart the ministry. Burke, after all, is the Whig politician who had Parliament laughing out loud when he parodied Burgoyne's 1775 speech to the Indians ("my sentimental wolves, . . . go forth," and by the way, be sure to "take care not hurt man, woman or children"). This is also the man who had drawn "*iron tears*" from hardened MPs a few months earlier when he vividly described Jane McCrea's death.

Regardless, in 1780 Burke assisted Burgoyne in writing a 251-page brief, *A State of the Expedition from Canada*, which he dedicated "TO THE OFFICERS OF THE ARMY HE COMMANDED." In it, he printed "authentic documents . . . which were prevented from appearing before the House." Burgoyne visited Burke at his house in Beaconsfield in order to work on the manuscript. As a result, some of the tract has a Burkean flair for the sublime, especially Burgoyne's description of enemy fire flying overhead while he was burying General Simon Fraser at Saratoga, a passage that bears resemblance to scenes from Shakespeare's *Othello*.[26]

Most of *State of the Expedition* is a transcription of the detailed House of Commons testimonies of a string of military men: General Guy Carleton, commander of British forces in Canada; the Earl of Balcarras, a major commanding the right flank of Burgoyne's advanced corps; John Money, quartermaster and captain in the 9th Regiment; Gordon Forbes, a major in the same regiment; Thomas Bloomfield, a captain in the artillery; and Robert Kingston, a lieutenant-colonel and Burgoyne's secretary, all taken verbatim from their appearances in the House. Testimony mostly concerned Burgoyne's tactical and strategic moves between Ticonderoga and Saratoga, as well as the failed connection with Howe. Finally, during the questioning of Charles Stanhope, the Earl of Harrington, captain of the 29th Foot, and Burgoyne's aide-de-camp, the topic turned to the Native American auxiliaries and the killing of Jane McCrea.

Question: "What was the tenor of General Burgoyne's speeches and injunctions . . . respecting the restraint of barbarities?"

Answer: "He absolutely forbid [Indians] scalping, except their dead prisoners, which they insisted on doing, and he held out rewards to them for bringing prisoners, and enjoined them to treat them well."

Q: "Does your Lordship remember General Burgoyne's receiving at Fort Anne, the news of the murder of Miss M'Rea?"

A: "I do."

Q: "Did General Burgoyne repair immediately to the Indian camp, and call them to council, assisted by Brigadier General Fraser?"

A: "He did."

Q: "What passed at that council?"

A: "General Burgoyne threatened the culprit with death, insisted that he should be delivered up; and there were many gentlemen of the army, and I own I was of the number, who feared that he would put that threat in execution. Motive of policy, I believe alone, prevented him from it; and if he had not pardoned the man, which he did, I believe the total defection of the Indians would have ensued, and the consequences, on their return through Canada, might have been dreadful; not to speak of the weight they would have thrown into the opposite scale, had they gone over to the enemy, which I rather imagine would have been the case."

Q: "Do you remember General Burgoyne's restraining the Indian parties from going out without a British officer or proper conductor, who were to be responsible for their behaviour?"

A: "I do."

Q: "Do you remember Mr. St. Luc's reporting discontents amongst the Indians, soon after our arrival at Fort Edward?"

A: "I do."

Q: "How long was that after enforcing the restraints above mentioned?"

A: "I can't exactly say: I should imagine about three weeks or a month."

Q: "Does your Lordship recollect General Burgoyne's telling Mr. St. Luc, that he had rather lose every Indian, than connive at their enormities, or using language to that effect?"

A: "I do."

Q: "Does your Lordship remember what passed in council with the Indians at Fort Edward?"

A: "To the best of my recollection, much the same exhortation to act with humanity, and much the same rewards were offered for saving their prisoners."

Q: "Do you recollect the circumstance of the Indians desiring to return home at that time?"

A: "I do, perfectly well."

Q: "Do you remember that many quitted the army without leave?"

A: "I do, immediately after the council, and the next morning."

Q: "Was it not the general opinion that the defection of the Indians, then and afterwards, was caused by the restraint upon their cruelties and habits of plunder?"

A: "It was."[27]

State of the Expedition contains accurate transcriptions of testimony. At the same time, because it was Burgoyne's book he got the opportunity to end it with a long essay explaining and often justifying himself in his own words. He could see that "my errors may have been numberless," further conceded he might have placed too much trust in the French Canadians whom he had hired to handle the Western Indians, and finally admitted that his declaration of principles had failed to restrain the warriors. At the same time, he could now project blame on his auxiliaries. "Their evil passions were fomented" by the "cabals of the Canadian interpreters," who were miffed at having to defer to Burgoyne. Saint-Luc, put in the position of having to repress the "accustomed horrors" of the Indians, could no longer gain favor with them by simply distributing "necessaries and presents," and as a result he subversively encouraged "dissention, revolt, and desertion" and indulged "their most capricious fantasies," much to "the dishonour of the King's service and the disgrace of humanity."[28]

Throughout the months of debate, testimony, and interrogation, Burgoyne never took full responsibility for civilian deaths under his command. Instead, he made Saint-Luc the scapegoat just as Germain had made Burgoyne his. Indian marauding, Burgoyne said, had been fomented by the "Canadian interpreters," who were themselves motivated by "rapacity" and "self-interest." Burgoyne's only regret was ever taking Saint-Luc's advice.[29] He also accused "that wily partisan" of supplying false information to a Tory government too eager to hear "any whispered intelligence, in contradiction to that received from the General himself." The "system of deception which has so long and so fatally influenced his Majesty's advisers" was, Burgoyne thought, threatening all of Britain's plans to retain America.

The Ministry's withering campaign took its toll on Burgoyne, expanding at times into farcical scenarios intended to shut him up. In a number of letters, Burke speculated on the true motivation for government's endless animosity toward Burgoyne. It had nothing to do with the general's action in the field or the use of Native Americans, yet everything to do with his special ability to expose Britain's total misjudgment and mismanagement of the American war.[30] In spite of that insight, for as long as government continued to blame Burgoyne, it could survive another day.

Burke's theory may be true. Nevertheless, Burgoyne's case against the government was as inconclusive as Germain's was against Burgoyne. The crux of Burgoyne's self-defense was his claim that his strict orders from Germain were to arrive in Albany, set up a communiqué with Howe, and wait for the assault from New York City. Yet Burgoyne knew by mid-July 1777, and perhaps as early as April, that Howe intended to invade Pennsylvania and not push to Albany, as Burgoyne hoped he would.[31] Howe had acquired pre-approval for a Philadelphia campaign from Germain, with the ridiculous expectation that he would conclude that invasion "in time for you to cooperate with the army ordered to proceed from Canada."[32] Burgoyne received written confirmation of the Philadelphia plan from Lieutenant-General Henry Clinton.[33]

That conflicted with Burgoyne's original "Thoughts for Conducting the War from the Side of Canada." In that proposition, a timed "junction" with Howe in Albany was the preferred option; Philadelphia was not part of the scheme. Should the "junction" in Albany be "impracticable or too hazardous," the other option for Burgoyne was "turning the expedition eventually towards Connecticut" with the idea of joining another British army moving westward from its position in Rhode Island.[34] Burgoyne had insisted on being granted "latitude" in making on-the-ground decisions, because perfect timing with Howe was near impossible and because he could not predict conditions as he progressed south, deeper into enemy territory. Making matters worse, the messengers shuttling between Burgoyne and Howe were mostly being caught and hanged.[35]

But during the parliamentary review, Burgoyne insisted—and published documents to support his claim—that Germain deviated from the original "Thoughts for Conducting the War from the Side of Canada." In Germain's first statement, Burgoyne was, "by the most vigorous exertion of the force under his command, to proceed with all expedition to Albany, and put himself under the command of Sir William Howe."[36] The option of proceeding toward Connecticut had been taken off the table. In Germain's new orders, Burgoyne gets "possession of Albany," and then—and only then—"open the communication to New-York," and wait patiently for some future action from Howe who might, or might not, move up the Hudson. In his defense, Burgoyne stated that "*every discretionary latitude which I had proposed was erased*." In effect he felt marooned: "I little foresaw that I was to be left to pursue my way through such a tract of country, and hosts of foes, without any co-operation from new-York."[37] In short, he felt compelled to get to Albany, whatever it took.

Buried in his orders, however, Germain had indeed provided Burgoyne with a "saving clause."[38] Until Burgoyne heard from Howe he would be empowered to "act as exigencies may require, and in such manner as they shall judge most proper for making an impression on the rebels, and bringing them to obedience."[39] To be sure, Burgoyne "must never lose view" of the "intended junctions with Sir William Howe."[40] All the same, until orders were received from Howe, Burgoyne had the authority to re-jigger his course of action. It seems that Burgoyne either overlooked the "saving clause" provision while he was in America, or he was now deliberately minimizing its importance in order to reduce his culpability.

Ignoring or misinterpreting the "saving clause" during his defense, he mused over what that could have been. "Had I latitude in my order, I should think it my duty to wait in this position [north of Saratoga] or perhaps as far back as Fort Edward, where my communication with Lake George would be perfectly secure, till some event happened to assist my movement forward," such as news of Howe's full army heading up the Hudson.[41] As Burgoyne phrased it, the "saving clause" was weak, related only "to such collateral and eventual operations as might be advisable in the course of my march" to Albany.[42] Yet, instead of exercising the on-the-ground decision-making vested in him, he recklessly pushed head-on into the morass of Saratoga, stacked up against Gates's 20,000 men, claiming he had no choice, orders were orders, Albany or nothing.

The question was asked of Colonel Kingston, during the Parliamentary hearing, whether a junction of Burgoyne's and Howe's armies would have avoided the "disaster" at Saratoga. That is, what might have happened if Howe had gone up the Hudson instead of down to Philadelphia? Kingston, who was Burgoyne's secretary, was of the opinion that a "great army" storming up the Hudson would have "dislodged Gates," and "the misfortune at Saratoga would not have happened." Kingston was further questioned about the size of Burgoyne's army. In his opinion, it was "not to be equal to the forcing our way to Albany, without some co-operation" from Howe.[43]

The question remains, whether ultimate fault lay with the generals in New York, with the ministers in London, or with Burgoyne. The House committee that had exhaustively investigated Burgoyne's conduct never issued a final report because Parliament adjourned for the spring session. In the November session, the debates remained partisan and thus inconclusive. The Whigs—Burke, Wilkes, Fox, William Petty, and others— endorsed Burgoyne's account of government malfeasance because it was in their political interest to do so. Petty, the Earl of Shelburne, said of Burgoyne's predicament: "He was charged with carrying measures into execution, which were wild, romantic, and impracticable."[44] Prime Minister North and Secretary Germain argued the opposite. One Tory MP, looking at the Whigs' newfound political embrace of Burgoyne, said sarcastically that they had "elevated him to the rank of a martyr."[45] In the end, as one historian has put it, "it was parliamentary theater at its best."[46]

Burgoyne turned sixty in 1782, when he was released from his five years of parole and technically exchanged for Henry Laurens, the former president of the Continental Congress who had been arrested at sea and jailed in the Tower of London. James Sayers, a political caricaturist sympathetic to the Tory ministry, pictured Burgoyne in Parliament, transformed from the dashing hero of the Seven Years War into a fragile, older man who continued to wear his general's uniform while defending himself. When the war effectively ended in 1782, everyone, including Burgoyne, began the difficult process of moving on with their lives. Even John McCrea, Jane's grieving brother, told Burgoyne he no longer blamed the general for his sister's death.[47]

Burgoyne's life went through a transformation. The military and political men who had dominated his career started walking offstage, while stepping onto it were new friends: William Jackson, composer of operas, anthems, and hymns; Richard Brinsley Sheridan, the Irish playwright who was the renowned owner of the Drury Lane Theatre and a recently elected Whig MP; and Susan Caulfield, a married actress and singer with whom he had four children. After years of defending himself against blame for the death of Jane McCrea and his mishandling of the Northern Expedition, and having always been a dramatic personality, even on the battlefield, Burgoyne returned to acting and writing. *The Heiress*, his 1786 hit comedy, went through multiple editions and was performed on the Continent. John Adams considered the theater too frivolous to attend when he was Minister to the Court of St. James, but his son, John Quincy Adams, praised *The Heiress* while a student at Harvard. "A good play," he wrote of it in his diary, "much more regular; and more chaste, than those that are acted on the English stage."[48]

However far Burgoyne's life may have accelerated away from the ignominy of Saratoga, he might have still heard Shakespeare's lines from act V of *Richard III*, when Richard is haunted on Bosworth Field by the ghosts of those who perished because of him: "Have mercy, Jesu! I did but dream. O coward conscience, how dost thou afflict me!" Burgoyne died in 1792, at age seventy, while editing a Shakespearean play for future production. After a private funeral, he was interred next to his wife in the North Cloister of Westminster Abbey, in a grave left unmarked until 1960.

9.

THE TABLES TURNED

WHILE JOHN ALMON was publishing Burgoyne's *State of the Expedition* in 1780, three years after Jane McCrea's death, the debacle of Saratoga was already old news in London. A new cause célèbre had emerged in Tappan, New York, 172 miles down the Hudson from Fort Edward. On October 2, 1780, British Major John André, a dashing twenty-nine-year-old adjutant-general to Lieutenant-General Henry Clinton, was death-marched to freshly constructed gallows on a hill, where, surrounded by five hundred American infantry and fourteen generals, he was hung for espionage on the orders of George Washington. When word spread across the Atlantic, André instantly became Britain's martyr, the riposte to Jane McCrea, another pretty youth cruelly cut down.

Major André's execution while in American hands did two things for the British. First, it had enough emotional power for Britons to mourn one of their own, at last. Five years of warfare had not produced a martyr or even a hero. The Americans had Joseph Warren shot dead at Bunker Hill, Richard Montgomery dying in a snowstorm below the ramparts of Quebec, and Brigadier-General Hugh Mercer falling at Princeton, all of them honored as brave officers who sacrificed for the cause and inspired others to walk in their paths. Jane McCrea was America's sweetheart martyr, inconsequential in a military sense, yet an appealing wartime innocent capable of evoking intense feelings of loss and regret. André's awful hanging, which created howls of protest and outpourings of sympathy, finally gave the British the opportunity to distract themselves from the mortification they had felt for pitiless American civilian deaths—most notably McCrea's—during Burgoyne's Northern Expedition.

Second, André's hanging allowed the British to turn the moral tables on the Americans. Instead of listening to the outcries of Americans, especially Gates, reproaching them for being barbarians guilty of using wanton auxiliaries to rip apart their American cousins, it was now Britain's chance to accuse the Americans of flagrantly ignoring the principles of *jus in bello* for having punished a senior officer with hanging. Captured British and American officers were, as a rule, not executed during the Revolution.[1]

The Americans had caught André in the midst of the most audacious intelligence operation of the Revolution. Three American militiamen intercepted him in Tarrytown, New York, on September 23, 1780, three days after he had met secretly with Benedict Arnold, then the commander of West Point, the key American fortress on the Hudson. The perpetually irate Arnold, linchpin of the American victory at Saratoga where he was severely wounded, long felt that Congress and his fellow officers had overlooked, bypassed, and disdained him.[2] Out of bitterness in 1779, he began passing to André coded intelligence on American troop strength and locations, often via his Loyalist wife, Peggy Shippen, whom André had known while stationed in Philadelphia. André's September meeting with Arnold, fifteen miles south of West Point, centered on plans to surrender the fortress to the British, which, had it taken place, would not only have been the most flagrant act of treason committed during the Revolution; it would also have given the British the control over the Hudson that had eluded their grasp in 1777.

When news of André's capture reached Arnold, he immediately boarded the fourteen-gun British sloop *Vulture*, appropriately named, on which he made his escape to headquarters in New York. Whereupon, Arnold had the temerity to write an open letter "To the Inhabitants of America," which attempted to justify his treason. The British rewarded Arnold with a commission at the rank of Brigadier-General, after which he went on to capture Richmond and burn New London to the ground, a few miles south of where he grew up in Connecticut.

A Board of General Officers, comprising fourteen generals, including the Marquis de Lafayette, Friedrich von Steuben, and Nathanael Greene, condemned André to the most humiliating and unusual death available: a vulgar hanging, more suitable for an ordinary criminal. Efforts were made to negotiate his release, to exchange André for Arnold, and to reduce the sentence. In response to every plea for clemency, Washington turned a deaf ear.

The gruesome details of André's death, like McCrea's, amplified the sense of tragedy. After asphyxiating, the mortifying body, clothed in a dress uniform of "the brightest scarlet" and faced in "the most beautiful green," hung motionless for half an hour in front of 2,000 onlookers.[3] Soldiers cut André down and laid him on the ground. "Spectators were permitted to come forward and view the corpse."[4] Most of his clothing was then removed, leaving him exposed in undergarments, whereupon the stiffening body was placed in a black coffin and buried in a shallow unmarked grave.[5]

As with McCrea, the execution of André stirred an extraordinary flood of emotions. Most exceptional—even inexplicable—was the universal level of sympathy among American soldiers, officers, and civilians for a spy caught red-handed in an attempt to flip West Point to the British. Lafayette, who helped condemn André, wept at the gallows. Lieutenant-Colonel Richard Meade, who supervised the execution, said André elicited "the compassion of every man of feeling and sentiment."[6] James Thacher, a surgeon in the Massachusetts 16th Regiment who had reported McCrea's death in his military journal, now observed André, one moment "in the bloom of life," then lying on the ground dead; he said, "the spot was consecrated by the tears of thousands."[7] Joel Barlow, a chaplain in the 3rd Massachusetts Brigade, visited André during his imprisonment. Writing to Ruth Baldwin, his fiancée, Barlow described something like a momentary love affair with André: "A politer Gentleman or a greater character of his age perhaps is not alive . . . My heart is thrown into a flutter My dear at the sight."[8]

André's handler, Major Benjamin Tallmadge, was overcome with grief, wondering if the major had "been tried by a Court of Ladies, he is so *genteel, handsome, polite* a young gentleman that I am confident they would have acquitted him."[9] Tallmadge was smitten with André: "From the few days of intimate intercourse I had with him, which was from the time of his being remanded to the period of his execution, I became so deeply attached to Major André, that I could remember no instance where my affections were so fully absorbed by any man. . . . I walked with him to the place of execution, and parted from him under the gallows, entirely overwhelmed with grief; . . . all were overwhelmed with the affecting spectacle, and the eyes of many were suffused with tears. There did not appear to be one hardened or indifferent spectator in all the multitude."[10]

Colonel Alexander Hamilton, Washington's aide-de-camp and a toughened veteran of the Battle of Princeton, visited André during his imprisonment, after which he wrote unfathomably touching words for an enemy spy attempting to deliver a fatal blow against the United States. André, he wrote Lieutenant-Colonel John Laurens in an extraordinarily long letter that was reprinted in many newspapers, had "a composure that excited the admiration and melted the hearts of the beholders." He "died universally regretted, and universally esteemed."[11] Hamilton believed he had briefly but intensively been in the aura of someone special. "He united a peculiar elegance of mind and manners, and the advantage of a pleasing person. It is said, he possessed a pretty taste for the fine arts. . . . His knowledge appeared without ostentation, and embellished by a diffidence that rarely accompanies so many talents and accomplishments. . . . His sentiments were elevated, and inspired esteem; . . . His elocution was handsome; his address easy, polite."[12] When Henry Cabot Lodge wrote André's biography, he extravagantly compared the major to Orestes, Hippolytus, and Oedipus.[13]

Americans were mourning André as a man of exquisite sensibility. To be sure, they were not admiring a great military leader from the opposition. Quite the contrary. André had not been especially accomplished as an officer, having been captured in 1775 by Richard Montgomery and held prisoner in Lancaster, Pennsylvania, where he was free to enjoy the town. He was an administrative officer in Philadelphia during the British occupation, where he stood out as a heartthrob, charming in manner and artistic by nature. There, he acquired fame as the organizer of the Meschianza, a mammoth all-day-and-night public extravaganza celebrating the British occupation of the city. While the American army starved and froze at Valley Forge, André planned a fête never before seen, complete with parades, mock jousts, balls, fireworks, and a regatta on the Delaware.[14] He designed the women's Turkish outfits and took the time to pin pink bows to his own regimentals during the event. He was sensitive, aesthetic, and foppish, all in all an improbable military man. Yet, in spite of his inherent aesthetic flair, there were Hamilton and Lafayette sobbing at his execution, a British major captured in a mortal plot against the United States. The seeming contradiction raises the question, why?

André was a focal point in the great age of sensibility, which Samuel Johnson defined as "quickness of sensation." Feeling and sensitivity were not only lauded in the late eighteenth century, they were publicly flaunted. The ability to be affected, to possess the capacity to experience deep feeling and then express it openly was magnified during a war that was at once stir-

Major John André, *Self Portrait*. 1780. Pen and brown ink. New Haven, Yale University Art Gallery, Gift of Ebenezer Baldwin, B.A. 1808.

ring, impassioned, fanatical, and deadly, when every overwrought emotion was enlarged by the cruel and pathetic.[15] Women had long been thought to possess sensibility, while men were just beginning in the eighteenth century to plumb their hidden reservoirs of emotion.[16] "The man within," in Adam Smith's words, was free to express himself. "Our sensibility to the feelings of others, so far from being inconsistent with the manhood of self-command, is the very principle upon which that manhood is founded."[17]

André may not have had many military credentials, yet he exemplified the modern man of feeling. His extraordinary self-portrait, drawn the day before his hanging, in fact radiates gentlemanly grace in the face of dire circumstances: elbow lightly draped on the crest rail of a Chippendale chair, uniform rakishly unbuttoned, legs fetchingly crossed, and right arm stretched out toward a quill pen.

Not only did he express sensibility, he was himself the ultimate object of other men's deepest emotions. Seasoned American officers quickly found themselves in André's thrall, unavoidably pouring out their own feelings of sadness and regret. Though he was sentenced to hang for an unspeakable crime, that did not prevent Tallmadge from admiring André's unflinching composure in the face of death, nor Hamilton from not only listening attentively to André, but also cherishing his courage and humility.

British reactions in London and at military headquarters in New York bordered on the histrionic for the emotions generated. The wife of one member of Parliament said that "Major André's fate has been the universal topic of conversation" in London.[18] Upon hearing the news, Samuel Johnson compared Washington's heart to the Emperor Nero's.[19] Much of the British press wanted to canonize André, some newspapers committing a Freudian slip by calling him St. André.[20] He was akin to the "undaunted spirit . . . of a Citizen of Rome or Athens," said to be "universally beloved" by all: "The feeling heart will not fail to lament the deplorable end of a deserving young Officer, whose name will be handed down to posterity in the shining list of self-devoted Patriots."[21]

Instead of the traditional masculine standards by which the public hero had been measured, André seems to have possessed new attributes—refinement, wit, impeccable manners, accomplishment in music, poetry, and art, and, most especially, physical grace and vulnerability—all of which one historian likened to his "erotic appeal."[22] In written accounts and engraved portraits, he was always a pretty boy, more dandy than warrior, a sensitive soul who won over strangers and even antagonists with his personality. As a result, Britons promoted André to the temple of fame not only for the extraordinary awareness and susceptibility he evinced on the threshold of his execution, but also for the empathy he elicited from other people.

Anna Seward, an important British poet known as the Swan of Litchfield, immediately began writing a thirty-page elegy on "murder'd ANDRÉ" that resembles the agitated emotions expressed in romantic pieces composed after McCrea's death. It first establishes the Americans as the true barbarians, a reversal of 1777 when it was the Britons who were accused of resorting to monstrous measures. Washington, whom Britons had much admired, took the brunt of Seward's anger: "O Washington! I thought thee great and good, Nor knew thy Nero-thirst for guiltless blood! Severe to use the pow'r that Fortune gave, Thou cool determin'd murderer of the brave! . . . O dark and pitiless! Your impious hate, O'er whelm'd the hero in the ruffian's fate! . . . Remorseless WASHINGTON!" Britons, Seward wrote, will be inspired to seek revenge for "the sacred life you stole; . . . When injur'd André's memory shall inspire, A kindling army with resistless fire." The dust of his dead body, "like Abel's blood, shall rise, And call for justice from the angry skies!"[23]

At headquarters in New York, James Rivington, the leading Loyalist printer, republished Seward's poem, giving the British there an occasion to be further galvanized and unified by the loss. On a dedication page to General Clinton, the crestfallen British commander in the city, Rivington called André a "murdered Saint" who "fell a Martyr in the cause of his King and Country with the intrepidity of a Roman, and the amiable resignation of a Christian hero."[24] British troops stationed in New York "on hearing of his execution raised such an outcry for vengeance . . . that the Commander-in-Chief could hardly keep them within the bounds of discipline. . . The universal cry of the soldiers at New York is, REMEMBER ANDRÉ . . . no language can describe the mingled sensations of horror, grief, sympathy, and revenge that agitated the whole garrison."[25] Repurposing the cry, "REMEMBER JENNY MCCREA," the grief-stricken Clinton considered hanging American prisoners in retaliation.[26] Even Arnold threatened Washington, "I shall think myself bound by every tie and honour to retaliate on such unhappy person of your army as may fall within my power. . . . I call heaven and earth to witness that your Excellency will be justly answerable for the torrent of blood that may be spilt in consequence."[27]

In London, George III was so distressed by André's death that he immediately hired Robert Adam to design an eight-foot-tall monument to be installed in the nave of Westminster Abbey, which was the prestigious home to statuary remembering the greatest defenders of Britain. Further amplifying André's glorification, Edward Barnard, a historian at Eton, published his monumental *History of England* in 1782, complete with engravings of the nation's greatest figures. King Alfred, William the Conqueror, Queen Elizabeth, and George III come to visual life on Barnard's pages. The Magna Carta is signed, the battle of Agincourt is waged, Charles I is executed, London burns, Admiral Rodney defeats the French. And, disproportionally, John André is hanged. Based on a painting by William Hamilton, known for his Shakespearean subjects, the print shows André hanging from the gibbet. American soldiers, dressed in blue, flank him on each side, while an American flag, missing its starred canton, waves behind.[28]

André was an unlikely candidate for martyrdom by any traditional standard. He never directed troops and did not win a battle, or die in one either. The qualifications for monumental treatment of a military hero, such as General James Wolfe, were entirely absent. British history could easily have consigned him to the scrap heap. After all, his one major espionage assignment, the delivery of West Point, had been a complete failure. His capture had been the result of bungling every aspect of the rendezvous with Arnold. General Clinton told him not to penetrate enemy lines, not to remove his uniform, and not to carry incriminating papers, all of which he did anyway. And then the Americans hanged him.

Nonetheless, in the fifth year of the war, Britain had few military heroes to honor.[29] Burgoyne, Howe, Clinton, Gage, and Cornwallis were under investigation, not candidates for apotheosis. Though André's military credentials might have been meager, he at least attempted to do something heroic and died in the process. Britons could embrace him as an emotional hero because he helped distract the nation from the lowering trajectory of the American war.

In some ways, André and McCrea were similar: two unlikely figures who nonetheless received high honors and eternal fame in their home countries.[30] The criteria for their enshrinement were not tangible deeds or contributions to the causes that had ensnared them. Instead, they soared in the popular imagination because of the surge of feelings produced by two gorgeous persons, both young and not especially savvy, killed when the correct victim should have been someone else—the satanic Arnold in the case of André or the American pickets around Fort Edward in the case of McCrea. Heightened descriptions of André's beauty and innocence were eerily similar to the loving words written about McCrea: "His beauty shone with an unnatural distinctness that awed the hearts of the vulgar."[31] People commented that he "had a long and beautiful head of hair, which, agreeably to the fashion, was wound with a black ribband, and hung down his back."[32] Even one of the American sentinels on duty at the execution said that many had exclaimed, "He was the handsomest man I ever laid my eyes on."[33]

André and McCrea both inspired pilgrimages. André's adherents traveled to the tulip tree where he was caught, gathered around his cenotaph in Tappan, and visited the monument in Westminster Abbey. McCrea's devotees trekked to Fort Edward to stand quietly at her fenced gravesite and to pause in the shadow of the old pine where she was said to have been slaughtered. Some visited Tappan first and then moved on to Fort Edward. The objective was to be overcome with emotion. Weeping pilgrims could rehearse in their minds—or discuss in tragic conversation among themselves—what those last sublime moments felt like, and in doing so, uncover their own feelings of vulnerability, love, and sorrow. One out-of-town visitor to Westminster, a Mrs. Mary Shackleton, stopped at Joseph Wilton's gigantic marble memorial dedicated to the transcendent General Wolfe. She then walked to the thirty-three-foot monument to William Pitt, the late great prime minister, both impressive and moving. Suddenly, Mrs. Shackleton wrote, "a desire to behold Major André's monument seized us." Though André was not of the stature of the other men, she nonetheless gravitated to the man of sensibility. "We love his character," she noted, "which was brave & amiable."[34]

As McCrea's and André's renown grew, their deaths intertwined. James Fenimore Cooper incorporated them in his novels. First, André inspired the character Henry Wharton in his 1821 espionage novel, *The Spy: A Tale of the Neutral Ground*, and then McCrea was the model for the captured sisters Cora and Alice Munro in his 1826 historical novel *The Last of the Mohicans: A Narrative of 1757*.[35] In two other instances André and McCrea are coupled. An engraving on one side of a revolutionary era powder horn depicts André's capture on one side, while a picture of McCrea's murder is on the other.[36] In 1839, Delia Bacon audaciously presented McCrea (renamed Helen Grey) and André as friends in her Shakespearean play, *The Bride of Fort Edward*.[37] André is stationed with the British party that discovers McCrea mortally wounded in the woods, and when she dies in her lover's arms, André intones, "This was Love."

To be sure, there were important differences. André's death was well documented. But in McCrea's case, the facts were ambiguous, which only inflamed the desire of mourners hungry for every new tidbit of information, however speculative. One story would beget the next two, each doubling, pushing her further into the realm of the mythological. Though we can never know exactly what happened to her the morning of July 26, 1777, we can say with certitude that McCrea's last moments penetrated to the heart of the American revolutionary soul: the young, beautiful woman whose tragic death inhabited the romantic imagination like no one else's.[38]

Sensibility's antagonist is sense, the two locked in an eternal battle staged between heart and head. Though the André monument in Westminster was a sacred shrine, not everyone was moved to tears. John Adams, Minister to the Court of St. James, and his sixteen-year-old son, John Quincy Adams, both men boastful of unflinching rationality, were demonstrably angered by the monument when they visited in April of 1784. "I felt a painfull Sensation," John Quincy wrote with negative sensibility, "at seeing a superb monument, erected to Major André . . . how much denigrated that

Nation must be, which can find no fitter Object for so great an honour, than a Spy, than a man whose sad Catastrophe, was owning to his unbounded Ambition, and whose only excuse for his conduct, was his Youth; as if youth, gave a Man the right to commit wicked and Contemptible Actions."[39]

Where André provoked anger from the Americans in London, heartbroken Britons demanded revenge against the Americans. That was logically supposed to occur in America, where, perhaps, there would be another effort to capture the Hudson, or to hunt down an American officer and lynch him. Instead, the revenge scenario took place in London. John Adams first heard news of the intended target in 1780, while he was in Holland looking for Dutch support. His undercover agent in London, Thomas Digges, wrote that, "nothing has been talk'd of here but 'making Examples,' acts of retaliation." Digges continued, "A person of the name of Trumbull was taken up for high Treason on Sunday night and committed to Prison. . . . It is impossible to say to what lengths they will go against Mr. Trumbull. . . . Reports say . . . his own papers are quite sufficient to hang Him, and hang him they certainly will if they can." The British "seem to thirst after blood most exceedingly since André's execution."[40]

John Trumbull, son of the Revolutionary governor of Connecticut and Washington's aide-de-camp in 1775, had once been, as he put it himself, a favorite of Horatio Gates, serving as his trusted deputy adjutant-general with the rank of colonel. Trumbull and Gates had sailed by sloop up the Hudson to Albany in 1776, then went overland through Saratoga and Fort Edward to join the Northern Army at Fort Ticonderoga, where both men encountered the beaten-down survivors of the failed military expedition to Quebec. While he was there, Trumbull had occasion to meet Dr. Stephen McCrea, Jane's brother, who was tending to the soldiers. We cannot know whether they talked about the McCrea family, or if Trumbull heard stories of Jane's life on John McCrea's farm south of Fort Edward, or of her romance with David Jones, who had, by that point in time, joined the British. But, to be sure, Trumbull's experience along the northern Hudson lingered in his mind.

Trumbull suddenly quit the Continental Army in February of 1777, just before Burgoyne's assault on New York from Canada. In retrospect, the cause seems trivial, a petty dispute with Congress regarding his rank. Persistent entreaties by Congress were ineffectual in changing his mind. Whether his ultimate motivation was public honor or personal fear, he moved on to recently liberated Boston, where he embarked on, of all things, a career in the arts. He copied old master pictures and tried to paint new ones in the style of the inimitable John Singleton Copley. Then in 1780, the revolution still raging, this former army officer with the rank of colonel made an audacious, improbable, and surely reckless decision to travel to George III's London to study painting under the tutelage of Benjamin West, the Pennsylvania-born artist who held the high position of official historical painter to the king.

Trumbull had received assurances from contacts in London that Secretary Germain, minister for the American war, would tolerate his residency if he avoided "all political intervention."[41] However, that détente evaporated when news of André's hanging reached London on November 15. Within days, police arrested Trumbull, escorted him to the Bow Street station, then remanded him first to New Prison Clerkenwell, and finally to Tothill Fields Bridewell prison. The charges were espionage and treason, which if proven required death as the punishment.

The evidence against him was flimsy at best: an innocuous letter from William Temple Franklin, the nephew of Benjamin Franklin, another one from his father, and a third letter cryptically referring to France, "our dear and great ally," and the procurement of "camp equipage."[42] In fact, Trumbull had violated the no-politics rule by attempting to raise money for American prisoners on British ships, and to acquire British textiles in order to ship them to the Continental Army, via France, which had recently joined the war.

Trumbull quickly realized that the arrest was not for the letters in his possession or plans to acquire supplies. Instead, he was, in his own words, the "perfect *pendant*" for André's death.[43] "The resentment of government [over André's execution] marked me as an expiatory sacrifice. I had no idea of the storm."[44] Trumbull would be due revenge for André, who was in turn the perfect pendant for the sorrow stirred up by McCrea. Trumbull, André, and McCrea were links in an emotional chain that crisscrossed the Atlantic.

London newspapers, the same ones that previously featured André and McCrea, started spotlighting Trumbull's story. Gates, Benjamin Franklin, and Adams received news of Trumbull's situation, but were powerless to help. Over the seven months he spent in prison, unfounded rumors spread through Britain and over the Atlantic that he had been executed, like André.[45] In the end, Benjamin West used his special relationship with the king to plead for leniency, and Edmund Burke, not knowing Trumbull personally though always looking for an opportunity to undermine the Tory government, persuaded the Privy Council to release Trumbull in June of 1781. After a brief stop in Amsterdam, he returned to America.

Undaunted, Trumbull booked passage back to London late in 1783, immediately after news of the Treaty of Paris reached America. He quickly became studio assistant to West, who instilled in his young protégé the idea that an artist ought to value momentous historical events over other kinds of subjects, such as portraiture, still life, or landscape. The "Great Style," according to Sir Joshua Reynolds, president of the Royal Academy, required a subject that is epic and that "powerfully strikes upon the public sympathy."[46] West himself was Trumbull's professional model, having painted the most admired modern historical subject, *The Death of General Wolfe*, which shows the British general heroically expiring on the plains of Abraham, outside Quebec, at the end of the climactic battle of 1759, during the French and Indian War.

Inspired by West, Trumbull would dedicate himself to "painting the great Events of the Revolution."[47] In short order, he finished two brilliant pictures while in London, *The Death of General Warren at the Battle of Bunker's Hill, June 17, 1775* and *The Death of General Montgomery in the Attack on Quebec, December 31, 1775*. Looking ahead, he imagined dozens more pictures, including the battles at Trenton, Princeton, Saratoga, and Eutaw Springs, the sieges at Savannah and Charleston, the Declaration of Independence, the Treaty of Paris, the surrenders at Saratoga and Yorktown. And, too, the capture and death of Jane McCrea. After all, she was at the confluence of all his wartime experiences on the Champlain and Hudson corridor in 1776, involving Gates, Burgoyne, André, Stephen McCrea, and Fort Edward.

Trumbull produced two drawings for a picture on Jane McCrea.[48] The more legible one presents a stunning scene.[49] To the right of center, three Indians seize a naked and terrified Jane McCrea. In the tightly knotted tangle of legs and arms that form that group, one warrior wraps an arm around her waist, while another pulls back her hair. A third warrior, taller than the others, raises a knife high overhead. McCrea fruitlessly tries to run, throws her arms wide, and opens her palms to heaven, her white body contrasted against the inked-in torsos of the Natives. In the right distance can be seen a house, presumably that of Sarah McNeil, where McCrea was found. To the left is a sketchy cluster of six or seven men, one of whom is frantically running, arms stretched into the air, toward Jane. That, we can infer, represents Lieutenant David Jones. A second, fainter drawing is similar, except that in the right distance there are two added figures, one in

John Trumbull, "Miss McCrea, Fort Edward," ca. 1790. Sepia. Bennington, VT, Bennington Museum, Gift of Hall Park McCullough.

pursuit of the other, presumably another scene of butchery near Fort Edward. For unknown reasons Trumbull never commenced a full-scale painting. Nonetheless, by including her story he had vaulted the young betrothed daughter of a New Jersey minister into his monumental pantheon of American fame.

He returned to the upper Hudson in 1791 to make sketches of the Saratoga battlefield in preparation for a colossal painting, *The Surrender of General Burgoyne*, which would eventually be installed in the Rotunda of the United States Capitol. In it, Gates, his former commander and mentor, stands tall at center stage, while on the right, American officers witness history being made. Behind him, the vast expanse of the Saratoga battlefield stretches toward the horizon, as storm clouds push away to reveal a new sunny day. A glum Burgoyne, emptied of charm, stands left of Gates, handing over his sword as a mangled branch of a fallen tree in the lower left seems to snap at him like a wooden crocodile. Scattered throughout are men Trumbull knew while posted in the Northern Department. To the right of Gates, Daniel Morgan, dressed in his rifle company's distinctive

John Trumbull, *The Surrender of General Burgoyne at Saratoga, October 16, 1777*, c. 1822. Oil on canvas. New Haven, Yale University Art Gallery, Trumbull Collection.

white woodsman garb, turns directly toward the audience, as if this were the curtain call for the Saratoga stage production. Trumbull tastefully omitted Benedict Arnold, once the military hero of the Saratoga battles, but now a reviled traitor.

Also omitted was Jane McCrea. Of course, even if she had lived past the summer of 1777, she would never have been present at the Saratoga battlefield. Yet, by the time Trumbull painted *Saratoga*, McCrea had become so fundamental to the Saratoga narrative—thought to have been an inspirational ghost pushing men onward to victory—that Trumbull, were he a more freewheeling artist living in another time and place, might have been tempted to paint her into the heavens. Though the conventions of American art of the eighteenth century surely would have disallowed it, Trumbull could have tucked her between the banks of clouds, peering down on the profitable results of her death, the watchful patron saint of the Saratoga victory.

10.

IN FRANCE

"The shot heard round the world," wrote one historian, "sounded as sharp and clear in the Garden of the Tuileries as if it had been fired on the Place Louis XV."[1] The French were transfixed by the Revolution and America in general. They avidly read Jefferson's *Notes on Virginia*, Franklin's *Autobiography*, the *Constitution* and *The Federalist*; Thomas Paine's *Rights of Man* went through eleven French editions.[2] When the war was over, Lafayette, J. Hector St. John Crèvecoeur, and François-Jean Chastellux published accounts of their time with the American forces. Newspapers, such as *Le Courier de l'Europe*, *Gazette de France*, and *Les Affaires de l'Angleterre et de l'Amérique*, regularly printed war dispatches and translated articles from the American press into French, including ones on Jane McCrea.[3]

The French love affair extended into comprehensive histories of the Revolution by Paul Dubuisson, Joseph Mandrillon, and Guillaume Raynal, as well as translations of American documents and newspaper articles. By 1790, the French had translated David Ramsay's *History of the American Revolution* and Thomas Anburey's *Travels*, both volumes containing accounts of McCrea's killing.[4] Some Frenchmen became so hungry for information about her that they solicited information from the American envoys to France—Benjamin Franklin first and then Thomas Jefferson and Gouverneur Morris.

While Franklin was minister, François Godefroy, the royal engraver to Louis XVI, began work on sixteen remarkable prints on a variety of subjects from the Revolution, eventually publishing them as a suite titled *Recueil d'estampes representant les differents evenemens de la guerre, qui a procure l'indépendance aux Etats Unis de l'Amerique.* To be sure, Godefroy was not able to take direct portraits of officers, knew little of their uniforms, lacked access to the American terrain, worked with sketchy knowledge of military events, occasionally got dates and spellings wrong, and indulged in head-spinning tangents. Yet, his project was one of the first efforts to visualize the Revolution for French audiences.

One print depicts Burgoyne surrendering to Gates at Saratoga. Below the image itself, Godefroy printed a military synopsis of the entire Saratoga campaign. Under that, he added a few lines about Jane McCrea, the sentimental heroine of Saratoga: "The death, above all, of the young and beautiful Miss MacRea fills all hearts with horror. Daughter of a very rich subject of the King, she was massacred by the savages the day of her marriage with an English officer of the army of Burgoyne."

More expansively, Michel-René Hilliard d'Auberteuil, a lawyer who held controversial opinions on the colonization of the New World by European powers, in 1784 turned his attention to the American Revolution in a detailed two-volume *Essais Historiques et Politiques sur less Anglo-Américains.*[5] In a chapter on the year 1777, Hilliard narrated the Saratoga campaign and made a point of condemning Burgoyne's Native auxiliaries by using McCrea as his primary example. He mangled some facts along the way, even though he had made a research trip to the upper Hudson in 1778. Hilliard inaccurately wrote that McCrea was the sixteen-year-old daughter of a rich New York merchant, was in love with a British officer, not an American Loyalist, and while heading into his camp was assaulted, stripped, carried into the woods, and killed by Indians, who then paraded her scalp in front of the British army and her lover.[6]

Hilliard was besotted with McCrea. He bombarded Franklin with letters introducing himself, his new book, and his infatuated thoughts about her. At one point, so enamored with her story, he told Franklin that he wanted to make a "petit monument" to the "mémoire de la pauvre mis Mac Rea."[7] That urge morphed into a fantastical seduction novella of 1784, in which he took even more liberties with her story. In it, Jenny, a sweet and pious girl living in New York with her father, meets the wounded "Captain Belton," a cunning and exploitative British rake who stands in for the benign David Jones. Belton wins Jenny's heart, but—because he is a British man

François Godefroy, *Sarratoga*, c. 1784. Engraving. New York, Metropolitan Museum of Art. Bequest of Charles Allen Munn, 1924.

in a French novel—he is cast as a libertine, intrinsically insincere and false. In words that equally fit the glamorous descriptions of Major André, Belton "was a man of intelligence, he had traveled, and he possessed to an eminent degree that false good breeding and dexterity of language."[8] The naïve and smitten Jenny, however, imagines Belton to be in possession of "the dignity of Mars and the beauty of Apollo," despite the fact that he tries to rape her at one point.[9]

That notwithstanding, she is so dazzled by the regalia of Belton's British uniform and the strict protocols of high-born officers that she decides to abandon her father's homespun simplicity in favor of her lover's aristocratic allure. Putty in Belton's hands, Jane forsakes "American innocence," as Hilliard put it, for "European vices."[10] She and her Irish servant gallop north to the British camp for a rendezvous with her beloved, whereupon, Mohawks capture her in the deep woods.

Hilliard indulged himself with a graphic sex scene in which the Indians, having "received a double ration of brandy this day," surround Jane and her servant. "The Indians stripped them completely naked, tied them to trees, and divided their clothes and baggage among themselves. . . . The most important of them, taken with her beauty, stared desirously at her charms. . . . Her anguish added to her beauty; her hair, long enough to serve as a veil for her modesty, made the whiteness of her skin appear lustrous."[11] They kill and scalp Jane, notwithstanding the attempt of Kiashatu, a noble chief, to stop the tragedy. Kiashatu ferries her scalp to Belton, who, Hilliard emphasizes, is feckless enough to refuse suicide, which would have allowed him to live forever with his sweetheart in the afterworld.

Hilliard's novella is riddled with historical inaccuracies, all of which were deliberate and purposeful. The indecent assault on a white woman by dark "savages," he wishes to say, was the criminal result of the systemic European exploitation of Native Americans, all hopped up on imported liquor. These were just "simple people," who "did not love cruelty for its own sake." But because they were "continually intoxicated in order to increase their ferocity and to encourage them to murder and commit atrocities," the ultimate responsibility for civilian deaths falls squarely "upon the nations that provoked them, nations that dared to call themselves civilized."[12] Hilliard, a deep critic of France, had adapted and altered the McCrea story in order to condemn not only Britain's destructive presence in the New World, but also his own imperial nation's ruinous colonization of Haiti and the Caribbean. The "civilized" ancien régime, like the British in his novella, was guilty of having warped native societies that would have been, if left alone, virtuous, a concept that shows the influence of Jean-Jacques Rousseau. *Mis Mac Rea* is his disguised political commentary on what happens when white Europeans enter the socially and racially complex societies of the New World, in particular the French Caribbean, and twist its values, habits, and balance by importing Africans, imposing their imperialistic ways, and waging war.[13]

Mis Mac Rea's claim to fame was its status as the first prose treatment of McCrea's life and death. Hilliard proudly sent a copy to Franklin as soon as it was published in 1784, and two years later he received a note from Jefferson, who had succeeded Franklin at court, thanking him for all the "immortal" ways he was contributing to the "memory of the American revolution."[14]

Hilliard, Godefroy, and dozens of other writers, artists, and *philosophes* paved the way for the arrival in Paris of the American painter John Vanderlyn, who would turn Jane McCrea's story into a haunting spectacle of violence, eroticism, and politics. Vanderlyn himself had grown up on the Hudson.[15] When he was two years old, in 1777, British General Henry Clinton tried to halt Burgoyne's October collapse at Saratoga by means of a distraction eighty-five miles downriver, in Vanderlyn's hometown of Kingston, then New York's capital in exile. Clinton had instructed Lieutenant-General John Vaughan to invade Kingston with a force of 1,600, and to rout the state legislature. This he did, but then acting on his own Vaughan burned the town to the ground, all 326 houses, including Vanderlyn's, in hopes of pulling Gates away from Saratoga. The 4,000 citizens of Kingston, including the Vanderlyns, who lived on Green Street at the edge of the original Dutch settlement of Wiltwyck, were suddenly homeless as they faced winter. For them, the trauma of the British invasion forever etched itself into family memory.

Though John Vanderlyn's family was among the "principle sufferers" of the burning, his parents "were still able to afford him, at the proper age, the benefits of a liberal education."[16] After classical studies at Kingston Academy, he moved in 1794 at age seventeen to the city of New York where he began art instruction at the Columbian Academy of Painting while lodged with the supremely talented painter Gilbert Stuart. He joined the Tammany Society, a workingman's club named for Tamanend, a legendary Lenape chief. Members pretended to be Indians, dressed the part, invented secret rites, and whooped and hollered in unison. Tammany was a politically powerful organization in New York, opposed to reconciliation with Britain, hostile to Alexander Hamilton's federalism, and smitten with France, America's first and foremost ally. He also met Colonel Aaron Burr, a recently elected United States senator who intended to be a candidate for the presidency.

In 1796, Burr hosted Vanderlyn at Richmond Hill, his twenty-six-acre estate on Varick Street in southern Manhattan, and offered to finance his first trip to Paris in order to be trained properly, in the French way. He enrolled as a student at the Académie de Peinture, where he studied under François-André Vincent. In 1800 Vanderlyn painted his self-portrait as a serious young man and gave it to Burr, who pronounced him, without doubt, "the best painter that now is or ever has been in America."[17] Vanderlyn debuted his self-portrait at the prestigious Salon in 1800, after which he made a brief return visit to the United States, during which time Burr became vice-president under Jefferson. Vanderlyn returned to Paris in May 1803, this time as a representative of the American Academy of the Fine Arts, a new art school in New York founded by Edward and Robert Livingston, the latter serving as American minister to the First Republic of France. Vanderlyn had arrived the very month in which Napoleon sold the Louisiana Territory to the United States and Britain declared war on France.

Vanderlyn's arrival coincided with his fellow citizen Joel Barlow's effort to commission artists to illustrate his epic 8,350-line poem, *The Columbiad*, a hymn to American history and destiny, which he thought would be nothing less than the new republic's equivalent to the *Iliad* and the *Aeneid*. Barlow had originally come to France on a business trip in 1788, and during the French Revolution was one of a handful of Americans to declare solidarity with the National Assembly that successfully toppled the ancien régime. He was involved with the moderately republican Girondists and actually sought election, unsuccessfully, to the ruling National Convention.

In recruiting an artist to illustrate *The Columbiad*, Barlow had first turned to Robert Fulton, who had been living in Paris with his wife Eliza since 1787. Fulton was an accomplished painter, yet he had to turn down Barlow's offer because he was also an engineer too busy designing submarines, experimenting with torpedoes, and testing a sixty-six-foot-long steamboat on the river Seine. On Fulton's advice, Barlow turned to Vanderlyn, who was affectionately called "Toot" by the young artist.[18]

For *The Columbiad*, Barlow assigned two scenes to Vanderlyn to illustrate, one of which was the killing of a young woman—a fictionalized Jane McCrea—during the Saratoga campaign. Vanderlyn was especially well-positioned to produce such a picture. His Hudson Valley upbringing made him familiar with McCrea's tale and all the variations on it. He also had some knowledge of Indian dress, in part from the Tammany Society. Psychologically, he was motivated to illustrate McCrea because he held a long-festering grudge against the British for the damage inflicted on his family and his fellow citizens in 1777 when they burned Kingston. Now, in 1803, with Napoleon intent on crushing Britain, the usually quiet Vanderlyn vocally supported France, as did Barlow, declaring, "Preparations for the Desscent on England are going on bravely. . . . Haughty Britannia already trembles I don't doubt."[19]

Vanderlyn had been waiting for the opportunity to paint a subject from history, which was de rigueur for a budding artist in Paris. Vincent, his mentor, was already a leading historical painter, and because of France's expanding empire, war subjects were the rage. The French minister of war,

John Vanderlyn, *Portrait of the Artist*. 1800. Oil on canvas. New York, The Metropolitan Museum of Art, Bequest of Ann S. Stephens, in memory of her mother, Mrs. Ann S. Stephens, 1918.

Alexandre Berthier, expressly urged artists to depict scenes of contemporary conflict, preferably Napoleonic.[20] As a result, some mammoth war paintings emerged, such as Louis-François Lejeune's *Battle of Marengo* of 1801, a giant panorama with thousands of French soldiers battling the Austrians in Piedmont. Colossal pictures usually contained subplots, one of the most absorbing and common being women in distress, unfailingly flanked on one or both sides by assailants, the vignettes meant to be illustrative of the dire consequences of war.[21]

At age twenty-six, Vanderlyn may not have been ready to attempt a complicated, large-scale scene, but the commission from Barlow did allow him to isolate a single, up-close encounter from within a war zone, and move it to center stage. Vanderlyn's job was to illustrate a passage still in manuscript form, from Barlow's sixth book of *The Columbiad*, where he tells the tale of the upper Hudson in 1777, beginning with a chilling political insight: "Cold-blooded Cruelty" had now joined the British advance.[22]

Barlow took poetic license when he composed the romance between Jane McCrea and David Jones, changing their names to Lucinda and Heartly, the latter evocative of true love. Lucinda risks everything to arrive at her fiancé's camp for a wedding ceremony, whereupon Heartly, "in youth's o'erweening Pride," has decided to reschedule because he feels compelled to follow his "valorous heart" into a battle that day. An anxious Lucinda, sensing death, ties a feather to Heartly's cap, a "mystic knot, the knot of love," that will allow her to spot him from a distance.[23] The battle becomes apocalyptic, stained with "thick flames" and "sulphureous clouds" wafting atop a field "sheeted o'er with blood." Lucinda catches sight of Heartly, then suddenly he "vanish'd in the warrior cloud."[24] Thinking him dead, she recklessly abandons camp and drifts into the woods, bewildered.

Heartly fruitlessly searches through the night for her, only to discover that "sweet" Lucinda has already encountered two Mohawk warriors. In an extended passage, Barlow detailed the pathos of her murder:

> She starts, with eyes upturn'd and fleeting breath,
> In their raised axes views her instant death,
> Spreads her white hands to heaven in frantic prayer,
> Then runs to grasp their knees, and crouches there.
> Her hair, half lost along the shrubs she past,
> Rolls in loose tangles round her lovely waist;
> Her kerchief torn betrays the globes of snow
> That heave responsive to her weight of woe.

Sexual suggestion intended, Barlow then pointed an accusatory finger at the British:

> Does all this eloquence suspend the knife?
> Does no superior bribe contest her life?
> There does: the scalps by British gold are paid;
> A long-hair'd scalp adorns that heavenly head;
> And comes the sacred spoil from friend or foe,
> No marks distinguish, and no man can know.

Barlow's heroic couplets—technically, rhymed iambic pentameter—created a metrical tom-tom beat, suitable for Lucinda's inexorable march toward death.

> With calculating pause and demon grin,
> They seize her hands, and thro her face divine
> Drive the descending ax.

When readers arrive at this passage, they would have already known the sad end to the tale because Jane McCrea was such an international sensation by the first decade of the nineteenth century. So, Barlow ginned it up and pulled Heartly into the murder scene.

The shriek she sent
Attain'd her lover's ear; he thither bent
With all the speed his wearied limbs could yield,
Whirl'd his keen blade, and stretch'd upon the field
The yelling fiends; who there disputing stood
Her gory scalp, their horrid prize of blood.
He sunk delirious on her lifeless clay,
And past, in starts of sense, the dreadful day.[25]

Finally, Barlow admonished his readers never to forget "Lucinda's fate; the tale, ye nations hear; Eternal ages, trace it with a tear."[26]

The ever-pedantic Barlow outfitted *The Columbiad* with sixty-seven pages of footnotes. Note 47 provides a history lesson, where we hear about Burgoyne's "unjustifiable" hiring of "ferocious" Indian auxiliaries. In the footnote, Barlow credited Burgoyne for his attempts to control predations, then condemned him and the British ministry for not knowing that "indiscriminate and ungovernable ravages" were inevitable. His case in point: "The tragical catastrophe of a young lady of the name of Macrea, whose story is almost literally detailed in the foregoing paragraphs of the text, is well known." Her killing, Barlow added, "made a great impression on the public mind at the time, both in England and America."[27]

As Vanderlyn worked on his picture through the summer of 1804, he received word that his friend and patron, Aaron Burr, the standing vice-president and candidate for the governorship of New York, had on June 11 crossed the Hudson to the New Jersey Palisades for a fatal duel with Alexander Hamilton, the former secretary of the treasury. Burr fled to South Carolina, replaced in Jefferson's cabinet by his archrival, George Clinton.

Vanderlyn could have just made a pencil drawing to satisfy Barlow's commission for a sketch that would lead to an engraved print, but instead he produced a finished painting. Before delivering it, he submitted the picture to the Salon of 1804, held in the Musée Napoléon (the Louvre was temporarily renamed when Napoléon declared himself emperor in the spring). His painting, number 495 out of the 691 entries, was thoughtfully

John Vanderlyn, *The Murder of Jane McCrea.* 1804. Oil on canvas. Hartford, Wadsworth Atheneum Museum of Art; purchased by subscription.

hung near Jean-Antoine Houdon's sculpted busts of Fulton and Barlow. Small compared to the French blockbusters, in part because it was meant to be transferred into an engraved print that would be published in a book, it nonetheless attracted some critical notice: "A young American artist, Vanderlyn, presented a proof of his talents."[28]

Left, Greek hoplites attacking an Amazon. Tomb of Mausolus, c. 350 BCE. London, British Museum. Right, Wounded Niobid, c. 440 BCE. Parian marble. Rome, Palazzo Massimo alle Terme.

To be sure, one of Vanderlyn's goals in painting the picture, besides the fulfillment of Barlow's commission, was to prove his legitimacy as a serious artist in Napoleonic France. He accomplished that by making a show of how much he knew of the classical past, which was considered an artistic requisite and a national imperative. He based the overall staging on sculpted panels on the ancient tomb of Mausolus, where Greek men subdue Amazon women.[29] For the two warriors, Vanderlyn adapted a famous statue of a Greek athlete that was something of an obsession among French painters.[30] He took McCrea's pinwheel pose—down on one knee, arms splayed—from an ancient Greek statue of a dying Niobid.[31]

By incorporating motifs and images from the classical past, Vanderlyn made McCrea's death timeless, as if it too were a tale from classical mythology reenacted in the Hudson Valley during the American Revolution. Even McCrea's Directoire gown had a classical flair. As was the *mode* in Napoleonic Paris and elsewhere, women were busy "making themselves into *Greeks* or *statues*."[32] The thin blue material that clings to Jane's body, as well as the low-cut bodice and lack of structured undergarments, echo the dress of antiquity, in particular the Greek *chiton*, in effect transforming an American country girl of 1777 into a stylish woman of 1804.

Exposure was in. Eighteenth-century corsets, stays, paddings, stiff stomachers, long sleeves, and poufy coiffeurs were out. In Vanderlyn's modern take, the sensual contours of Jane's thighs were not to be hidden beneath a wall of impenetrable fabrics. Instead, we trace her body beneath the blue drape and spot bits of underwear: a red underskirt below her right knee, and a thin, almost see-through, muslin chemise that, were it not being pulled apart by the struggle, would barely conceal her bust. Because the fabrics are so lightweight and the whole ensemble so unfortified by protective undergarments, McCrea looks especially defenseless in Vanderlyn's painting, her safety ironically endangered by a silky modern gown donned for Lieutenant Jones's lovelorn eyes.

If he has imagined McCrea as a Greek figure or a version of Napoleon's Josephine, who modernized the risqué Greek mode, then Vanderlyn has made her assailants into the opposite: dark-skinned barbarians from the deep forest, like what the Goths were to the ancient Romans. French paintings during the Napoleonic era, especially those depicting scenes from the Egyptian campaign dominated the exhibition that September. The critical favorite, Antoine-Jean Gros's massive *Napoleon Visiting the Victims of the Plague at Jaffa*, was a striking scene of Bonaparte's 1799 trip to a pest house in Syria. In it and others set in the Middle East, light-skinned Europeans contrast with exotic dark-skinned Muslims, the differentiation intended.

Conflicts in faraway places were pointedly focused on the contrast between Europeans and "uncivilized" Ottomans, Egyptians, Africans, Asians, Haitians, African Americans, or Native Americans.[33] Painters in Paris, like Vanderlyn, had learned from the anatomists teaching in the Louvre that skin color—*couleur de peau*—was not merely a physical trait. Instead, it was fundamentally cultural, indicative of temperament, behavior, and morality, all of which was innate to the race.[34] As a result, audiences understood that paintings like *Jane McCrea* were comparative studies of race and behavior, cautionary tales of what awful things can happen when cultures collide. Vanderlyn's eyepopping picture played to white fear.

Were we to think of Vanderlyn's stunning dance of death as a theatrical production with the three lead actors placed downstage and spotlighted against a darkened background, we would instantly know that we are nearing the harrowing climax of the play. This is the point where the strands of the plot—Jane's arrival in Fort Edward, David Jones's quest to retrieve her, Burgoyne's auxiliaries fanning out in front of the main force, and the anticipation of a wedding between separated lovers—all culminate in the form of a nightmare come terribly true. This would be the unforgettable set-piece that closes act four and that lingers in every theatergoer's mind long after the curtain has come down.

Vanderlyn knew that the sight of McCrea's torment a moment before death had more shock value and would elicit more pathos than if the scalping were actually taking place.[35] He also knew that he could maximize the impact of the picture if he made Jane's demise suggestively lascivious and positioned it voyeuristically close to the audience. As an audience, we get to feel McCrea's horror because Vanderlyn was so effective in allowing us to inhabit the vocal gasp, the body tremor, the tight grip, and the palpable dread, all our senses having been recruited and linked together in sublime empathy.[36] In Vanderlyn's visual snapshot, we cannot escape the tangle of arms and hands, the contrast between dark and light flesh, and the fatal clash between savage and civilized. Sexual innuendo is conspicuous in her slack jaw, supplicating hand, and exposed breast. A pink sash suggestively hangs between her thighs, while her white body nestles softly below her attacker's dark legs. In Vanderlyn's compression chamber, we nervously scan across an active crime scene forever frozen in time.

Because the action is large and looming, anguished French viewers were ushered into front-row seats in the woodland theater of death. The picture may cause a few of us merely to reflect dispassionately on the plight of a woman who was accidentally caught up in the violence of the American Revolution. But most will experience an emotional wallop of the most visceral kind, namely the frightening possibility of ourselves—or our sisters, our wives, and our daughters—suddenly assaulted by strange men intent on ending our lives.

Intriguingly, in 1804 Vanderlyn did not display the picture with any reference to Jane McCrea, or Lucinda, or Joel Barlow. Instead, the title at the Salon, translated from French, was *A Young Woman Slaughtered by Two Savages in the Service of the English During the American War. Historical Event Documented in the Sixth Book of The Columbiad, American Poem.*[37] Vanderlyn had turned his debut as a history painter into a timely political statement, the key word in the title being "English." Because he desired success within the French art world and was living in expansionary France, and because France was in the midst of an all-out war against Britain, and because Vanderlyn despised the British for the burning of his childhood home, there could not have been a better subject than one showcasing murderers in British employ, scalping and killing a young, beautiful, and innocent woman who never deserved such an awful fate.

Tellingly, Vanderlyn painted Jane's Directoire gown in the colors of both France and the United States. He further decided not to paint the tiny figure of Heartly/Jones in a British officer's red, but in American blue. He must have reckoned that in France there would be no sympathy for a woman who was, in reality, a British sympathizer, like the real Jane McCrea, in love with a Loyalist officer. In his effort to maximize the desired indictment of the hated British and their auxiliaries, Vanderlyn made the victim an American woman engaged to an American rebel officer.

Finally, when the time came to deliver the picture to Barlow, Vanderlyn was cheeky enough to ask for more money. It was so much more that Barlow felt justified in not paying. Instead of the original 384 French livres stipulated in the contract, Vanderlyn demanded an additional 688. Barlow was civil in his response to Vanderlyn's extravagant—almost extortionate—demand, perhaps because he could see that the picture was perhaps *too* terrifying for his poem. Barlow walked away, left the picture in Vanderlyn's studio, and wished this "man of genius" well, hoping him "success & prosperity equal to your merit, which I really think is very great. . . . I do not pretend to say that the picture in question is not worth more . . .; my moderate fortune will not permit me to give whatever maybe its value."[38]

Barlow quickly hired another artist, Robert Smirke, an Englishman ironically, to produce a more decorous image for *The Columbiad*.[39] Eventually Fulton, friend to both Barlow and Vanderlyn, purchased Vanderlyn's painting in 1805 and gave it to the American Academy of the Fine Arts in New York, which was led by Robert Livingston.[40]

A bizarre postscript to the story of Vanderlyn's *Jane McCrea* occurred in April of 1836, at a time when the painting was in the possession of the American Academy. The *New York Herald*, one of the city's penny press newspapers, famous for gorging readers with kinky crime coverage, carried a disturbing feature on the grotesque murder of a twenty-three-year-old prostitute who had come to the city from Maine. Helen (also referred to as Ellen) Jewett had been sleeping in her mahogany bed at Rosina Townsend's upscale brothel at 41 Thomas Street, near City Hall. In the early morning hours of April 10, an intruder bludgeoned her to death and then set fire to her bed. Police arrested Richard Robinson, an ardent nineteen-year-old

Anker Smith, after Robert Smirke, *The Murder of Lucinda.* Etching and line engraving. New Haven, Yale Center for British Art, Paul Mellon Collection.

"john," who claimed innocence. Six weeks later at a circus trial at City Hall, presided over by a judge who was Aaron Burr's cousin, the jury found Robinson not guilty for lack of evidence. Both the murder and the trial became front-page news in the city, especially in the tawdry hands of James Gordon Bennett, the *Herald*'s editor, who proclaimed "this tragedy and the accused have occupied every tongue—been the topic of every conversation—is discussed in every drawing room and gin shop throughout the extent of New York."[41]

At a time when countless illustrations and theatrical reenactments were picturing Jane McCrea's death in Eastern cities, Jewett's slaying became national news. Nathaniel Hawthorne, a devotee of stories about female slayings, noted the killing in a journal entry after a visit on his thirty-fourth birthday to the wax effigies of Jewett and Richardson then on display in Salem. "Ellen Jewett and R. P. Robinson, she dressed richly, in extreme fashion, and very pretty; he awkward and stiff, it being difficult to stuff a figure to look like a gentleman. The showman seemed very proud of Ellen Jewett, and spoke of her somewhat as if this wax-figure were a real creation."[42] Jewett's murder later would become the subject of a serial novel in the *National Police Gazette*, and eventually she appeared as a character in Gore Vidal's 1973 novel, *Burr*.[43]

As part of the *Herald*'s salacious reporting of a "Most Atrocious Murder," Bennett narrated his visits to the crime scene, which included a necrophilic description of the corpse, "the most remarkable sight I ever beheld." Though the body had been partially burned by the fire and hacked to the bone by both the murder and the autopsy conducted on site, Bennett headlined "BEAUTIFUL WORK OF ART," the "perfect figure, the exquisite limbs, the fine face, the full arms, the beautiful bust, all surpassed in every respect the Venus de Medici."[44] In a coarsely pornographic merger of violence and beauty, he described Jewett's corpse "as white, as full, as polished as the purest Parian marble."[45]

As Bennett was combing through the brothel, he discovered in the parlor a picture "representing the murder of a beautiful young woman, by an Indian with a hatchet," namely Jane McCrea and the Indians. "It represented a beautiful female," Bennett wrote of the picture, "in disorder and on her knees, before two savages, one of them lifting up a tomahawk to give her a blow on the head." That was either an 1839 copy of Vanderlyn's original, or a picture derived from it, or the actual 1804 Vanderlyn.[46]

John Robert Livingston, scion of the powerful New York Livingstons, was the wealthy property owner of Townsend's brothel and a member of the American Academy, which owned Vanderlyn's original *Jane McCrea*. Livingston presented himself to the world as a businessman, but more accurately he was a sex racketeer, known as New York's "Lord of Vice," or, even less generously, as the city's "whoremaster."[47] He oversaw dozens of brothels, run by notable madams, including Rosina Townsend's, and he was himself once accused of murder during the Revolution for ambushing and killing a British captain whose son-in-law was Horatio Gates. By 1836, the American Academy had fallen into a moribund state and most of its collection was in storage. That means Livingston could have retrieved Vanderlyn's painting and loaned it to the brothel that he owned and Madame Townsend ran.

In pointing out a connection between Jewett's and McCrea's killings, both by hatchet, Bennett was suggesting that Vanderlyn's graphic spectacle of brutality may have entered the warped mind of the killer. "What a remarkable type," Bennett wrote of Vanderlyn's picture, "or hint—or foregone conclusion of the awful tragedy perpetrated upstairs. . . . Would not that picture perpetually hanging there—visible at all hours," suggest "the very act that was perpetrated?"[48]

Vanderlyn's painting was the most reproduced and most influential image of Jane McCrea's killing in history. In addition to all its reproductions in books and essays, it made an exquisite appearance in Martin Scorsese's 1993 film adaptation of Edith Wharton's *The Age of Innocence*, set in New York during the Gilded Age. A voiceover narrator tells us of the upcoming marriage between Newland Archer, a young lawyer whose life was being orchestrated by his family, and May Welland, a young, correct, yet dull daughter of a scheming mother. Setting the stage for the wedding, the Welland family hosts a reception for the couple in their elegant New York mansion. Meant to be a celebration of the engagement and the joining of two prominent families, Scorsese's camera glides through room after opulent room, stuffed with European and American paintings that speak to good taste and refinement.

The thrust of both film and novel is the slow uncovering of Newland's deep and previously repressed passions, which slowly bubble into his mind, causing him to doubt the wisdom of a polite marriage and to pursue the mysterious Countess Olenska. Scorsese expresses the unruly desires that threaten Newland's unalterable engagement to May in a scene where the camera moves from one soothing landscape painting to another, and starts to ascend a staircase whereupon the chain of delirious pictures cracks. The camera stops moving and fixes on Vanderlyn's *Jane McCrea*. Its raw dissonance—its vista of ravishment—clangs amidst the polite gems of the Welland mansion. The visceral image of a young woman attacked unmasks the hidden viciousness within New York society and portends the dark and soon-to-be unharnessed forces lodged deep within Newland Archer's heart. It is a disruptive departure into sublime terror, a peek into the uncharted territory below the genteel surfaces of life.

II.

TOURISTS

Rashomon, Akira Kurosawa's celebrated film of 1950, tells five contradictory accounts of an eighth-century murder of a samurai in a bamboo forest near Kyoto. A woodcutter, a priest, and a bandit, as well as the samurai's wife and the deceased samurai himself, offer their versions of the terrible crime, each story narrated in convincing detail. However, instead of one story building upon another, leading to an ever more complete picture of the murder, the accounts veer away from and mostly contradict each other, thus clouding the facts, scrambling the story, and confounding the viewer. All the narrators prove to be unreliable (and that includes the dead samurai himself, speaking through a medium). By the end of the film, the objective truth of the crime has become impossibly murky and, ultimately, unknowable.

After the Revolution, McCrea's death took on *Rashomon* dimensions in America, the stories of her last hours multiplying at an ever-increasing clip and gathering in a heap of conflicting accounts told by former soldiers and officers, as well as dozens of townsfolk eager to regale listeners and readers with their versions of what each claimed really happened that day in 1777 in a wood near Fort Edward. In short order, the original facts, insofar as they could ever be ascertained, drifted into folklore. McCrea, who had the bad fortune to be in the deadly path of Burgoyne's march, ultimately had the good fortune to be the subject of enduring curiosity, conversation, and controversy. As a result, in the decades after her killing she became the sentimental icon of the American Revolution.[1]

The first tourists began arriving while the Revolution was still active. François-Jean Chastellux, a major-general serving in the French expeditionary force under the Comte de Rochambeau, took a circuitous route to his destination in Yorktown after his landing in Newport in 1780. In order to grasp the magnitude of the war, he traveled to meet great figures and visit famous battle sites. In Albany he dined with General Schuyler and in Saratoga he reconstructed Burgoyne's epic defeat.

He could have stopped there. Instead, he pressed northward, "benumbed" by ice and snow, nonetheless determined to get to Fort Edward, where he arrived at the house of "the unfortunate *Miss MacRea*, who was killed by the savages."[2] Chastellux wondered if her death was some kind of "Divine vengeance" for having turned against the American cause. Had Lieutenant Jones "triumphed over her virtue, and her patriotism." Why did she stay in Fort Edward while everyone else evacuated, mused Chastellux. Perhaps it was because "she wished to see him again as a conqueror, to marry him, and then partake of his toils and his successes." After the Indians "pillaged" and "carried her off," a "dispute" over the spoils forced them to "terminate the quarrel" by killing her. Chastellux reflected on this "sad catastrophe," felt for Lieutenant Jones, and accurately predicted that "a death so cruel and unforeseen, would furnish a very pathetic subject for a drama, or an elegy. . . . Nothing short of the charms of eloquence and poetry is capable of moving the heart." After all, "such is the true character of love."[3]

Henrietta Marchant Liston, an heiress married to a Scottish-born diplomat who was British minister to the United States, traveled widely in America, collecting botanical specimens and observing American culture with a keen eye. In June of 1799, traveling up the Hudson with her husband, she visited "the small town near which poor Major Andree was taken, the very Tree (a Tulip Tree) beneath which he was seized and searched is plainly to be seen." She then pushed on to Albany, staying at Platt's Inn, before moving north to Fort Edward, where she colorfully imagined Jane McCrea's last day.

> On a rising ground about a mile further on, the spot is shown on which the unfortunate Miss McCray was murdered by an *Indian.*— Her lover, Capt. Jones, to whom she was immediately to have been married, was in *Burgoyne's* army; He sent two *trusty Indians* to

> the House of an Aunt, with whom she lived near Fort-Edward,—promising them a barrel of *Rum* if they conducted her safely to the Camp;—This was perhaps the greatest reward an *Indian* could receive.—The agreement was overheard by two *Indians* of another Nation, who setting out soon after met this unhappy young Woman, with her two Escorts—at the top of the Hill,—the two Natives disputed the Prize,—concluding, that the Rum would be given to whomever delivered the Lady into the hands of Capt. Jones.—the combat was most violent, & one of the Strangers, finding that he & his Companion were likely to have the worst of it, ran up to Miss McCray, who had clung to a Tree trembling with apprehension, & raising his *Tomahawk* killed & scalped her in the course of a few minutes.—A spring issues near the Tree.[4]

The source of Chastellux's information is unknown, but Liston's slightly skewed narrative came from Fort Edward's citizens upon her request for insider knowledge.

Everyone in town would have noticed—and initially might have been surprised to see—that their otherwise inconsequential town was becoming a tourist destination. McCrea's notoriety , villagers came to realize, had the power to confer fame on the town and the site of the killing, and sometimes on those who said they knew her, professed ownership of hidden facts, and claimed to know the truth about what really happened on July 26, 1777. As a result, the citizens of Fort Edward began spinning fabulous stories that contributed to the timeless legend of their most famous daughter, and in the process, they inevitably converted facts, such as they were ever determinable, into folklore.

Occasionally there arrived a tourist inured to legend-making. Benjamin Silliman, an eminent professor of chemistry and geology at Yale, traveled through the upper Hudson in 1819, while en route to Canada. He stopped in Fort Edward where he "saw, and conversed with a person, who was acquainted with her, and with her family."[5] After hearing one of the typical stories about Jane McCrea, namely that Lieutenant Jones had sent two parties of warriors to fetch her, leading to a feud that resulted in her murder, Silliman, a man of science whose mind trafficked in rational thought rather than emotion, stepped back and asked some tough questions: "Where were his affection and his gallantry, that he did not go himself, or least that he did not accompany his savage emissaries!" Was this a case of criminal neglect? Was David Jones really so callow as to jeopardize the life of his beloved with such a preposterous plan? Equally troubling to a skeptical Silliman was the seeming stupidity of McCrea herself, who agreed to consign "herself to the care of these fiends." Could anyone be so naïve? Was it her "strange infatuation in her lover, to solicit such a confidence—stranger presumption of her, to yield to his wishes." And then, upon agreeing to a plan that Silliman thought suicidal, "what treatment had she not a right to expect from such guardians!"

For most, however, mythologizing had greater allure than prosaic fact-finding, and no one in Fort Edward was immune to it. In the 1830s and 1840s, Doctor Asa Fitch, a professional entomologist and amateur historian, meticulously collected and recorded oral interviews from elderly neighbors in and around Fort Edward who remembered the Revolution or knew people alive at that time.[6] When he asked townsfolk about Jane McCrea, Fitch, whose scientific papers on pests are housed in the Smithsonian, frequently encountered citizens who not only recalled her death, but seemed to also have well-rehearsed answers, suggesting they had been in the habit of expounding on the subject for a long time and with self-assured authority.

Fitch acquired a recollection of how McCrea journeyed from her brother's house to Sarah McNeil's on the fateful day. In one account, she was said to have left her brother John's farm on July 25, traveled up the west side of the Hudson to the home of her fiancé's mother, who ran a ferry to the east side. After spending the night, McCrea entered Fort Edward "to go to her aunt Campbell's." That is, Sarah McNeil, who was not her aunt. The ferryman reputedly said McCrea was dressed in "her best suit of clothes" and "her wedding cap."[7]

A man named Robert Blake told Fitch in 1847 that McNeil had long ago described for him the events of July 26. According to McNeil's account—relayed through Blake and recorded by Fitch—McCrea had indeed left her brother John's farm on the west side of the Hudson, and waited at McNeil's house on the east side, hoping "for a chance to get from there into the British camp." McCrea and McNeil were just "sitting outside of the door, in the shadow on the north side of the house, it being a warm summer's day, engaged in sewing." In "a jocular way" they conversed about their "forsaken situation," everyone else having evacuated in anticipation of the British advance. The "rattling of musket shots among the bushes" a half mile away, however, disrupted their sewing, whereupon they saw a "party of Americans pursued hotly by a band of Indians." As the two women sought shelter in the house, "a half dozen Indians" approached, "jumping and yelling." The women opened a trapdoor and "jumped into a small cellar," along with a young man named Norman Morrison. McNeil's black servant also tried to enter the cellar with her child, but McNeil pushed her back and closed the trap door. According to Blake, the invading Indians then opened that door and pulled McCrea, McNeil, and Morrison out by their hair. Another of Fitch's interviewees, Samuel Cook, described McNeil's house as a simple log cabin. "It had an old fashioned fire-place, in one end the fire-place without jambs. There was a loft over head, and ladder, or ladder like stairs leading to this loft, the stairs being on one side of the fireplace.... There was a cellar hole under the house ... entered by a trap door."[8]

Returning to Blake's packaging of McNeil's story, the Indians then ran with Morrison up a hill. McNeil followed. The warriors forcibly mounted McCrea onto a horse that Lieutenant Jones had sent and ran alongside her while the aroused Americans from the nearby fort started shooting. A second set of Indians, having heard of the reward for "bringing Miss McCrea into camp," overtook the first party and "snatched the rein of the horse on which Miss McCrea rode." The "bridle was snatched backwards and forth several times," until an Indian of the first party, "vexed to be thus foiled,... ruthlessly drew up his gun, and shot Miss McCrea." It was Blake's understanding that McCrea was not scalped. He supposed the body was left on a hill north of town, near a spring and a pine tree, and covered there by local Loyalists before it was taken downriver to the Black House for burial. Blake also did not believe there was ever an American soldier—namely Lieutenant Van Vechten—found there.

Fitch recorded an interesting variant of Blake's story from an unidentified source. Instead of a sewing party on the porch, McNeil was in bed when the Indians arrived. There was no Norman Morrison. McCrea and McNeil jumped into the cellar, whereupon the band of Indians pulled them out. McNeil reputedly said, as "big and heavy as my arse is, my hair was stout enough to sustain the weight" of being pulled up from the cellar. Fitch said he ran these new details by Robert Blake, who "denies them all in toto."[9]

The lack of agreement between the stories—in fact, among all the accounts—circles back to McNeil, who survived her ordeal and subsequently, as Fitch humorously put it, became "the oracular authority on Miss McCrea's death."[10] A local celebrity, McNeil habitually "varied the story afterwards; she was a great talker and would tell a story very well."[11]

Fitch accurately pegged McNeil as the ultimate unreliable narrator. After recording dozens of stories that all had their root in McNeil's chattering, Fitch reckoned:

> It is easy to perceive that such a person would soon become weary of iterating and reiterating the same statements, and, on coming to notice how eagerly attentive her hearers became, and how deeply interested if anything was given them as being new and never told before, and that mere surmises and conjectures, which had on reflection been formed in her mind but never till then communicated to anyone, were received with more satisfaction than any other part of her recital, the temptation was strong and to her it was irresistible to interpolate some novelty into each successive rehearsal of the story.

After McNeil repeated the new storylines a few times, they "were liable to become wrought into her mind as being authentic facts which she well remembered and had often told before." As a result, the stories "told in her later years came to be wholly unlike that which she at first was accustomed to give."[12] Of the "one hundred and one variations" she told, one of the last—completely fictional—was the "sensational" assertion that the Americans killed McCrea. To Fitch, "this was the last brilliant vagary of Mrs. McNeil's feeble imagination—like the flame of the exhausted candle blazing brightly forth just as it is expiring."[13] Memory, Fitch knew, was a nebulous thing, and when one's memory is addicted to fame, anything is possible.[14]

Thus, when Timothy Eddy gave his own account to Fitch, he too was dependent on McNeil for the "facts." In his accounting, via McNeil, the Native Americans in question were Mohawks from St. Regis, or Akwasasne, a location along the Saint Lawrence River. These warriors, Eddy said, "crept along" the banks of the Hudson (more likely they followed established trails), whereupon they were spotted by a boy who ran to McNeil's house shouting "Indians! Indians!" McNeil's black slave was said to run into the house with her baby, which she sat on the floor before she "turned a large kettle over it, thus adroitly hiding it and insuring its safety." At this point in Eddy's story, Asa Fitch could not resist some sarcastic remarks on the ridiculously good behavior of the baby underneath the kettle. That kettle, said Eddy, was later stolen and hidden in the top of a tree near Fort Anne.

The baby safely tucked away, the black woman then raised the trap door and jumped in, followed by McCrea. McNeil, however, was so overweight that the Indians caught her on the way down, then pulled out McCrea, and never discovered the "wench," as Eddy put it. Fitch appended to that statement two exclamation points to indicate its implausibility. The Indians then ran with the two women to the base of a hill north of town where they "found two horses." With a wink and a nod, Fitch confessed his profound incredulity that they "found" horses. The Indians, Eddy continued, mounted McCrea on one of them when an American detachment began firing on them. One shot killed McCrea. After McNeil made her way to the British camp, she identified "Jane's scalp among the number."[15]

The major narrative twist in Eddy's account, based on McNeil's new story, was the claim that the cause of McCrea's death was an American musket ball, not an Indian hatchet. That switch, with all its serious political implications, echoed for years as a primary variant. Fitch thereupon ran Eddy's account by Robert Blake, who started to doubt his own "facts." A frustrated Fitch, in his utmost effort to make sense of what had become local folk tales, surmised that when it came to the subject of Jane McCrea, "impression and statement may have been derived from subsequent hearsay information, inwove with [everyone's] original knowledge."[16]

The number of stories—and the minute details within those stories—multiplied like a Fibonacci sequence. David Wilson, a mid-nineteenth-century New York politician, published several widely read books on historical subjects, including *Henrietta Robinson*, the "veiled murderess" who was hanged in 1855, and *Twelve Years a Slave*, the harrowing tale told by Solomon Northrup, a free-born African American who was drugged, kidnapped, and sold into slavery on a Louisiana plantation. Wilson's *Life of Jane McCrea* was yet another eye-popping "story of the unfortunate girl" who is "so interwoven in our history that it has become a component part."[17]

Wilson claimed to reject hearsay, though he was guilty of depending on preposterous anecdotes. One was Lieutenant Jones running to the crime scene, where he "tore away the leaves and earth, clasped the bleeding body in his arms, and, wrapping it in his cloak, bore it to a place of secrecy." Wilson described McCrea as "uncommonly beautiful," and Jones as "brave and generous," a man "distinguished for his truthfulness," of "easy affability and grace of manner," whose "heart overflowed with tenderest emotions," and who liked to accompany Jenny on horseback along the Hudson's shoreline. Wilson also printed a spurious letter Jones supposedly wrote to McCrea as he was approaching Fort Edward in 1777, and referenced other correspondence about their pending marriage, none of which is extant. In those letters, Jones offered "such an alluring and romantic proposition, and abounded with so many warm and endearing terms, that the confiding but distracted girl" decided to wait in Fort Edward while everyone else sought shelter toward the south. "It was Love's reinforcement."[18]

According to Wilson's "history," gleaned from local sources and David Jones's nephew, the plan was to have McCrea leave McNeil's house on July 26 and walk alone, "beyond the American out-posts, without any *visible* attendant," to a northerly location where ten or fewer trustworthy Indians, led by the warrior "Duluth," acting as Jones's emissary, would escort her toward the British camp. Meanwhile Jones "would advance to meet her," the rendezvous to be immediately followed by a wedding service. Jane accepted the plan with "unhesitating alacrity" and "laughed at the idea of personal danger."[19]

Wilson described how that plan dissolved, according to his unnamed sources. While walking northward, a group of "flying Americans were seen rushing down the hill directly towards her, followed, like bloodhounds, by screeching and painted savages," led by the warrior "Le Loup," who had already massacred the Allen family in Argyle. McCrea ran back to McNeil's house "with the speed of an affrighted fawn," whereupon she, McNeil, "two small children and a black servant girl hastily descended to the cellar." The new band of Indians pulled Jane out, rushed her toward the pine tree north of town, and seated her on a horse. When Duluth arrived and confronted Le Loup, "angry words were exchanged." As the Americans were closing in, Le Loup, "in a boiling and sudden flood of passion," leapt "like a maddened tiger towards the object of contention, and whirling his tomahawk with inconceivable dexterity, buried its glittering blade deep within her side!" He scalped her, held the scalp aloft "with a look of ferocious and infernal triumph!" as others "tore the dress from her lifeless body." Duluth had the difficult task of reporting Jane's death to the "horrified lieutenant," while Le Loup escaped with her scalp and proudly danced with his trophy at the Indian camp.[20]

Wilson was not alone in publishing a bewildering account. William Leete Stone, a lawyer and editor of the New York *Journal of Commerce*, said that McCrea and McNeil were intending, on the advice of Benedict Arnold, to flee southward from Fort Edward, instead of waiting for the arrival of the British and David Jones in particular. Arnold supposedly dispatched twenty men to board the women onto *bateaux* and row them to the town of Fort Miller. Impatient, however, the women thought to find horses and head toward the ferry so that they could proceed to John McCrea's farm. Before they could embark, the arrival of Burgoyne's auxiliaries forced McCrea and McNeil into the basement with a slave, now named "Eve." The "Panther" found McCrea and said: "My squaw, me find um agin—me keep um fast now." Panther threw McCrea onto a horse and led her up a hill, whereupon pursuing Americans accidently shot her. No longer anticipating a reward for his captive, Panther took her scalp. Meanwhile, McNeil made it to the British camp, where she quickly recognized the scalp of "poor Jenny" because "the hair was unusually fine, luxuriant, lustrous, and dark as the wing of a raven."[21]

As Asa Fitch bluntly phrased it, every statement in the "Galaxy" of wild accounts told by local folks or written by historians was incorrect. "Even if a sentence commences with a truth, the writer, before he comes to a period, invariably manages to weave in some matter which is apocryphal, and what are mere inferences and conjectures of the writer are narrated as being authentic and well ascertained facts. A candid, correct writer of history never abuses his readers in this manner."[22]

Not only the particulars of McCrea's killing, but subsequent events also became murky as time went on. Her burials, exhumations, reburials, hair color, clothing, skeleton, and skull became latter-day subjects of inquiry and controversy. Even arcane issues, such as who had the honor of participating on the burial teams, led to public argument. Individuals always claimed to possess incontrovertible facts.

The site of the killing, for example, was a hotly contested subject. Caleb Baker, according to Asa Fitch's interview with Samuel Cook, pinpointed the "very spot where the body of Jane McCrea was found," at the "orchard back of the Widow Case's house." The murder occurred "on the old road just at the summit of the hill" north of Fort Edward. Baker's father claimed to have helped remove her body. "There was blood, and some locks of hair that were being cut off as they were making the incision to remove the scalp." Baker added, "After she was scalped, she was dragged over the flat land N. W. some 20 rods in a direction towards the famed tree and spring, and was there left by the side of a log, and some brush thrown over the body, partly hiding it from view."[23]

Fitch knew all along that local accounts were full of "highly poetical embellishment."[24] Some "wiseacre"—or many of them—might identify a particular pine tree as the murder site, next to a "limpid spring," claiming the Indians "stopped to drink" there with McCrea. The tree and the spring, Fitch sarcastically noted, "are a short distance from the highway, easy of access, without danger of soiling the polish of my gentleman's boots, or exposing the *muston de lain* of my lady's dress." That is, it was a convenient site for tourists. Soon, a roadside shrine appeared, far enough from the actual murder site to prevent a farmer's orchard from "being clubbed by the thousand and one visitors that annually frequent this locality to 'drop a silent tear in token of the inward workings of a sensitive mind,' as one of the latest writers expresseth it."[25]

Though Fitch's interviewees were sincere in their accounts of 1777, he knew that "the tree and the spring where Jane McCrea was not killed, and where her 'reeking corpse' was not found, have been accurately described by tourists, floridly descanted upon by novelists, fervently sung by poets, and vividly pictured by artists, for half a century, until it may now with safety be affirmed the tree and spring have hereby become objects of tenfold more interest than anything whatever that visitors can discover at the spot where the maiden fell, or where her body was found." Fitch enjoyed mocking the romantic tourists who were suckered in by a faux sacred site. He caricatured "the sentimental boarding-school miss" who sees her own "fair features distinctly mirrored in that smooth surface of that limpid pool." Rattled, she shrinks "back with horror as the thought flashed to her mind that the same waters erst reflected the stern hideous and paint-begrim'd visages of the 'bloody savages.'"[26]

Tourists in the mid-nineteenth century often had their minds and itineraries shaped by travel guides and popular histories of the Revolution, the most famous being Benson Lossing's widely read, 1,500-page *Field-Book*, which escorts readers on journeys through the "History, Biography, Scenery, Relics, and Traditions of the War for Independence."[27] Lossing traveled 8,000 miles in 1848 and 1849 to sites big and small, where he interviewed aging locals who provided entertaining anecdotes to supplement his otherwise conventional historical narrative. In chapter four, having already told a rousing patriotic story of the battles at Saratoga, Lossing embarked on a picturesque journey by steam packet farther up the Hudson, stopping here and there to delve into "the half-buried, decaying past."[28]

He "landed at Fort Edward at midnight, and took lodgings at a small but tidily-kept tavern close by the canal."[29] First stop the next morning was "the venerable and blasted pine tree," where "the unfortunate Jane McCrea lost her life while General Burgoyne had his encampment near Sandy Hill." The tree trunk, Lossing informed the prospective tourist, "is engraved, in bold letters, Jane McCrea, 1777." At the time of his journey in the 1840s, the tree was eerily dead but still standing, and also carved, he added, with the names of "many ambitious visitors."

Lossing noted that McCrea's story "is told with so many variations, in essential and non-essential particulars, that much of the narratives we have is evidently pure fiction; a simple tale of Indian abduction, resulting in death, having its counterpart in a hundred like occurrences, has been garnished with all the high coloring of a romantic love story." To be sure, "it seems a pity to spoil the *romance* of the matter." On the other hand, "truth always makes sad havoc with the frost-work of the imagination, and sternly demands the homage of the historian's pen."[30]

To his credit, Lossing advocated for high factual standards, yet he proceeded to track down Sarah McNeil's granddaughter, who served up another helping of hearsay. Figuring, like every other tourist, that he had discovered a previously untapped vein of truth, Lossing acquired erroneous news that McCrea was from Jersey City, was twenty years old, and first met the elder McNeil in New York City. The younger McNeil told Lossing that the Americans shot Jane, that Lieutenant Jones purchased Jane's scalp and then deserted Burgoyne's army and fled to Canada. From other sources, Lossing relayed accounts of Jones shot at Bemis Heights or dying in Canada, "heart-broken and insane."[31]

Lossing also visited the wife of a judge in nearby Glens Falls, who was related to Jones by marriage. In Jones family lore, the lieutenant purportedly "lived in Canada to be an old man, and died but a few year ago." He "avoided society as much as business would permit," and "toward the close of July in every year, which the anniversary of the tragedy approached, he would shut himself in his room and refuse the sight of any one."[32]

A wood engraver by training, Lossing illustrated the *Field-Book* with dozens of his own pictures, which added to the charm of the historical narrative and at the same time showed readers where to go and what to do on their travels. A small print shows McCrea's gravesite, from which he said he took away a bouquet of flowers, as if she were a relative. On another page he engraved a full-page illustration of the pine tree under which she died, complete with tourists no doubt chatting about Jane's demise.

The tree itself was felled shortly after Lossing's visit, and the landowner, George Harvey, hired a local sawmill owner, J. M. Burdick, to convert the wood into souvenirs for tourists coming to Fort Edward in search of McCrea. He advertised "elegant canes and boxes manufactured from this world-renowned tree," believing that "an event fraught with so much interest . . . will meet with a hearty response from every American." The cane featured an ivory handle and metal collar, beneath which a label pictures McCrea under attack in front of the very tree that made up the wood of the cane.[33] From that tree, Burdick also produced small souvenir panels printed with the same scene. On the back he assured authenticity: The tree, "after having grown more than 70 years, marked the spot where the unfortunate JANE MCCREA WAS MASSACRED BY THE INDIANS."

In 1853, the enterprising Harvey and Burdick rented space at the Crystal Palace in New York City, a gigantic international exposition of manufacturers. Tucked in between Julius Dessoir's rosewood furniture, William Jeffers' Side-Stroke Fire Engine, and William Colt's firearms, they set up a small exhibition of McCrea souvenirs. Anticipating the market for fakes, Harvey certified that he is "the owner of the land on which grew the tree. . . . All other parties offering Canes for sale, representing them to be made from the renowned Jane McCrea Tree, are counterfeits, and will be dealt with accordingly."[34] A state historian of New York sarcastically noted that "almost a whole pine grove was used up in making these souvenirs."[35]

After the tree was gone, the hallowed locus of tourist interest shifted to an adjacent spring and springhouse, leading entrepreneurs with new technology to market stereoscopic photographs that could make the scene come to three-dimensional life in the comfort of one's parlor. William Wirt, a loquacious United States Attorney General under James Monroe, wrote of the spring in a letter to a friend while he was making his own journey through Fort Edward. Wirt and his wife Elizabeth were "shown the spring at which the Indians who had charge of Miss McRae, stopped to drink when they were discovered and fired on by the whites; and the tree, on the root of which she was found sitting, . . . tomahawked and scalped and tied to the tree." Wirt's engrossment did not stop there. He needed something special, even sacred, to take away so that he could continue to savor the historical moment. "I borrowed an axe and cut a chip out of that identical root, . . . which, with some other holy relics, I shall send you by the first opportunity."[36]

Wirt, like other tourists, valued relics that were not only associated with historical figures, but that were also thought to be material evocations of them. In the hands of an inspired collector, a bit of purloined wood or a cane carved from the McCrea tree—or, more unethically, pieces stolen from her skeleton—had the capacity to stimulate deep emotion. They accessed the past, brought it momentarily into the present, and awakened in the owner a sense of the sufferings of a young woman from the Revolution.[37]

Reliving Jane's McCrea's death, in one form or another, was a journey into the revolutionary sublime. In the first years of the new republic, emotion-hungry tourists might indulge themselves closer to home, rather than making a pilgrimage all the way to Fort Edward. New Yorkers could visit the Park Theatre, which featured a performance of "Indian Cruelty, the Death of Miss McCrea," a "grisly tale of a frontier woman captured and killed by Indians."[38] Baltimoreans might visit a waxworks ensemble of "The Murder of Miss McCrea."[39]

Philadelphians attended John Bill Ricketts's circus. British-born Ricketts had come to America in 1792 with a plan to make money from a vast repertoire of stunt horsemanship, including an ability to ride two horses simultaneously while standing on their backs. He could also run alongside a galloping horse while vaulting into the saddle, jump down, and vault up again.

In 1793, Ricketts opened a circus on Market Street, succeeded in 1795 by a 1,300-seat Art Pantheon and Amphitheater on Chestnut Street, which he exotically topped with a fifty-foot-high conical roof and fronted with a stately colonnade.[40] Though he was the headliner, he often complemented shows with tightrope walkers, jugglers, clowns, dancers, magicians, singers, dramatic acts, and patriotic reenactments.[41] In 1798, along with John Durang, his deputy manager, he produced a pantomime of the Battle of Trenton, complete with real snow falling on the Americans as they marched toward the Hessian encampment. Ricketts and Durang continued to expand the number of acts the following season, to include a staging of *Don Juan* and pantomimes performed by horses.

In the spirit of never overlooking a lucrative entertainment possibility, they also offered on January 23 and 26, 1799, a new act written by John B. Rowson: "A Representation of the Murder of Miss McCrea." Mrs. Rowson played McCrea. Totomahow, an actual chief with hatchet in hand, performed the mock killing and scalping, and a variety of actors, including Ricketts himself, played other roles, presumably one of them being Lieutenant David Jones. Reviews lauded it as "among the best exhibitions of this season." The performances "approached reality as close as it was possible for acting to do."[42] A few nights later, Ricketts's troupe reenacted "The Death of Major André."[43]

By mid-nineteenth century, the American entertainment business was booming. Working-class audiences flocked to the melodramatic and the spectacular, the violent and the lurid, often with some politics smuggled in.[44] Shipwrecks were reenacted, Pompeii was buried, Huguenots were massacred, and Marat stabbed by Charlotte Corday. Women were of particular interest, especially pious saints, unreformed sinners, innocent victims, surprising heroes, nurturing mothers, mutilated corpses, and Jane McCrea, who never failed to fascinate antebellum Americans.[45]

At the New York Museum in 1841, five Indians performed "a scene depicting her tragic death. A young lady and a young gentleman participated as the hapless Miss McCrea and her grief-stricken lover."[46] A year later, the Grand Saloon of the Arcade in Philadelphia advertised "Scenic Scenes of the Murder of Miss M'Crea," with "Real Indian Warriors and their Squaws." In addition to "Exhibiting the various Modes and Ceremonies of Savage Life," the show promised a "beautiful young Lady" in the role of the maiden, who, night after night, "fell prey to the Savages during the dark days of the American Revolution."[47]

George Mastin, once a shopkeeper in Cayuga County, New York, commissioned country artists to produce a suite of gigantic paintings—one of them depicting McCrea—that he took on a paying tour through central New York in 1846, "Admission, 25 Cents." In country sheds and assembly rooms illuminated by candles at night, and accompanied by moralizing lectures, double clog dancing, and comic singing, Mastin comingled biblical stories with scenes of American violence. Audiences could revel in the temptation of Adam and Eve, the Crucifixion and Resurrection, an American burned at the stake, the Van Nest family being killed by "a Negro," and "the Murder of JANE McCREA."[48]

Never to be outdone, P. T. Barnum, the greatest showman of the age, opened his American Museum in New York in 1842. A large-type broadside trumpeted, "Indians & Squaws!" and a "Variety of thrilling Indian Pantomimes!!," one of which was "a scenic representation of The Murder of Miss McCrea!"[49] Barnum's friend and rival, Moses Kimball, wowed audiences at the Boston Museum on Tremont Street in 1841 by treating them to a menagerie of stuffed animals, ancient Greek fragments, sentimental musicales, elocutionary readings, vaudeville performers, the mind-bending "Feejee Mermaid," almost two hundred paintings by John Singleton Copley, Gilbert Stuart, and others, and all kinds of scenes sculpted in wax, so "Natural and Lifelike as to Mock Reality."[50]

For the "God-fearing folk of Boston," Kimball touted a Christian playing chess against Satan and a three-dimensional replica of Leonardo da Vinci's *Last Supper*, followed by an array of women in danger. An enslaved African-American girl will be beaten, a wife is to be killed by her husband, and ultimately, there will be the "MURDER OF MISS MCCREA." A "thrilling group showing the characteristics of the Red Men" was intended to incite

"The Murder of Jane McCrea," c. 1846. George Mastin, commission. Oil on bed ticking. Cooperstown, Fenimore Farm, Museum Purchase.

in viewers "tender feelings and moral sentiments."[51] In one of the special live shows, beginning on December 4, 1841, and continuing for two months, Kimball's troupe of Iowa Indians performed a live reenactment of "the terrible and savage murder of Miss McCrea near Sandy Hill, N.Y., July, 1777."[52]

The mid-nineteenth-century entertainment landscape thrived on Jane McCrea's killing, and no matter how many times it was performed, in however many variations, Native warriors were unfailingly exotic and preternaturally dangerous, while Jane was always sweet, innocent, and sexually vulnerable.[53]

For those history tourists not wanting to visit Fort Edward or even venture out in order to experience a reenactment of Jane McCrea's torment, they could attend an at-home parlor spectacle, complete with music, costumes, sets, and inspired direction.[54] Parlor subjects were typically taken from history ("Ethan Allen at Ticonderoga") or from works of art ("The Death of General Warren"). In one nineteenth-century do-it-yourself book on how to stage a tableau at home, "The Death of Edith" is offered as one of ninety-nine suggested subjects. The scenario sounds much like McCrea's demise. "A young and beautiful maiden was taken captive"; the "scenery in the background should represent woods and rocks"; the victim should wear "a loose white dress, sleeves five inches long, hair done up loosely in the neck, and face and neck made as white as possible"; the bodies of the Indians "stained light brown"; and the "music soft and plaintive."[55]

A satiric short story written by Nathaniel Deering and published in the *Knickerbocker Magazine* in 1839, "Tableau Vivant 'Down East,'" poked fun at the growing Victorian vogue for parlor theatricals.[56] An aging spinster, a Miss Mercellina Peebles, known as "the *arbitress elegantarium*" of a rural town in Maine, wishes to introduce the homespun locals to the sophisticated pleasures of the tableau vivant. Her directorial preparations were lengthy and detailed, though her "corps dramatique" was not well suited to certain themes, such as the time when an enactment of the *Laocoon* sculpture had to be aborted because the only available older man in town was, alas, "stiffened with rheumatism."

Not only the corps, but the audience too was ill-prepared for the centerpiece production on one winter night. A few moments before the curtain rose, the "long parlor was crowded with guests" who were being warned by young Mr. Snoodles, an assistant as well as an actor, that what they were about to see is "all illusion; that there was nothing real in it." Despite the advisory, or because of it, guests steeled themselves for an "irreparable shock" to their "exquisite sensibility," which in turn led anxious ladies to sniff a precautionary solution of hartshorn, which, they possibly were unaware of, is made from the horns and hooves of red deer. Drugs aside, "many a heart was palpitating," and when the curtain rose, "there were at least two shrieks that mingled with the involuntary groans. The tableau was the murder of Miss McCrea." Miss Nancy Bean, a middle-aged friend of Miss Peebles, played the part of the poor maiden, the role having been deemed inappropriate for young women. Dressed revealingly in a sheer white cotton fabric, Miss Bean posed "on her knees," "blood splattered around," her hands "upraised as if her only hope were in a higher power than man."

Mr. Snoodles stood over her "in the garb of an Indian, having in one hand her auburn locks, and in the other a scalping-knife." His "breast was ornamented with a platter of bright pewter, suspended from the neck by strings of beads, and his face was covered with alternate streaks of lampblack and red ochre." Over his shoulders, "a horse-blanket partially enveloped his person," but "beneath it were seen his pants of red flannel."

"The Murder of Jane McCrea." Original artwork for George P. Morris and Henry Russel, *The Soldier and his Bride.* 1841. Notated sheet music. The Miriam and Ira D. Wallach Division of Art, Prints and Photographs, The New York Public Library.

Though the actors were supposed to remain frozen in place for the duration of the tableau, Mr. Snoodles became unexpectedly "intoxicated" with his role. "He forgot himself. He was no longer Snoodles, and lost his identity in that of the savage. Flourishing his knife, he drew back as if to give a more effectual blow," at which point "a heart-rending shriek burst from the lips of Miss Bean, which was answered in full chorus by the fairer portion of the spectators." If that were not enough, the now traumatized Miss Bean "rushed from the scene of her expected triumph, and from the village," not to return for months. Afterward, Miss Peebles, the host and producer, "mortified at the total failure, has announced her determination to give no more parties."

Miss Peebles had arranged to have music performed at her parlor theatrical. No specific number is mentioned in the *Knickerbocker* story, but she might have played a popular tune from mid-century, "The Soldier and His Bride," a morose ballad about Jane McCrea in A-flat for piano and voice.

The lyrics, by George Pope Morris, whom Edgar Allan Poe considered America's best songwriter, tell us

The red-men of the woods were sent;
They led her where sweet waters gush;
Under the pine tree bough!
The tomahawk is raised to crush;
'Tis buried in her brow!
She sleeps, she sleeps,
beneath that pine tree now!
Her broken-hearted lover
in hopeless conflict died!
The forest leaves now cover
That soldier and his bride!

The sheet music featured a gruesome cover that depicts the stream, the pine tree, and two Indians about to bludgeon and slash Jane. For those not already acquainted with her story, a long preface on the next page not only tells her tale, but also adds a concocted tourist memoir in which two men, presumably the lyricist and composer, have come to Fort Edward, "seated ourselves in the shade of the large pine tree and drunk of a spring that gurgled beneath it." Nearby, a group of Indians "gave a groan, and turn their faces from the water," not wanting to "drink of the spring nor eat in the shade of the tree" because, they explain, "that place is bad for the red man; the blood of an innocent woman, not of our enemies, rests upon that spot . . . she was there murdered."

Proposing a Poe-like curse, the Indians tell the tourists, "No one avenged her murder, and the great Spirit was angry. That water will make us more thirsty and that shade will scorch us. The stain of blood is on our hands, we know not how to wipe it out." As a result, in subsequent battles the Indians "were sadly cut up; the Americans attacking them most furiously whenever they could get an opportunity. The prophets of the Indians had strange auguries; they saw constantly in the clouds the form of the murdered white woman invoking the blast to overwhelm them, and directing all the power and fury of the Americans to exterminate every red man of the forest." The passage proposes that Native peoples, who at the time were subjected to the government plan to uproot them from Eastern lands and deposit them west of the Mississippi, had brought their demise upon them-

Nathaniel Currier, *Murder of Miss Jane McCrea A.D. 1777*, c. 1846. Lithograph. Washington DC, Library of Congress Prints and Photographs Division.

selves because of Jane McCrea, "whose spirit still called for revenge." One grievous error has pushed them all to the edge of extinction.

A flood of pictures, encountered in illustrated magazines and books, and for sale as fine prints suitable for framing, descended on antebellum America. Nathaniel Currier, soon to be a principal at Currier & Ives, the colossus of popular prints in New York, mass-produced lithographs for the booming home market. Like Barnum, Kimball, and others, Currier tapped into the thirst for tragic sentiment in 1841 by refashioning John Vanderlyn's famous painting. To be sure, he was smart to make the scene more palatable to a middle-class market. Indians still manhandle Jane, but the three figures are less compressed and more separated, and Jane's Victorian dress is less revealing than Vanderlyn's Greek-style *chiton*. The famous pine tree, true to form, stands in the distance like a witness.

To amplify the melodrama, Currier added an explanatory text at the bottom: "She was dressed to meet her bridegroom, and accompanied her Indian conductors;—but by the way, the two chiefs disputed which of them should deliver her to her lover. The dispute rose to a quarrel, and according to their usual mode of disposing of a disputed prisoner one of them cleft her head with his tomahawk." Hanging as it would, in the safety of a parlor, the print was available as an object of conversation. It transported ladies and gentlemen back to the days of the Revolution when Indians freely roamed the Eastern forests, and reminded them that they now lived in a time when that threat had been all but extinguished.

Because there were dozens of differing stories of how McCrea met her end, there were dozens of variations on how artists depicted it. John Warner Barber, a popularizer of religious stories, traveled around America in a one-horse wagon in order to collect material for his illustrated *Historical Scenes in the United States*. Published for "the youthful reader," his book contained crude but well-intentioned engravings, which he hoped "will be of much utility in assisting the memory to retain the *facts* mentioned." Barber's illustrated "facts" put McCrea on a horse when a second set of Indians intercepts the first, leading to her killing near the famous pine tree. Barber added a quiz at the end of the book to test readers on how much they had absorbed. "Where did Miss McCrea and her lover reside? What method did he use to convey her to the British camp? Describe the manner of her death. What effect did this murder have on the Americans?"[57] Correct answers were not provided.

Curiously, in future books, he changed the image, even though the text remained the same. For his *Incidents in American History* of 1847, he dropped McCrea to one knee and pulled the Indians closer, and for an 1851 history of the state of New York, he eliminated the competing band of Indians altogether.[58]

William Dunlap, a prominent New York playwright and artist, extracted the Christian parable from McCrea's death. In a two-volume history of New York, written for young students of American history, he not only told McCrea's story, he also accompanied it with an illustration that shows her submissively praying rather than actively struggling. He asked young readers to look closely at it and discern what happens when "savages are left to follow the dictates of uncontrolled passion." The image, he wrote, "might disgust you, and make you abhor all scenes of strife, battle, bloodshed, and murder." To his credit, Dunlap extended his moral condemnation to "the European soldier," the so-called "civilized man, the man calling himself

Christian," who also "sacks cities, burns villages, murders females and aged men and women."[59]

Dizzying variations on the McCrea theme proliferated. An 1849 edition of the *Pictorial National Library* printed an illustration in which one humane warrior tries to protect McCrea by pushing his colleague away.[60] Benson Lossing came back to McCrea's story after the Civil War in a new publication, *Our Country*.[61] As before, he promoted one of Sarah McNeil's more inventive stories, namely that American fire killed Jane. This time, Lossing hired Felix O. C. Darley, a talented artist who had made prints for books by Washington Irving and James Fenimore Cooper, to illustrate this rare variant of her death narrative, which shows McCrea struck by a musket ball in the chest while seated on the getaway horse, next to the famous pine tree.

Naturally, McCrea was a difficult subject in Britain.[62] John Cassell, a midcentury social reformer, book publisher, and first London printer of *Uncle Tom's Cabin*, began a multivolume *History of England* that featured 2,000 original illustrations, the first edition of which sold more than a quarter-million copies. Readers could learn about the Saratoga campaign from a British point of view. Burgoyne, "a very brave officer" who was "miserably betrayed" by Howe and Germain, can be seen in one illustration informing Native Americans "of the principles which guided Christians in making war."[63] Cassell then directed the reader to the "case of one Jenny McCrea," killed by Burgoyne's auxiliaries. The adjacent illustration is one of the most vivid among the thousands contained in the volumes, as she is seen bracing herself against a pine tree while Indians, nine in all, circle round for the kill. A few pages later, Cassell moved on to Major André arrested and hung.

The most unusual variation belonged to Edward Henry Corbould, a notable British painter and drawing master to Queen Victoria's household. He avoided the murder scene entirely and moved the narrative back about an hour to show a group of five Indians pulling Jane out of the cellar by her hair. A second figure, most likely McNeil, can be seen below, ready to be yanked out.

For history tourists, both those sitting in the comfort of a parlor and those on travel itineraries through the Revolutionary landscape, the story of Jane McCrea stood out as an emotional high point. The amateur historian might not only reconstruct the complicated moves of the British and American armies on the Saratoga battlefield, but also enter into endless debates over how, where, and by whom McCrea was killed on that Saturday in July of 1777, and whether she did or did not inspire thousands of men to come to the Saratoga battlefield.

The history tourist might also acquire vertigo from all the competing stories, each vying to be the true one. Of all the Revolutionary subjects described and depicted, from Concord to Princeton to Yorktown, McCrea's killing was by far the most unstable, about which there was the least agreement, the one most likely to fluctuate from one source to another. That instability, however, was part of her fame. It drew attention to her, and whichever school of thought one subscribed to, it launched readers and viewers on a frightening yet emotionally charged sojourn into the gothic corners of the American Revolution.

12.

REVOLUTIONARY PATHOS

In the world of popular writing and public entertainment, Jane McCrea's death often took on an emotionally tawdry aura. Palpitating hearts, uncontrollable sobbing, and muttered expressions were common responses. Professional historians, however, while also interested in the drama of her killing, tried to place her within the overarching narrative of the Revolution, usually assigning her to a distant but distinct role behind Warren's bravery, Arnold's treason, Jefferson's Declaration, Franklin's diplomacy, and Washington's leadership.

David Ramsay—Charleston doctor and Continental Congress delegate—devoted a part of his *History of the American Revolution* to the "universal horror" of McCrea's capture and slaying. Publishing his book in the first year of Washington's presidency, he accurately portrayed her as a "young lady" with British sympathies, her death having helped to extinguish any lingering notion that the Crown and its government had ever been benevolent fathers protecting their American children. On the day of her "intended nuptials," she was "massacred by the savage auxiliaries attached to the British army," the homicide, he qualified, "though true, was no premeditated barbarity." That is to say, it was a misfortune, just as Burgoyne had said it was. For Ramsay, the Indians attacking McCrea were to be understood as cold instruments of British military policy, rather than innate monsters. In flatly refusing to be party to the expanding pathos and propaganda surrounding McCrea and her assailants, Ramsay was unique among the early historians.

On the other hand, Parson Weems, Washington's first biographer, struck histrionic notes in the five sentences he published on McCrea in 1800. Always striving for the moral lesson, he warned that Indians were—and continued to be—the lethal beasts of the North American wilderness, but noted that McCrea's killing at their hands had inspired victory at Saratoga: "The hatchets of the Indians were drunk with American blood. No age, no sex could soften them. The widow's wail, the virgin's shriek, and infant's trembling cry, was music in their ears. In cold blood they struck their cruel tomahawks into the defenceless head of a Miss M'Rae, a beautiful girl who was that very day to have been married. Such acts of inhumanity called forth the fiercest indignation of the Americans, and inspired that desperate resolution of which the human heart is capable, but which no human force can conquer." Weems, a master of exaggeration and invention, promoted the fiction that "the New Englanders, who were the nearest to these infernal scenes, turned out in mass."[1] That dubious notion of her as a linchpin of victory became a common feature of American histories.[2]

Positioned somewhere between Ramsay and Weems, Mercy Otis Warren, a leading poet, playwright, and historian living in Boston, featured McCrea in her magisterial 1,298-page *History of the Rise, Progress, and Termination of the American Revolution*, published in 1805. For Warren's "tragic theater" approach, McCrea was "a blooming beauty," whose "heart glowed in expectation of a speedy union with the beloved object of her affections." Dressed that day in her "bridal habiliments," in preparation to be "married the same evening," she instead found herself "shivering in the distress of innocence, youth, and despair." She was "massacred on the way, in all the cold-blooded ferocity of savage manners, . . . her bleeding corpse left in the woods." Warren's entire project in the *History* was to see the war as an existential fight for survival between American patriots and the dark forces of the morally bankrupt British and their Native American henchmen. She offered no shades of gray, only stark contrast. Warren's McCrea allowed Americans, still adjusting to their newly minted identity as citizens of the republic to precisely discern the dividing line between British evil and American good. At the same time, Warren refused to write off Native Americans entirely. "Nature has been equal in its operations," endowing Indians and Europeans with the same raw material. It would be foolish to think they "cannot be civilized." Instead, every measure must be taken to instruct them in "arts, manufactures, morals, and religion."[3]

In a more psychological vein, Emma Willard, the pioneering women's rights activist who founded the groundbreaking Troy Female Seminary in 1821, wrote about McCrea in her *History of the United States* in 1843. The primary difference between Willard and other historians was her effort to probe inner feelings. "Confiding love," Willard wrote, must have "prevailed in her mind over her strong fears" of her Indian escorts. Soon, competition between the parties spun out of control, leading to McCrea's unintended murder. When the Indians presented David Jones with the scalp, he collapsed, "withered and blasted." Willard, who for years lived downriver from Fort Edward, implored her readers to feel McCrea's death viscerally. She asks us to pause for a moment to put ourselves in the shoes of Jones and all those who lived within a hundred miles of the incident. Imagine "what every man could feel, what it would have been, or would be to him, to have his bride torn, as it were, from his arms, shrieking, and murdered in the hour of his love."[4]

All the dominant American historians of the nineteenth century—William Gordon, Theodore Dwight, Jared Sparks, William Dunlap, William Cullen Bryant, Washington Irving, Richard Hildreth, George Bancroft, Henry Cabot Lodge, and Woodrow Wilson—would continue to narrate McCrea's tale in one account or another. For them, she was the sad human-interest story set apart from the masculine dramas unfolding at Independence Hall and on blood-soaked battlefields. For some, she shined as the inspiration behind the victory at Saratoga, while demonstrating the dangers all white women faced in hostile Indian country. To be sure, these histories of the United States were inherently incomplete, insofar as they uniformly omitted the point of view of Native Americans who never had an opportunity to narrate their side of story, or tell of the savageries conducted against them.[5]

In poetry, some of what was written in the immediate aftermath of McCrea's killing was outright treacly. Wheeler Case, a Presbyterian minister and amateur poet, published "The Tragical Death of Miss Jane M'Crea" in 1778, a year after the event. In Case's doleful verse, Jane pulls the deepest sympathies from readers. "As I advanc'd along, before me lay/ A lady richly dressed, her name M'Crea," it turgidly begins. Case spoke of "The cursed Indian knife" and the blood "gushing forth from all her veins."

Throwing away all emotional discipline, he injected McCrea's father into the poem, though he had died and been buried in New Jersey eight years earlier.[6]

Ann Eliza Bleecker, a professional poet, was living on an estate thirty miles south of Fort Edward when McCrea died. Surrounded by the fertile lands that were formerly Mohawk territory, she had her "Eden," as she put it, shattered by Burgoyne's assault from the North in the summer of 1777. Like many others, she decided to abandon her home and flee southward toward Albany as Burgoyne's advanced guard approached. Prospects of slaughter at the hands of Burgoyne's warriors fueled her panic, as it did other women from the area.[7]

After Burgoyne's surrender in October, Bleecker turned personal tragedy into tragic poetry.[8] In "The Hudson," her 152-line poem, the river weeps for Jane McCrea:

But wherefore river creep thy waves so slow?
Or why so mournfully pursue their course,
As though thou here had'st known some scene of woe,
Whose horrors fain would fright thee to thy source?
Alas! alas! the doleful cause is known;
'Twas here M'CREA, guided by savage bands,
Fell, (oh sad suff'rer!) by their murderous hands,
And this flood heard her last expiring groan!
This flood, which should have borne the nuptial throng,
Found her warm blood deep tincturing its streams!
These woods, which should have heard her bridal song,
Wildly responded all her hopeless screams!
CRUEL in MERCY, BARBAROUS Burgoyne!

Bleecker, taking full poetic license, brought David Jones to the side of Jane's mangled corpse:

Hear a distracted lover's frightful voice.
See, as he bends to kiss the clotted gore
Senseless he sinks! but Death hath clos'd thine eyes,
And Mem'ry weeps, but will reproach no more.

By far the finest poet of the Revolution, Philip Freneau, in 1778 composed "America Independent, and her Everlasting Deliverance from British

Tyranny and Oppression," a 448-line political poem in which a wicked George III, "the Nero of our times," has goaded "the fierce Indian," who "with scalps and tortures aggravate our woe." Upon the "soil of blood" of America, "full many a corpse lies mouldering on the plain." Pointing an accusatory finger directly at America's British oppressors, Freneau made Jane McCrea exhibit A in his case that independence was inevitable and right. She "yonder lies, all breathless, cold and pale, drenched in her gore."[9] She was irresistible in the role of tragic heroine.

The cruel Indian seized her life away,
As the next morn began her bridal day!
This deed alone our just revenge would claim,
Did not ten thousand more your sons defame.

Writing in the year of the Massachusetts Banishment Act that excommunicated Loyalists, Freneau requested bloody retribution for McCrea's killing.

Americans! Revenge your country's wrongs;
To you the honour of this deed belongs,
Your arms did once this sinking land sustain,
And saved those climes where Freedom yet must reign—
You bleeding soil this ardent task demands,
Expel yon' thieves from these polluted lands.

Freneau would later learn firsthand of British cruelties when he was captured at sea in 1780 and incarcerated on the *Scorpion*, one of the most notorious prison ships anchored in New York Harbor.

McCrea also appeared in short stories and novels, putting her squarely in the center of nineteenth-century American literature. Hartford's leading woman of letters, Lydia Sigourney, writing in 1824 in her *Sketch of Connecticut, Forty Years Since*, tells the hallucinatory story of Kehoran, a Mohegan now known by his Christian name, Maurice, who is wracked with guilt over an episode from the Revolution. Confessing to the Reverend Sansom Occom, he asks, "Heard you ever the name of M'Rae? Yes! M'Rae! M'Rae! McRae! For years I have not dared to pronounce that name. Even now, the demons shriek it in my ears. They write it in flame upon the walls. It scorches my heart."[10]

Maurice tells Occom of his youthful embrace of Christianity, and then of his fateful service under John Burgoyne. Under British command, he had acquired a reputation for bravery, which led him to the tent of the fictionalized Lieutenant David Jones. Would Maurice help him? "We are within a league of Fort Edward," the fictional Jones explained. "It is to be attacked. The inhabitants have fled,—all, save one whom I hold dearer than life. . . . She waits me there, though all her household have departed. Such faith hath she in my truth. But when the ravage commences, how can I save her? She must be brought hither, and the priest must unite us."[11]

Jones would have fetched her himself but would be considered "a traitor to my king" for crossing enemy lines. However, "thou mayest go with safety. I have chosen thee for this embassy. . . . Take with thee ten associates, whom I will amply reward. Lead for her my own horse." Maurice promised, "that no hand but mine shall present her unto thee," as the "Holy Mother of God be my witness."[12] Maurice was to rescue Jane and meet Jones "at the door of my tent with a holy man, who, in making us both one, shall remove from my soul every earthly fear. Have I said that her name is M'Rae?" She "hath the heart of a lion, though the glance of her eye is like that of the dove."

"Attired for war," Maurice "arrived at the house of the fair-one," whose "long hair, black as the raven's wing, was folded in braids around her head." He lifted her onto a horse, "her lips smiled fearlessly when she spoke, and on her cheek trembled something, like the glow of the morning sky when it expects the Sun." Just then, "a party of Canadian Indians intercepted our path." They had heard of the reward. "Cutlasses clashed, and blood flowed upon the earth" from "hatchets each in the other's head." When the rival chief took the bridle of the horse, Maurice took it upon himself to "cleft that beautiful head with my hatchet." The chief then tore off Jane's scalp, "with its shining tresses." Maurice attacked, killed the chief and cut him into pieces, before he snatched Jane's scalp from "his dying hand."

Upon arrival at the British camp, Maurice approached Jones and "held the scalp." Jones instantly recognized "those dark locks, and fell to the earth, as if in death." Maurice's arrest followed, along with his puzzlement. Shouldn't he have been commended for courage and "firmness in his cause"; hadn't he "done my duty in being faithful to my vow, that no hand but mine should bring the maiden, whether living or dead?" A fanatical Jesuit priest, Father Paul, visits Maurice whom he considers a true "son of the holy Church," receives his confession, and plots how he shall escape. Namely, he arranges to have another Indian, one who had not accepted Christ, to be drugged and substituted for Maurice. There was only one condition:

Maurice must distance himself from the Revolution and live a solitary life where he will spend every day and night crouched with crucifix in hand, and visited by the "fiery eyes" and "hellish laughter" of the dead.[13]

Sigourney's head-spinning adaptation of McCrea's death featured a religious conversion, a twisted Catholic priest, a penitent murderer, and an Indian who is fated to die because he had not embraced Christianity. Published during the emerging national debates over what to do with the Native peoples who populate the East, Sigourney's Maurice, try as he might to be a good Christian, could not control his innate passions and thus is doomed to self-punishment and the fires of hell. Further along in the novel, anticipating federal policy, half of Maurice's fellow Mohegans emigrate from New England to western lands because they know they can never assimilate fully.

The greater the liberties writers took with McCrea's story, the more likely they would present her in a fictional guise. Edgar Allan Poe's literary colleague and good friend George Lippard wrote a more fantastical fiction about McCrea's death than Sigourney had. In full gothic splendor, "The Bridal Eve" transports us to "an old mansion, perched yonder among the rocks and woods" of Lake Champlain, where "on a summer night" a party of British officers assemble to discuss "the comparative beauty of the women of the world." Italians, Hindus, and English are heartily proposed, but a young captain, the fictionalized Lieutenant David Jones, adds, "*American.*" In fact, the next day he is about to marry one, the literary stand-in for Jane McCrea, "the most beautiful in the world," who will soon arrive to join a festive dance underway in an adjacent room that is "thronged by fair ladies and gay officers." The other officers wonder how she will be able to cross "the rebel lines" to get to the party. Not a problem, for the captain assures his colleagues that he has made arrangements with "a friendly Indian chief, on whom I can place the utmost dependence."

Out of nowhere, a ghostly premonition suddenly seizes the captain. His face turns "pale as a shroud, his blue eyes dilated, until they were encircled by a line of white enamel." Minutes later, "a bold Indian form came urging through the crowd of ladies, . . . advanced along the room, and stood at the head of the table. There was no lady with him!" Perplexed, the captain wonders if she had been left in the next room, or perhaps had "refused to obey her lover's request—refused to come meet him!" Ominously, in "the deep silence that reigned through the room," "the solitary Indian stood there, at the head of the table, gazing silently in the lover's face."

"*Where is she?*" For a moment, "the strange horror of that lover's face" froze the Indian. A crowd gathered around. The Indian then drew his hand from a war blanket, his fingers clutching "a bleeding scalp, and long and glossy locks of beautiful dark hair!" The Indian had grossly mistaken his orders to fetch the young woman. The crowd turned funereal and stood in "the silence of that dreadful moment. Look there! The lover rises, presses that long hair—so black, so glossy, so beautiful—to his heart," and then he fell to the floor. This evening was to have been their bridal eve. With trembling lips, the captain conjured his lover's final moments: "The red forms of Indians going to and fro, amid flame and smoke—tomahawk and torch in hand! There, amid dead bodies and smoking embers," he visualized his bride, "kneeling, pleading for mercy, even as the tomahawk crashed into her brain." Lippard then turned to address his readers directly to reveal that this gothic tale is in fact true. "This is the simple history of David Jones and Jane M'Crea," he reveals, a story "with which you have all been familiar from childhood, that I have given you."[14]

Lippard was a popular niche writer, but his older colleague James Fenimore Cooper was the dean of American literature. Having grown up on former Iroquois lands, Cooper located his Leatherstocking novels in central New York. *The Last of the Mohicans, a Narrative of 1757*, a novel of 1826 that was set during the French and Indian War, centers on the transport of two sisters, Cora and Alice Munro, from Fort Edward to what their father, British Lieutenant-Colonel George Munro, thought was the superior safety of Fort William Henry on the southern shore of Lake George. The young women's escort is Hawk-eye, a frontiersman who is accompanied by a British officer, two friendly Mohicans named Chingachgook and Uncas, and a Huron secretly working for the French, the villainous Magua.

Despite the fact that the historical novel takes place in the 1750s, when the French and the British were fighting over control of the American northeast, Cooper wrote it from a post-Revolutionary perspective; the 1770s informed characters and events that took place two decades earlier. Cooper's noble and selfless Mohicans resemble the Oneida who fought with General Gates in the Revolutionary period; they are accustomed to Western ways, have acquired Christian values, were thought to be on the right side of history, and in Burgoyne's terminology, have been "domiciliated." Cooper's Hurons, and Magua in particular, are the opposite, demons who revel in dashing "the head of an infant against a rock." They are much like the Great Lakes Indians that Burgoyne recruited to his campaign, the ones, he said in retrospect, whose "only preeminence consisted in ferocity," that is, the ones who killed and scalped Jane McCrea.

After being exposed as an enemy agent, Magua abducts Cora and Alice, whose lives can be spared only if Cora marries Magua, the thought of which, she exhales, is "worse than a thousand deaths."[15] A harrowing roller-coaster ride ensues, involving rescues, recaptures, torture, disguise, deception, and even a horrific recounting of the Fort William Henry massacre that was, in reality, the handiwork of La Corne Saint-Luc. Repeatedly, Cora confronts situations in which she must choose between Magua and death.

In fashioning the scenes of Cora's mortal plight in 1757, Cooper tapped into the Revolutionary story of Jane McCrea in 1777. Cora's father is Scottish, like Jane's, and both are marooned in Fort Edward. Cooper, who was close friends with American painters, also turned to Vanderlyn's painting, which he had seen exhibited in New York, for inspiration.[16] In an early scene with Magua, the similarities between Vanderlyn's Jane and Cooper's Cora are evident: "Seizing Cora by the rich tresses which fell in confusion about her form, he tore her from her frantic hold, and bowed her down with brutal violence to her knees. The savage drew the flowing curls through his hand, and raising them on high with an outstretched arm, he passed the knife around the exquisitely molded head of the victim, with a taunting and exulting laugh."[17]

Unlike Jane, Cora does not die quickly. She is rescued by Uncas, only to be recaptured by Magua and the Hurons, who toss her body around like a doll as they run through the forest. In the penultimate chase, Hawk-eye and the Mohicans draw close to the fleeing Magua and spot Cora, who "will go no farther. . . . Kill me if thou wilt, detestable Huron." Magua offers his final ultimatum: "Woman. . . . Choose; the wigwam or the knife." Again, like McCrea in Vanderlyn's painting, Cora falls "on her knees, with a rich glow suffusing itself over her features, she raised her eyes and reached her arms toward heaven." Just then, Uncas attacks and is mortally wounded, while one of Magua's Hurons, knowing that the abduction plan can go no further, "sheathed his own knife in the bosom of the maiden." Cora's death elicits from the Huron "a cry, so fierce, so wild, and yet so joyous, that it conveyed the sounds of savage triumph to the ears of those who fought in the valley, a thousand feet below."[18]

Because McCrea was so well known in the 1820s, readers were already familiar with Cora's mortal plight and could easily predict her ultimate fate. More than that, Cora, like McCrea, was a template for all white women—past, present, and future—who were, are, or ever will be, besieged by forces that endanger their lives and, by extension, threaten the expansion of American civilization.

Readers of *Last of the Mohicans* might have noticed that artworks illustrating Cora's final scene were variations on Vanderlyn's *Jane McCrea*.[19] Thomas Cole, emerging as America's great landscape painter, channeled Vanderlyn as he was preparing to depict the climactic fight scene from chapter 32, in which Cora dies. Like Cooper, Cole was already familiar with Vanderlyn's painting before he made a research trip from New York to the upper Hudson and Fort Edward in 1826, just as locals were regaling tourists with overheated stories of McCrea's death. Cole showed Cora on her knees, like Vanderlyn's Jane, as Magua grasps her hair and lifts a knife. Within a year, he exhibited *The Death of Cora* at the new National Academy in New York, only blocks away from Vanderlyn's painting at the American Academy.[20]

Jane McCrea's death echoed across American history. Though her name and fame rose and fell and rose again, her plight as a white woman, alone and under assault by evil forces, would prove to be politically useful during the administration of President Andrew Jackson, figuring in the nineteenth century's tortured debate over the fate of Native peoples in an expanding American republic.

13.

POLITICS

THE AUDIENCES that read Cooper's *Last of the Mohicans* in the 1820s were already drenched in the controversy over the removal of Native Americans to the western side of the Mississippi River. In the opening pages of the novel, Cooper was among the first to aver that Native Americans had been unnecessarily demonized and their culture grossly disfigured by the "magnifying influence of fear" that gripped white imaginations. As proof that Native peoples were not inherently bad, Cooper presented Chingachgook and Uncas as admirable characters dedicated to saving Cora. Yet, over the course of four hundred pages crammed with scenes of breathtaking violence, the image of the barbaric Magua—abducting Cora, insisting on sexual compliance, and bringing about her murder—haunted the imagination regardless of Cooper's stated interest in equanimity.

The case for removal had begun during Thomas Jefferson's presidency. To Jefferson, Native American ways were incompatible with the expanding American republic. He had envisioned the United States as a pristinely white, Anglo-Saxon homeland, generous enough to accommodate those who willingly consented to being assimilated by means of schooling and the acquisition of agricultural and household skills. Those who resisted, however, faced the harsh consequence of their decision: expulsion, extinction, or extermination. Jefferson's America, in the words of one anthropologist, "had no place for Indians as Indians."[1]

The Louisiana Territory, all 828,000 square miles that Jefferson acquired in 1803, offered the federal government the opportunity to divide the continent racially. Whites would congregate and advance their civilization on former Native lands east of the Mississippi River, while Eastern tribes not agreeing to assimilation would move to the West, where, the thinking went, they could continue to live in happiness. What Jefferson and his administration called "population transfer" was a euphemism for what we now call ethnic cleansing. The Louisiana Territory would in effect be America's Siberia.

In the same year that Jefferson hired Meriwether Lewis and William Clark to survey the newly acquired Louisiana Territory, Vanderlyn painted the *Murder of Jane McCrea.* The two projects—American expansion deep into Indian country and the frightening image of a white maiden butchered by Native peoples—were oddly connected. Originally, atrocities against civilians during the Revolution had energized Patriots to mobilize around the threats posed by the British and their Native American auxiliaries, and that, in turn, justified General Sullivan's backlash expedition against the Haudenosaunee in 1779. After the British were vanquished and expelled, however, the preternatural fear of "uncivilized" Native Americans lingered on and evolved into calls for radical resettlement.

During Jefferson's presidency, 1801–1809, Jane McCrea's tragic death, visually epitomized in Vanderlyn's painting, had become the most memorable example of what happens when discordant races collide.[2] In the emergent era of Indian removal, she served as the perfect example of the harm that unassimilated "savages" were purportedly inflicting on Americans. Her story encountered everywhere, she was a useful instrument for alerting the nation to the perceived dangers—to national wellbeing, to civil order, to Christian settlers, to domestic happiness, and to love itself—thought to be posed by Native peoples roaming freely across the continent.

Jefferson's stated rationale for removal was a paternal desire to protect a dying race that was ill-suited to an American society that was inexorably moving westward. Humanely pushing unrehabilitatable Natives out to pasture in supposedly lush Western lands, his logic went, would give them a better chance for survival. That was code for subjugation or eradication. Removal, plain and simple, would instead clear the way for white society. Since the arrival of the first Europeans the unchartered lands of North America beckoned as a promising Eden, but in reality, those "pioneers" mostly felt they were, as one historian phrased it, "poised on the edge of an abyss of barbarism," so threatened by dangerous forests and concealed Indian menace that ethnically clearing land was embraced as a legitimate goal of good government.[3]

In 1808, Jefferson received eyewitness news of that fear from Andrew Jackson, then colonel of the Tennessee militia, who wrote of the "savage cruelty" being perpetrated against "innocent Citizens" of the republic by "hostile murdering" Indians in the Southeast. Recalling Jane McCrea and others, Jackson noted, "These scenes bring fresh to our recollection the influence during the revolutionary War, that raised the scalping knife and Tomahawk against our defenseless women and Children."[4] Only removal would give homesteading whites an opportunity to fulfill their dreams without fear. Jefferson continued to ring the alarm after his presidency, writing to John Adams in 1812 that the United States needed to invade British Canada in order to save "our women and children forever from the tomahawk and scalping knife."[5] Like most leaders, he could never shake the notion that, in the words of one American historian, Indians were "founding traitors."[6]

Jeffersonian policy would soon deteriorate into President Jackson's Removal Act of 1830, which featured coercive expulsion, extortionist land acquisition, and outright war against those who resisted the government plan.[7] The false humanitarian rhetoric about saving a dying race would continue unabated, but a millimeter below the surface of that shabby rhetoric was a ravenous desire to secure Eastern lands. To be sure, the Choctaw, Cherokees, and every other displaced tribe understood that deportation was nothing other than deportation, a cruelty and not a golden opportunity. To them, their new Western home was "The Land of Death." As it came to be, over the 1830s and 1840s approximately 100,000 Native Americans would be uprooted, at the cost of 25,000 deaths. In turn, millions of acres of fertile land opened up to settlers and speculators who turned their southern windfall into profitable slave-labor plantations.[8] If we follow the money, American humanitarianism was never really in play.

Whatever the stated and unstated rationales, Jackson's Removal Act required legislators to obtain political consensus that Native Americans were hopelessly hardwired predators, and that despite earlier efforts they were unlikely to be assimilated in the East, or worse, that they presented an enduring threat to white populations. One United States senator who initially paid lip service to the notion of humanitarian expulsion finally admitted that removal was for the "advancement of the wealth and power of the Union." He baldly phrased the argument this way: There was little government could do in the old days when Indians "were strong enough to wage war upon the States, and to pursue their trade of blood with the tomahawk and scalping-knife." Now, however, when "their power has departed from them, and they are reduced to comparative insignificance," it was time for "a civilized and Christian people" to expand into, occupy, and profit from "this promised land of civil and religious liberty." Make no mistake, the senator continued, the United States was engaged in nothing less than an apocalyptic "struggle for *supremacy* between savages and civilized men, between infidels and Christians."[9] William Clark, the United States Superintendent of Indian Affairs, put the government's policy even more straightforwardly in a letter to one of his agents: a "*War of Extermination* should be waged against them" for predations against women and children; "the peace and quiet of the frontier, the lives and safety of its inhabitants *demand* it."[10]

Forced removal required the instillation of the fear that Native peoples were the devil's demons, posing an existential threat. Shelving all previous notions of voluntary assimilation, the new Jacksonian plan called for outright eviction, which was often accompanied by cases of rape and murder of Native women. In mounting their argument, Jacksonians could tap into a readily available stock of harrowing stories about Indian savagery, from hundreds of captivity memoirs to wartime accounts.[11] Among them, there could not have been better evidence for expulsion than the widely circulated memories, stories, and images of Jane McCrea, who loomed over the debates that culminated in the Removal Act of 1830. Though McCrea's story was not specifically invoked in congressional debates or newspaper editorials at the time, political figures in America—from Jackson and Vice-President Van Buren (who grew up in New York seventy miles downriver from where she was slain), on down to the 102 members of Congress who voted for the Removal Act—were aware of her killing, which had fully saturated American thought.

During a century of war waged against Native America, if there were moments when Jane McCrea was not on center stage in the white imagination, hundreds of understudies emerged to assume her political role.[12] One of them was Jane Wells. She and twenty-nine other civilians died in the Cherry Valley massacre of 1778 when Joseph Brant led a raiding party of Mohawk and Seneca into that sleepy village located near Lake Otsego, sixty miles west of Albany. There were no strategic reasons for the assault. Instead, it was pure retaliation for American destruction of Native American settlements, and that, in turn, was revenge for Indian atrocities in the Wyoming Valley of Pennsylvania. In the attack, the invaders burned Robert Wells's house and killed the entire household, including his mother, brother, sister, wife, three domestics, and four children, including Jane.

The ceaseless clash between races and civilizations, often with a white woman in the middle, caused renewed interest in the 1776 abduction of Daniel Boone's daughter, Jemima, an incident, like McCrea's, that reinforced the call for action to protect families and do whatever was necessary to secure the continent for American settlement. As the story was told, thirteen-year-old Jemima and two friends ventured from the protection of Boone's fort to canoe along the Kentucky River one afternoon. A war party of Cherokees and Shawnees, who had been engaged in guerilla skirmishes with the white settlers, followed the girls, and then kidnapped and marched them twenty-five miles through the woods for three days. A heart-thumping rescue ensued, led by Boone, who had long thought Indians were irredeemable savages. His party caught and routed the Indians, saving the girls from an uncertain fate.[13]

The story, like McCrea's, became legendary after the Revolution, and served the same political function, evoking the most heartrending sentiments from alarmed readers. Whichever variant of the story one may have read, as there were many, Jemima is always rescued at the last minute, her ordeal cast as a cautionary tale about fathers and daughters, civilization and savagery, predators and victims. Over time, the tale developed the traits of a good pulp novel, the Indians growing in fiendishness. In one lurid account, these "wolf-like savages" planned to sexually ravish the girls who, like McCrea, had ardent male suitors desperate to save them.

The racial logic leading to removal, subjugation, and ultimately decimation, needed a persuasive theory to propel it forward. Enter Manifest Destiny, first voiced in the 1840s as an evangelical belief in America's supreme place in the world, guided by God. In the words of the newspaper editor who coined the phrase, the goal, perhaps even the ethical obligation of the United States, was "to overspread and to possess the whole of the continent which Providence has given us for the development of the great experiment of liberty and federated self-government entrusted to us."[14] As American exceptionalism inched toward American imperialism, Manifest Destiny came to justify the annexation of western lands as a beneficial and inevitable way to further the divine cause, whatever that might require in the way of pacification, or if necessary, destruction of all barriers standing in the way.

Francis Parkman, the Boston Brahmin historian who authored an account of his own western sojourns, phrased the glowing prospect of America most succinctly in 1851: Native Americans are "destined to melt and vanish before the advancing waves of Anglo-American power, which now rolled westward unchecked and unopposed."[15] He knew that expanding nations need categorical enemies, so by constructing Native peoples as "them," Americans could acquire a clearer notion of who and what constituted "us." A rising United States believed it had to fight against foreign adversaries and irredeemable heathens intent on arresting its sacred appointment with destiny.

Jane McCrea still mattered politically after the cataclysmic Civil War, but the magnitude of that conflict—its staggering 700,000 deaths—dwarfed every casualty from the Revolution, including hers. Nonetheless, in spite of her exit from center stage, her storyline remained an active template—or what we could call a meme—for countless tales of frontier women endangered by Native peoples. During that postbellum period, the McCrea saga reverberated in the guise of other white damsels facing the Indian menace in dime novels, early burlesques, captivity memoirs, magazine illustrations, serious works of art, and eventually in Wild West shows and movies.[16]

One dime novel from 1873, a "True Narrative," breathlessly tells us that "a beautiful young lady has just returned East" after living through "stirring adventures," sure to be "of deep and entrancing interest." Mary Barber, a New England missionary, at age nineteen had willingly married Squatting Bear, a Sioux chief, and has now come to regret her naïve decision.[17] She attempts to escape from her "perfect tyrant" of a husband who regularly beats her, but is repeatedly captured and brought back. One preposterous scene follows another, including an abduction illustrated in the style of Jane McCrea. The Indians, both crude stereotypes, wrestle down the glamorous heroine, who might have been played by Hedy Lamarr if she were to adapt her role as Tondelayo in *White Cargo*, the steamy 1942 MGM film that ran afoul of the prurient Production Code.

Perhaps the most unusual variation on Jane McCrea's story occurred in Japan. In 1879, Tokyo's popular Shintomi Theater hosted former President Ulysses S. Grant, the first American chief of state to visit the country. The Japanese regaled him with a new play, *Chronicle of the Later Three Years' War in the Distant North*, which they hoped would allow him to recall the Amer-

Adachi Ginkō, "Act II, Scene 2: Along Train Tracks in America," from the series *The Strange Tale of the Castaways: A Western Kabuki*, 1879. Woodblock print (nishiki-e). New York, The Metropolitan Museum of Art, Bequest of William S. Lieberman, 2005.

ican Civil War. Grant thoroughly enjoyed himself at the theater, especially the part where seventy-two geisha walk on stage wearing kimonos bedecked with the stars and stripes.

In the wake of Grant's visit, the theater soon mounted a new play, *The Strange Tale of the Castaways: A Western Kabuki*, written by Kawatake Mokuami, the most famous dramatist in Meiji Japan, and illustrated by Adachi Ginkō, a *ukiyo-e* artist known for his woodblock prints. It tells the tale of a Japanese fisherman, Mihozō, who is adrift in the open sea and is then picked up by American sailors who take him to San Francisco. The Japanese consul there asks him to accompany his sister-in-law, Miss Wakaba, across the United States to New York in order to finish her education. In act II, while Mihozō and Miss Wakaba are en route, a band of Indians derails their train. They attack the Japanese passengers and abduct Miss Wakaba. Ginkō's picture of the attack shows the chief grasping the fallen

Miss Wakaba while in the foreground an Indian warrior prepares to strike Mihozō.

Both Ginkō and the playwright Mokuami were striving for American authenticity, which led to disparaging stereotypes picked up from American dime novels and various prints that depicted Jane McCrea, in particular the Robert Smirke print published in Joel Barlow's *Columbiad*, leading the Japanese to believe that this is indeed what Native Americans do. Ginkō encouraged the stereotype by writing "American savages" in Japanese script next to the two Indians. As for Miss Wakaba and Mihozō, they survive their American adventure and soon arrive safely together in Paris.[18]

14.

LEGEND

By the turn of the century there was no longer a reason for anyone to believe that Native peoples posed a mortal threat to the United States. The "Indian Wars" ended in 1890, when the 7th United States Cavalry killed three hundred Lakota at Wounded Knee in South Dakota. After that, Native peoples were too weak to mount further resistance. Yet, the fear, however false, was so ingrained that audiences continued to be gripped—and thrilled—by tales from the Old West, now as a form of entertainment. It was the never-tiring replay of the old story of white America's triumph over Native America.

The true master of that genre was Buffalo Bill. One of the endlessly repeated highlights of his Wild West show was the nick-of-time rescue of a white woman about to be scalped by Cheyenne warriors. The staging was based on a true story from 1869, in which the 5th United States Regiment of Cavalry attacked a Cheyenne encampment in Summit Springs, Colorado, in retaliation for raids in Kansas. Buffalo Bill took credit not only for killing Tall Bull, the Cheyenne leader, but also for rescuing two white women who were about to be killed.

Cody was indeed a scout for the 5th Cavalry, though most of the stories of his heroics were untrue. He did not kill Tall Bull. One of the women he supposedly rescued had her skull crushed beforehand. And the other woman was gravely wounded before she was saved. Nonetheless, Cody built his show around himself and the fierce contest between white and Native cultures. In the colorful poster of 1907, he is the gleaming white horseman in the center who races toward a captive white woman on the far right, down on her knee and reprising Jane McCrea's pose and imminent scalping, though with an altogether different ending implied.[1] David Jones may never have rescued McCrea in 1777, but in the mythic world of Buffalo Bill, an entire cavalry saves endangered white womenfolk.

Bill had to retire in 1910, only three years after printing the poster, in part because of silent movies, which required only one production that could be replicated on celluloid at little cost. Bill himself started appearing in short movies in 1894, and in 1908 he filmed and distributed the celluloid version of that Summit Springs extravaganza, with the two female hostages safely rescued.[2]

Much of the new media of the twentieth century gravitated to graphic images of murder, mayhem, and horror.[3] Rescues by heroic white men were prevalent in films when Indians, African Americans, trains, cowboys, or bad fathers menace a defenseless white woman, who might be played most vulnerably during the silent film era by Lillian Gish. In the 1930s and 1940s, distant reincarnations of Jane McCrea entered such Hollywood productions as *Custer's Last Stand* and Cecil B. DeMille's *Unconquered*, Paramount's highest grossing film from 1947. DeMille said he wanted scenes that would "grab me by the hair on my head . . . and yank me out of my seat."[4] Unwittingly, he was referring to both the scalping legend of Jane McCrea and to Cooper's Cora, the latter appearing in eight movie versions of *The Last of the Mohicans* before 1937. *Unconquered*, which starred Gary Cooper as Captain Christopher Holden, was set on the Allegheny frontier during the French and Indian War. The Seneca have captured Abby, played by Paulette Goddard, whom Chief Guyasuta, played by Boris Karloff, is about to have tortured. Surrounded by Indians who have pushed her to one knee, she "writhes exquisitely," in the words of James Agee, writing for *Time*. Agog audiences marveled at her low-cut dress that dropped lower with every passing minute. Agee knew *Unconquered* was a "florid" and "high-colored hunk of hokum," but thought the scenes with Goddard in the Seneca camp nevertheless "bulge with energy."[5]

Whatever the exact subject—whether it was Jane McCrea, Jane Wells, Jemima Boone, or Miss Wakaba, to name but a few—the conclusion to be drawn from the collision of races was always the same. Beyond a doubt, the stories confirmed the longstanding fear of the "ferociousness and destructive instinct of the savage," whose "nature is irreconcilable with society."[6]

Strobridge Lithograph Co., "Buffalo Bill's Wild West and Pioneer Exhibition." 1907. Lithograph. Cody, Wyoming, Buffalo Bill Center of the West.

And because of that, it was the enduring responsibility of government and society to do whatever was necessary to protect women and families. That was the flimsy cover story that justified a policy of extinction-in-slow-motion for those gullible white Americans who at some level knew better, but liked to congratulate themselves on their enduring fortitude and ingenuity.

In the twentieth century, Jane McCrea found new prominence in Kenneth Roberts's 1933 novel, *Rabble in Arms: A Chronicle of Arundel and the Burgoyne Invasion*. Roberts, a protégé of Booth Tarkington and a former correspondent for *The Saturday Evening Post*, began writing historical fiction in the 1920s. In novels such as *Northwest Passage*, he became famous for prodigious research and unwavering dedication to rousing historical epics set in eighteenth-century America. His 870-page *Rabble in Arms* narrates the Saratoga campaign in detail, the most familiar figures speaking to each other in vivid dialogue. *The New York Times* described its historical sprawl: "There are scouts, Indians, arrogant and foppish French officers, mercenary militiamen, patriots, and Tories, and the whole starving, grumbling, thieving ragged rabble in arms."[7] Graham Greene thought it a "vigorous, very readable" novel by an author "of wide rather than deep imagination."[8]

Generals Gates and Schuyler figure prominently, but Roberts's obsessive interest was in Benedict Arnold: "His eyes bored into mine," one character muses, "his mind worked like lightning, and somehow plunged straight to the heart of everything." He "was not tall, but he had the muscle, the nerve, the sturdiness, the endurance of a giant, . . . a stocky figure so full of energy that he seemed tense and resilient beside the calmer Schuyler." When Arnold walked into a room of underlings, "his eye fell on us at once and he showed his teeth in a smile that set us all to grinning like fools."[9]

In chapter 61, Roberts introduced three women in contrast to each other. One is the villainous Marie de Sabrevois, a double-agent femme-fatale and intimate acquaintance of George Germain, the British minister overseeing the war. Roberts described her in the novel as "artificial—oversweet, like the pink-frosted cake my mother makes. I stole one of them as a boy, and ate it all, and was sick for two days."[10] Her passing of nefarious misinformation damaging to General Schuyler's reputation is undermining his defense against the Burgoyne invasion, causing Arnold endless consternation.

A second woman is Sarah McNeil, the Tory "Widow," living in the town of Fort Edward, "as large as woman as ever I saw, having legs so vast that she found it difficult to stand on both feet at once, but must stand on one and thrust the other out to one side. Her bust was enormous, so that her arms were held out awkwardly by it; and she had a voice that sounded like shingles being ripped from a roof." She warns that "if any American soldier comes near her house, she would knock off his head with a hot poker."[11]

Cap Huff, a roughhewn American scout who always likes to provoke the "Widder McNeil," introduces the third woman. As the British advanced guard approaches Fort Edward, Cap, just returned from McNeil's cabin, tells old Doc Means, "They's a new girl come to stop with her!" Cap "raised his eyes to heaven and made caressing motions with his hands, as though he passed them over the surface of giant pumpkins perched atop of each other." Jane McCrea is Roberts's alluring damsel in distress, a real looker who warrants attention. "Hoy! Black eyes! Black hair! Name of Jennie McCrea! What some calls a ninf!" Cap explains, "when it comes to making a war rememberable, a dozen battles ain't to be compared with just one beautiful ninf!"[12] Roberts's exclamation points amply signaled sex appeal and impending danger.

A few days later, Burgoyne's Indians arrive like a demon force. Doc Means and Peter Merrill, the book's narrator, station themselves just north of Fort Edward in an observation post. They hear nearby musket fire and "exultant Indian whoops," followed by silence and then the sound of horses' hoofs. Mounted on one of them and surrounded by Indians "was a girl with long hair—long black hair. It hung below her knees, like a black veil. She was unbound, for we could see her, from time to time, push back the hair from her eyes."[13] This group was meant to convey Jane to British lines. Meanwhile, Means and Merrill could also see from their high perch an unrelated pack of Indians running from Fort Edward toward McCrea's group. "What happened then was unreal.... The Indians shouted and waved their arms. Their tones were angry."

Within seconds, the noisiest Indian "slapped the lock of his musket to jolt powder into the pan," then "jerked the muzzle against Jennie's breast and fired."[14] She fell forward onto the horse's neck, her hair tumbling down. "The Indian who had shot her dropped his musket, snatched at Jennie's hair and pulled her from the horse as though she were a sack of meal. She landed on her face. Another Indian shot her in the back."

The one who had first fired whipped his knife from his breast, where it hung by a string, and slashed the point across the back of Jennie's skull. Then he put his foot against her shoulder and dragged at her hair as one drags up a handful of grass. Again he slashed her—two slashes: above each ear; then leaned down, thrust his fingers into the first cut he had made, and pulled. Her whole scalp tore off, like a cap.

In Roberts's telling, they abandon the "mangled body" and run away as the Americans start to arrive.

Peter Merrill, the narrator, is injured that day and almost captured himself. A few days later, he argues with a militiaman over the reason why they are fighting the British. The shortsighted militiaman says it is purely for the money, a twenty-dollar bounty. Incensed by his money-grubbing motives, the wounded Peter upbraids him for not understanding the cause, which, he explains, is summed up in this young woman's awful death. "I do believe you need to be reminded about Jennie McCrea.... I saw her killed. The man that killed her was red, the color of a red fox. He wasn't any bigger than any of you. He and his friends got into an argument over her, so he shot her in the breast. He put the muzzle against her and blew the breast right out of her. Another shot her in the back. In the back! Understand?

He shot her in the back when she was lying on the ground. She hadn't done anything to any of 'em. One of the men put his foot on her and pulled off her hair. Understand? He tore it off her! Tore it off!"[15]

Peter and other true patriots "went into this war to stop the British! To stop the British!" His body shaking, hands trembling, and throat choked up, he indignantly "spoke with all my heart," explaining that they are sacrificing everything so that "you're safe and your homes are standing; and this morning your mothers put bread in the oven, and your sisters are tying ribbons in their hair and sleeping sound at night—because of what we did: because of what we've endured." The true patriots are the ones who stopped the British and their allies from "getting ready to shoot your mothers in the back and rip off your sisters' scalps the way they did Jennie McCrae's. She was a nice girl! She hadn't done anything to anybody, any more than your sisters have." Yet, all the militiamen care about is their twenty dollars, "and you can't see beyond it! . . . You'll let the British hack us to pieces and steal a nation away from us because you can't tell the difference between twenty dollars and justice—between twenty dollars and freedom—between twenty dollars and liberty! Between twenty dollars and your own country!"

Peter wants the departing militiamen to feel outrage over McCrea, and if they ever will, "there'd never be a red-coat get down the Hudson or back to Canada! They'd die right here! . . . There's no foreign force in the whole damned world strong enough to subdue America unless the corruption and the timidity of her own people first force her to her ruin." Peter is not successful in convincing the militiamen to stay, their contracts having expired, but generals Schuyler, Arnold, and Thaddeus Kosciuszko overhear the harangue and formulate a new assignment for Peter, proposed by Arnold: "I want you to start south the first thing tomorrow morning. I want you to tell the story of Jennie McCrae to the people that don't seem to understand this war. . . . Cross over into Massachusetts and work down into Connecticut—Peekskill, Hartford, New Haven, Providence, Taunton—make a circle that ends at Bennington. Understand?" He was to take a month or more, and take Doc Means: "stop at every settlement. Stop at every village. Call the people together. Tell 'em the story of Jennie McCrae. Tell 'em that if we don't get men, the same thing'll happen to their womenfolks that happened to Jennie McCrea."[16]

Arnold takes Peter aside to hammer home the point: "Coax 'em! Shout at 'em! Fight 'em! . . . Get men, and more men, and more men! . . . They can't stay back there, rotting in their feather beds, chewing and spitting and stuffing themselves with food while we're chased and shot at like a lot of rats!" Peter, along with other men recruited to the patriot mission, travel hundreds of miles and grow hoarse, begging "silent farmers to come to their country's aid," and all the while invoking the memory of Jennie McCrea. Like a latter-day Paul Revere or Saint Paul, Peter Merrill carries the word of the cause into the countryside and makes it urgent.

Roberts was not the kind of writer to venture into the inner thoughts of Peter Merrill or Arnold or Schuyler or Jane McCrea. Instead, Roberts's goal was to bring history to life, to give it human texture, and to allow readers to picture what it was like in 1777, as if they were there or watching a movie. He wrote *Rabble in Arms* at the nadir of the Great Depression and in the wake of World War I. His rally-round-the-flag passages, especially when Peter Merrill uses Jennie to explain why soldiers fight, are curiously similar to the familiar recruitment posters for World War I, which bluntly asked American men the same essential question that Peter Merrill had raised, "Hun or Home?" In times of national crisis, the core values of the Revolution have been the touchstones that remind Americans of the first principles that might be facing erosion or loss. Old stories, endlessly retold, including Jane's, have created the bonds that tie citizens to each other by providing compelling morality tales in which the United States repeatedly seeks to protect the innocent victims of a savage enemy.[17]

Roberts was the literary descendant of the hundreds of novelists, poets, historians, and artists, as well as the thousands of enterprising entertainers, hustling journalists, and sentimental memoirists who previously had invited millions of Americans to inhabit Jane McCrea's last day and to come away from the vivid accounts of her ordeal heartbroken, shattered, but also motivated. In the theater of revolutionary pathos, McCrea's terror is the dramatic scene that always provides an unnerving emotional experience deeper than any dry rational argument. Once internalized, no words are necessary.[18]

Rabble in Arms was the last great treatment of McCrea's life, love, and death. By the mid- and late twentieth century, she was mostly famous for having been famous. For some, she was another folk figure like Davy Crockett, Johnny Appleseed, Calamity Jane, Mike Fink, or Molly Pitcher, whose real lives and exploits faded while their fame grew to mythic proportions. Politics and patriotism for the most part faded from her aura in favor of a touching or inspiring tale. Folk musicians gravitated to Jane McCrea's tragic love story without appealing to the old anti-British, anti-Na-

Don Troiani, *The Murder of Jane McCrea*, 2018. Oil on board. (*Bridgeman Images*)

tive denunciations. Instead of Indian-bashing, Jane's sad tale became part of a long tradition of songs—such as *The Ballad of the Jealous Lover of Lone Green Valley*—where innocent women are inexplicably done wrong by bad men.[19]

Simple sadness also prevails in a watercolor design for a tattoo by Noryan Baker. He has adapted Nathaniel Currier's 1841 print of McCrea's killing and added a mourning woman, blonde hair flowing and tears draining from her eyes, while a resplendent sun pours forth from her broken heart. She is like the bereft Alice Munro, whose sister Cora is stabbed to death by Huron warriors in the climactic scene of Cooper's *Last of the Mohicans.*[20] The wide, wavy border, shaped for the back of a tattoo client, has an intricate pattern that Baker based on the bead patterns of the Great Lakes Indians who were responsible for McCrea's death.

For the painter Don Troiani, the goal was to set the record straight, or as straight as possible. Troiani and the historian Eric Schnitzer combed through military accounts and pension records in an effort to produce an updated image of McCrea's death. The resulting picture locates the attack on a hillside near a pine forest and includes the dead Lieutenant Van Vechten in the right distance. The most important revision to past treatments of the event is to Jane, who is not a waif. Pushing up the chain of events by a minute or so allowed Troiani to focus on the struggle rather than the murder. In every other historical account, Jane is a helpless victim facing her last few seconds. Troiani instead contemplates an earlier juncture, when Jane forcibly resists the assault. Though one Indian has grabbed her hair and the other one her wrist, she uses her weight to pull back against them. Ultimately, the outcome will be the same, but in this depiction, survival is on her mind, not capitulation.

15.

NECESSARY FICTIONS

"IN WAR," Aeschylus reputedly said, "truth is the first casualty." We will never know precisely how Jane McCrea lived or died. Military records, though closest in date to her death and thus most useful to reconstructing the events of July 26, 1777, were not eyewitness reports, except for Samuel Standish's deposition decades later. Other eighteenth-century accounts fulfilled agendas that were mostly political: Patriot newspapers obsessively sensationalizing the McCrea story because it was good for their partisan readers; General Gates shrewdly identifying her as a propaganda tool capable of mobilizing popular sentiment against the British and their Native auxiliaries; Whig politicians in London making her the perfect object lesson in their campaign to prove how the Tory government had conducted the war immorally. Subsequently, American historians, poets, and artists shaped the raw material of her death into an abundance of storylines, some wildly fictional. In American expansionist thinking and policy, she evolved into tangible proof that Native Americans were adversaries disrupting the westward march of American civilization.

As a result of all the improvisations and amplifications, truth capitulated to the wants and needs of the tale-teller. Jonathan Swift, author of *Gulliver's*

Travels, observed that distortion, rumor, gossip, legend, and outright imaginings were always more compelling than history could ever be. In 1710, Swift remarked that "falsehood flies," while the truth merely limps along. In fact, Swift, ever the social cynic, went on to say that falsehood does more than fly; it triumphs—and continually triumphs—over truth. Even at some later date, after people "become undeceived," he noted, "it is too late" to extinguish the sustained belief in the myth.[1]

Telling origin stories—the truthful, semi-truthful, and certifiably false narratives that explain and justify the beginnings of something significant—was a cultural necessity of the still-nebulous American republic because its integrity was unsteady, at times precarious.[2] The Revolution may have vanquished British rule, but that did not mean that a distinctive American culture was imminent or assured; it had to be made out of whole cloth.[3] Further, the Revolution had papered over the ingrained and deep divisions that existed among the thirteen states and their citizens. After the war was over, border disputes snapped back, religious affiliations multiplied, racial prejudices went unaddressed, Anglophilia lingered in some quarters, arguments over states rights became intractable, and sectional tensions returned unabated. The attempt to cement a republic spread over 1,200 miles was itself an inherently quixotic proposition. By 1800, discord and aimlessness having rebounded with all their old factious power, the infant union faced dissolution.

John Adams phrased the elusiveness of nation-making this way: "The colonies had grown up under Constitutions of government, so different, there was so great a variety of religions, they were composed of so many different nations, their customs, manners, and habit had so little resemblance, and their intercourse had been so rare, and the knowledge of each other so imperfect . . . that to unite them in the same principles in theory and the same system of action, was certainly a very difficult enterprise." Writing in 1818, with the benefit of hindsight, he thought it miraculous that somehow, "Thirteen clocks were made to strike together."[4]

In attempting to get those clocks synchronized, one of the first tasks of the post-Revolutionary era was to cajole still-discordant states to join the national project and to persuade newly minted Americans of their collective identity. Finding a new common cause involved not only the erasure of the British stories that Americans had told themselves in the past, but also the creation of new, irresistible American stories that would be rich in ideals, goals, heroes, and adversaries, and that could be shared across divides. The emerging American words, thoughts, beliefs, rituals, and images needed to be "unabashedly patriotic, teleological, partisan, and propagandistic," if the daring American experiment were to have a chance at succeeding.[5]

The Revolution itself had already produced a constellation of available origin stories and figures: George Washington's heroics at the battles of Princeton and Trenton, Thomas Jefferson drafting the Declaration of Independence in Philadelphia, Benjamin Franklin negotiating a French alliance at Versailles, Ethan Allen capturing Ticonderoga, the British surrenders at Saratoga and Yorktown, Joseph Warren and Richard Montgomery giving their lives on the battlefield, and the start of a new ritual, the Fourth of July, first staged in 1777.

To be sure, the abundance of compelling possibilities would not prevent federal and state legislatures from endlessly squabbling over who and what to commemorate.[6] But there was growing consensus on a handful of first heroes to be enshrined in what amounted to an American temple of fame. All nations had them, witness Romulus and Remus, El Cid, King Arthur, and countless others. Yet those were fictional characters. Here, we have enshrined real people, most especially the Founders, but also Jane McCrea.

Objectively examined, her claim to a pedestal was questionable. After all, she was engaged to a Loyalist officer in a company of rangers who fought against and killed Patriots. She had done nothing valiant in life. And unlike the men of the Revolution who were blessed with rich biographies and thick resumés, her life was anonymous, her death mysterious and debated. Yet, she touched sentimental hearts and was the most prominent female victim of the war for independence. For a young nation looking for stories to help define itself, a niche was available for a beautiful, young, white Christian girl murdered during the Revolution by America's stated adversaries.[7]

Let us speculate that within that imaginary temple of Revolutionary fame there is a smaller and more exclusive gallery of martyrs, the ones who died for America. That mythical place of fallen heroes, America's Valhalla, would be dominated by men. It would feature the transcendent generals Warren and Montgomery, both of whom died spectacularly for the cause. A respected physician and a fierce demagogue, Warren threw himself into the Battle of Bunker Hill, only to have his skull exploded by a British musket ball. The Dublin-born Montgomery led the quixotic American expedition up to the ramparts of Quebec, whereupon he was ripped apart by British grapeshot during a snowstorm on New Year's Eve. McCrea was indisputably the female martyr of the Revolution, the other women of note—Deborah Sampson, Margaret Corbin, Sybil Ludington, and Catherine

Barry—not qualifying for residence in the American Valhalla because the cruel precondition for enshrinement as a martyr was death.

The argument mounted for McCrea's induction was captured by the exuberant words of a nineteenth-century historian who lifted her up to a divine level. "The pathway of human progress has in almost all ages led upwards only through the blood of the martyrs." Because of McCrea, there resulted "a renaissance of patriotism, a reawakening of the public spirit, an arousing of the lion-heart in a dormant population." In her death, there thus arose "the birth of a new nation" of "nearly a hundred millions, with a dominion from the rising to the setting sun, controlling the destinies not only of our own but of alien peoples, that we belong to a land of liberty that has been made possible by the struggles, sacrifices and privations of a comparative handful of patriots." Would visiting her "quiet sepulchre beside the majestic Hudson," he wondered, inspire us to "pause a moment to drop the roses of love and the amaranth of remembrance." From her death there arose "the flowers and blossoms of progress," the seeds of which produced one of the "mightiest, wealthiest, most powerful nations of the earth."[8]

The author of that extravagant apotheosis had written nothing less than an American hagiography, a secular version of the stories of early Christian martyrs who died for their contributions to the faith. Saint Cecilia and Saint Catherine of Alexandria, both virgins and both beheaded, were often depicted in old master paintings like Jane, seconds before death. Both those saints, like Jane, had murky biographies, yet the means of their torture and forms of their martyrdom were always gruesomely explicit. We often encounter them in the same scenario in which McCrea was typically depicted: on their knees, centered in the foreground, and at the mercy of their executioners. Perhaps if Jane had been slaughtered in Catholic Italy, she would have had hovering angels preparing to escort her to heaven, but in Protestant America she would have to meet her end unaccompanied by divine emissaries.

If we extend the Christian analogy of McCrea having died a martyr for the cause, we would expect her to have performed miracles, either while living or after death. Catherine of Alexandria converted her adversaries to Christianity, and when she died milk ran from her veins.[9] Cecilia was meant to be burned alive but she miraculously survived and finally was beheaded, though only after numerous failed attempts.

In McCrea's case, the miracle attributed to her was the inexplicable turn of events against the vaunted British. General Howe never arranged an advance up the Hudson to squeeze the Americans, as Burgoyne had anticipated. The British battalions advancing eastward through the Mohawk Valley toward Albany met unexpectedly fierce American resistance and were stopped cold at the ferocious Battle of Oriskany in August 1777. And ten days later, a thousand of Burgoyne's men died at the ill-fated Battle of Bennington in Vermont. Perhaps most fatal to the British campaign, the further Burgoyne progressed southward, the more dependent his army became on an impossibly attenuated supply chain stretching 185 miles back to Montreal. By Saratoga, his soldiers were exhausted, starving, and vulnerable.

An equally striking series of miraculous events ensued on the American side. Just six days after writing to Burgoyne about McCrea, General Gates broke camp at Van Schaick Island, at the confluence of the Mohawk and Hudson Rivers, countermarched the Continental Army fourteen miles north to Stillwater and then Bemis Heights, where he waited to engage the British. He told his soldiers they had a sacred duty to avenge the slaying of innocent civilians. Previously haggard American troops surged to life and the British military behemoth staggered to epic defeat and final surrender at Saratoga on October 17.[10]

The epilogue to the miracle story was equally compelling: Because of the American victory, Benjamin Franklin was able to persuade Louis XVI and his foreign minister, the Comte de Vergennes, that the war was winnable and that France ought to commit its army, navy, and its ancient and fierce hatred of Britain to the revolutionary cause. Because of her place in the sequence of events and the desire to attribute those events to her in some measure, McCrea became "the Madonna of the North," a simple woman in possession of transformative powers.[11] Though her suffering may have been sublime, her ultimate reward was perpetual life as honored American heroine.

Saints often leave behind sacred relics, in the form of both personal effects and physical remains. The left hand and skull of Saint Catherine are said to be housed in a monastery on Mount Sinai in Egypt. Cecilia's body, claimed to be uncorrupted by time, lies in a crypt in the basilica of Saint Cecilia in the Trastevere section of Rome. Likewise, Jane McCrea's teeth, ribs, hair, vertebrae, and skull were thought to be so sacred that they were plucked from her skeleton during the ghoulish sifting through her grave in the nineteenth century. The rest of her remains lie in a palisaded grave in Fort Edward, which historically has been part of a pilgrimage tour that includes the spring and pine tree where she died.

The story of McCrea's revolutionary sacrifice also parallels another legendary martyr much older than the Christian saints. Lucretia, a married

Roman woman of the sixth century BCE, was raped by Sextus Tarquinius, the son of a tyrannical Etruscan king. Out of wounded honor and in an effort to prove she had tried to remain virtuous, Lucretia stabbed herself to death. Her appalled Roman brethren, galvanized by her suicide and the unspeakable violence committed by the Tarquins, banded together against the Etruscans—much as Patriots were said to against the British—"in defense of their liberty," determined never "to suffer such outrages to be committed by the tyrants."[12]

The rest of the Roman story, like the emerging American story against British tyrants, would be epic. The Romans raised a revolutionary army, overthrew the Tarquins, and established the Roman republic, which lasted 483 years. In countless old master paintings, such as Titian's, Tarquinius threatens Lucretia similarly to the way Vanderlyn and every other artist staged McCrea's capture. The eventual deaths of these women would provoke men to launch the republics of Rome and the United States.[13]

John Trumbull—who studied the classics at Harvard, served under Gates, knew Stephen McCrea, sketched Jane's murder, and painted Saratoga on a monumental scale—often gravitated to the striking parallels between ancient stories and modern America. He was not alone in making that analogy. John Adams also saw the "History of our own Country" as a reenactment of classical narratives. He wrote to Benjamin Rush that all one needs to do is "Change the Names and every Anecdote will be applicable to Us."[14]

As a young man, Trumbull painted the late Roman emperor Belisarius in a state of beggary, posed generals Joseph Warren and Richard Montgomery like Christ in Renaissance pietas, and in July of 1777—the month of Jane McCrea's death, the war still raging—he chose to paint Lucretia. Not her rape, but the moment when her husband Collatinus, her father Lucretius, and her cousin Lucius Junius Brutus, together swear revenge by the gods against the Tarquins with "whatever violence [they] may."[15] The Romans rally to the cause, fight fanatically, and overthrow the royal Etruscan house.

Trumbull's painting proposes a parallel between the Romans' collective response to Lucretia's rape and the American Patriots' fight to overthrow their British overlords. These were Lucretia's dying words, as written by a Roman historian: "If you are men and care for your children, avenge me," she beseeched, "free yourselves, and show the tyrants what manner of men

John Trumbull, *Brutus and His Friends at the Death of Lucretia*. 1777. Oil on canvas. New Haven, Yale University Art Gallery, Gift of the heirs of David Trumbull Lanman.

you are and what manner of woman of yours they have outraged."[16] If we do as John Adams suggested, we merely need to change the name from Lucretia to Jane in order to understand McCrea's symbolic importance to the Founding.

Trumbull and all the others who painted Lucretia knew that it was not her death that founded Rome; instead, it was the unity brought about by that unspeakable crime and the vengeance it provoked.[17] To be sure, Jane McCrea's assailed virtue was sufficiently appalling on its own terms to be noteworthy, but what made it memorable and important to the Founding was the unified American urge to punish those responsible for it—namely Native Americans and the British—and to commit to stopping them from ever inflicting future harm on the republic's civilian population.

One of the central imperatives of the American common cause was the protection of all Jane McCreas from such harm. As Tom Paine phrased the situation in *Common Sense*, "There are injuries which nature cannot forgive; . . . As well, can the lover forgive the ravisher of his mistress, as the [American] continent forgive the murders of Britain."[18] Jane McCrea was starkly alone when assaulted on that July 26, but her torment ultimately became a shared public ordeal, one that worked to forge citizenship in the new American republic. Vigilance was not just an ongoing security obligation; it was the essential quest that helped define the United States as a collective, first as a union, then as a nation.

NOTES

CHAPTER ONE: FACT AND FABLE

1. I use "Indian" and "Indians" when writing from the point of view of the eighteenth-century British and Americans. Otherwise, I use "Native American," "Native peoples," and "Native" when writing from a twenty-first-century perspective.

2. A letter purported to be from Jones to McCrea is in James Austin Holden, "Influence of the Death of Jane McCrea on the Burgoyne Campaign," *Proceedings of the New York State Historical Association* 12 (1913), 274–75.

3. Recent forensic evidence pegs her height between 5 feet 2 and 5 feet 4 inches; David R. Starbuck, *Archeology in the Adirondacks: The Last Frontier* (Lebanon: University Press of New England, 2018), 107–21. Judge William Hay (1790–1860), a respected citizen of the area who interviewed a number of locals in 1827—that is a half-century after the killing—said she was "a large coarse Scotch girl, very sprightly and with regular features and hazel eyes—not handsome but 'well-looking' and remarkable for a long thick head of black hair." William Hay to Lura Anna Boies, June 4, 1856; in Doris Putnam Lasselle, "Remembering Jane McCrea: A Newly-Discovered Correspondence from the 1850s," *Journal of the Washington County Historical Society* (2007), 75.

4. In the late nineteenth century, William Leete Stone painted a fictional image of her in words: "a young woman of rare accomplishments, great personal attractions, and of a remarkable sweetness of disposition. She was of medium stature, finely formed, and of a delicate blond complexion. Her hair was of a golden brown and silken lustre, and, when unbound, trailed upon the ground." *Ballads and Poems Relating to the Burgoyne Campaign* (Albany: J. Munsell's Sons, 1893), 131.

CHAPTER TWO: THE CLAN MCCREA

1. For an overview of the clan, see Alexander MacRae, *History of the Clan MacRae, with Genealogies* (Dingwall: Souter, 1910). For the Scots-Irish, see David W. Miller, "Searching for a New World: The Background and Baggage of Scot-Irish Immigrants," in *Ulster to America: The Scots-Irish Experience, 1680–1830*, ed. Warren R. Hofstra (Knoxville: University of Tennessee Press, 2012), 1–24.

2. George H. Ingram, "Biographies of the Alumni of the Log College: James McCrea," *Journal of the Presbyterian Historical Society* 13:5 (March, 1929), 217. Also, A. Van Doren Honeyman, "Two Bedminster Families: McCrea and Henry," *Somerset County Historical Quarterly* 7:2 (April, 1918), 81–97.

3. Thomas Murphy, *The Presbytery of the Log College: or, the Cradle of the Presbyterian Church in America* (Philadelphia: Presbyterian Board of Publication, 1889), 508.

4. Ingram, "Log College," 218.
5. R. Gloria Landers, *Pioneers, Pastors and Patriots: The 250-Year History of Lamington Presbyterian Church* (Bedminster, NJ: Lamington Presbyterian Church, 1990), 26.
6. Landers, *Pioneers*, 10; Ingram, "Log College," 221.
7. Landers, *Pioneers*, 45.
8. George H. Ingram, "The Story of the Log College," *Journal of the Presbyterian Historical Society* 12:8 (October, 1927), 487–511.
9. Horatio Gates to Benedict Arnold, August 23, 1776, in Peter Force, *American Archives*, fifth series, 3 vols. (Washington: St. Clair Clarke and Peter Force, 1848–53), 1:1129.
10. Jahiel Stewart, "A Most Unsettled Time on Lake Champlain: The October 1776 Journal of Jahiel Stewart," ed. Donald Wickman, *Vermont History* 62:2 (Spring, 1996), 92.
11. Stephen McCrea to Jonathan Potts, October 14, 1776, in Edward D. Neill, *Biographical Sketch of Doctor Jonathan Potts* (Albany: Munsell, 1863), 11. Joel Munsell, the publisher of this and numerous other books cited below, took a keen interest in Jane McCrea. His letters on the subject are in the William L. Clements Library, University of Michigan.
12. Lasselle, "Remembering Jane McCrea," 76. *New York in the Revolution as Colony and State* (Albany: Lyon, 1904), 15, 122. Asa Fitch, "Selections from the Correspondence and Papers," *Proceeding of the New Jersey Historical Society* 5 (1850–51), 165.
13. *Journals of the Continental Congress, 1774–1789*, ed. John C. Fitzpatrick, 43 vols. (Washington: Government Printing Office, 1933), 10:297.
14. E. Alfred Jones, *Loyalists of New Jersey: Their Memorials, Petitions, Claims, Etc., from British Records* (Trenton: New Jersey Historical Society, 1927), 137; Richard A. Harrison, *Princetonians, 1776–1783: A Biographical Dictionary* (Princeton: Princeton University Press, 1981), 75–77; Gregory Palmer, *Biographical Sketches of Loyalists of the American Revolution* (Westport, CT: Meckler, 1984), 527.
15. Landers, *Pioneers*, 46.
16. Yale professor Benjamin Silliman reprinted a statement from John McCrea in Silliman, *Remarks Made on a Short Tour between Hartford and Quebec, in the Autumn of 1819* (New Haven: S. Converse, 1824), 136.
17. S. DeWitt Bloodgood, *The Sexagenary, or Reminiscences of the American Revolution* (Albany: Little and Steele, 1833), 66.
18. "Two Old Wills—Van Horne's and McCrea's," *Somerset County History Quarterly* 4 (1915), 248–52.
19. Asa Fitch, "David Jones," *Orderly Book of Lieut. General Burgoyne: From His Entry into the State of New York until his Surrender at Saratoga*, ed. E. B. O'Callaghan (Albany: Munsell, 1860), 187–89.
20. Fitch, *Jones*, 188; Palmer, *Biographical Sketches*, 442. A purported biography, "Last Days of Jones, the Lover of Jane McCrea," by Julia Smalley and first published in 1882, is in Stone, *Ballads*, 319–28.
21. Palmer, *Loyalists*, 444. Recruiting Loyalists was difficult because of fear of Patriot reprisal; see Kieran J. O'Keefe, "Mass Incarceration as Revolutionary Policy: The Imprisonment of the Hudson Valley Loyalists," *Early American Studies* 19 (Summer, 2021), 495–527.
22. Lasselle, "Remembering Jane McCrea," 79.
23. Palmer, *Loyalists*, 442. Austin Holden, *History of the Town of Queensbury in the State of New York* (Albany: Munsell, 1874), 412.
24. Lorenzo Sabine, *Biographical Sketches of Loyalists of the American Revolution*, 2 vols. (Boston: Little Brown, 1884), 1:592. For Patriot treatment of Loyalists, see Philip Ranlet, *The New York Loyalists* (Knoxville: University of Tennessee Press, 1986), 153–62.
25. Sabine, *Biographical Sketches*, 2:180.

26. Mary Beacock Fryer, *King's Men: The Soldier Founders of Ontario* (Toronto: Dundurn, 1980), 188. See J. Fraser, *Skulking for the King: A Loyalist Plot* (Erin, Ontario: Boston Mills Press, 1985).
27. Theodore Corbett, *No Turning Point: The Saratoga Campaign in Perspective* (Norman: University of Oklahoma Press, 2012), 89.
28. Henry Griswold Jessup, *Edward Jessup of West Farms, Westchester Co., New York, and His Descendants* (Cambridge: Wilson, 1887), 226.
29. Holden, *Town of Queensbury*, 437.
30. John Burgoyne to George Germain, July 11, 1777, *Documents of the American Revolution*, ed. K. G. Davies, 21 vols. (Shannon: Irish University Press, 1972–1981), 14:140.
31. John Burgoyne, *A State of the Expedition from Canada, as Laid before the House of Commons* (London: J. Almon, 1780), 102.
32. Holden, "Influence," 261.
33. *Orderly Book of Lieut. General Burgoyne*, 189.
34. *Orderly Book of Lieut. General Burgoyne*, 187.
35. British War Office Records, 28, October 11 and 16, 1778; and May 2, 1779, David Library, Washington Crossing, PA.
36. Corbett, *No Turning Point*, 262, 300–304.
37. Corbett, *No Turning Point*, 302; Gavin K. Watt, *The Burning of the Valleys: Daring Raids from Canada against the New York Frontier in the Fall of 1780* (Toronto: Dundurn, 1997), 102. Asa Fitch prints the harrowing account of the panic that occurred at John McCrea's house, *Asa Fitch Papers*, ed. Laura Penny Hulslander, 2 vols. (Fort Campbell, KY: Sleeper, 1997), 1:52, 58.
38. *Report on Canadian Archives* (Ottawa: Queen's Printer, 1889), 696. Gavin K. Watt, *A Dirty, Trifling Piece of Business: The Revolutionary War as Waged from Canada in 1781* (Toronto: Dundurn, 2009), 247; Corbett, *No Turning Point*, 329.
39. Haldimand Papers, Loyalist Volumes, Public Archives List of Loyalists. Ms. group 21, b166, National Archives of Canada, Ottawa; thanks to Bruce A. Burton for a 2002 unpublished paper on the topic.
40. Gavin K. Watt, *I am Heartily Ashamed: The Revolutionary War's Final Campaign as Waged from Canada in 1782* (Toronto: Dundurn Press, 2010), 89, 126.
41. British War Office Records, 28, January 1, 1783, David Library, Washington Crossing, PA; David Jones, "A Description of the Country & Land on the River above Carryo etc, Vizt.," E. A. Cruikshank, ed., *The Settlement of The United Empire Loyalists on the Upper St. Lawrence and Bay of Quinte in 1784* (Toronto: Ontario Historical Society, 1934), 18–19.
42. *Report on Canadian Archives*, 755.
43. See Corbett, *No Turning Point*, 343–58.
44. *Proceedings and Transactions of the Royal Society of Canada*, ser. 2, vol. 9 (May, 1903), 151; Stephen A. Otto, *Maitland* (Erin, Ontario: Boston Mills Press, 1985).
45. *Report on Canadian Archives*, 14. Jones is listed as "Former Own Lands of Good Estate," in *Loyalist Lists: Over 2000 Loyalist Names and families from the Haldimand Papers*, ed. E. Keith Fitzgerald (Concord: Ontario Genealogical Society, 1984), 81, 83.
46. William Hay, in Lasselle, "Remembering Jane McCrea," 79.
47. *The Centennial of the Settlement of Upper Canada by the United Empire Loyalists, 1784–1884* (Toronto: Rose, 1885), 199.
48. *Report on Canadian Archives*, 80, 146. Cruickshank, *Settlement of the United Empire Loyalists*, 18–19.
49. *Report of the Public Records and Archives of Ontario* (Toronto: H. H. Ball, 1903). "The widow and children of Lieut. Jones are recommended for 2000 acres (including former

grants to himself) and also including former grants to the widow. The children (if of age) are recommended for 400 acres each, including former grants to themselves, but exclusive of their share in the 2000 acres and exclusive of such lands as they have by descent or devise from their grandfather Benjamin" (66). "Solomon Jones. Praying that the lands located by the late Lieutenant David Jones may be confirmed to him by His Majesty's deeds being duly authorised by papers from the heirs to receive the same. Recommended that the lands granted to him David Jones in his life time or in his right to his brothers and sisters since his death, do issue to Solomon Jones, he having produced this day releases from them of their rights to him" (161). All the Joneses are buried in Blue Church Cemetery in Leeds, Ontario.

CHAPTER THREE: THE LETTER

1. Many dates have been given, but Philip Schuyler's letter to George Washington, dated July 27, refers to McCrea's killing occurring "Yesterday"; Washington Papers, Library of Congress.
2. Horatio Gates to John Burgoyne, September 2, 1777. I am using Gates's draft of the letter; both the draft and the letter are in the Gates Papers, New-York Historical Society.
3. Horatio Gates to John Burgoyne, September 2, 1777, Gates Papers, New-York Historical Society.
4. The heat was noted by a German officer; *Letters from America, 1776–1779, Being Letters of Brunswick, Hessian, and Waldeck Officers with the British Armies during the Revolution*, ed. Ray W. Pettengill (Port Washington, NY: Kennikat, 1924), 82.
5. Gates to Jonathan Trumbull, September 4, 1777, Gates Papers, New-York Historical Society.
6. Gates to George Washington, August 22, 1777, Gates Papers, New-York Historical Society.
7. Gates to John Hancock, August 28, 1777, Gates Papers, New-York Historical Society.
8. McCrea had many spelling variants in the eighteenth century. John Burgoyne to Horatio Gates, September 6, 1777, Gates Papers, New-York Historical Society.
9. Philip Schuyler to George Washington, July 22, 1777, Washington Papers, Library of Congress.
10. Gates to Washington, July 27, 1777, Washington Papers, Library of Congress.

CHAPTER FOUR: MURDER MOST FOUL, STRANGE, AND UNNATURAL

1. Ivory Hovey to Horatio Gates, June 27, 1777, Gates Papers, New-York Historical Society. Hovey sent variants of the letter to his father, omitting some of the more harrowing encounters he was having with wounded men; see Hovey Papers, New England Historic Genealogical Society, Boston, and the Congregational Library and Archives, Boston.
2. O'Neil's house, according to Samuel B. Cook, a Fort Edward resident, "was a small house of round logs some 15 or 16 feet broad and somewhat greater in length. . . . It had an old-fashioned fire-place, in one end, the fire-place without jambs. There was a loft over head, and a ladder or ladder like stairs leading to this loft, the stairs being on one side of the fire-place. The door opened on the east side of the house, which was the only entrance. There was a cellar hole under the house, not walled up. This was entered by a trap door which was rather south of the middle of the floor;" Fitch, *Asa Fitch Papers*, 82–83.
3. James Wilkinson, *Memoirs of My Own Times*, 3 vols. (Philadelphia: Abraham Small, 1816), 1:231.
4. Unknown author's journal, July 27, 1777, *For Want of a Horse; Being a Journal of the Cam-*

paigns against the Americans in 1776 and 1777 Conducted from Canada, by an Officer who Served with Lt. Gen. Burgoyne, ed. by George F. G Stanley (Sackville, New Brunswick: The Tribute Press, 1961), 123.
5. Thomas Anburey, *Travels through the Interior Parts of America*, 2 vols. (London: William Lane, 1789), 1:371.
6. John Burgoyne, *The Substance of General Burgoyne's Speeches; on Mr. Vyner's Motion, on the 28th of May, 1778* (London: John Almon, 1778), 6.
7. John Burgoyne to Simon Fraser, July 26, 1777, in C. T. Atkinson, "Some Evidence for Burgoyne's Expedition," *Journal of the Society for Army Historical Research* 26:108 (Winter, 1948), 142.
8. Burgoyne's account seems to be confirmed by an entry for David Jones in a British army orderly book for money "paid for an Indian pilot to go for intelligence." Haldimand Papers, vol. B167, Part 1, 117m, National Archives of Canada, Ottawa; thanks to Bruce A. Burton for his unpublished paper on McCrea.
9. Stanley, ed., *For Want of a Horse*, 123.
10. John Burgoyne to Horatio Gates, September 6, 1777, Gates Papers, New-York Historical Society.
11. Roger Lamb, *An Original and Authentic Journal of Occurrences during the Late American War from its Commencement to the year 1783* (Dublin: Wilkinson and Courtney, 1809), 145.
12. Anburey, *Travels*, 373–74.
13. Josiah Bartlett to Jonathan Potts, July 26, 1777, in Edward D. Neill, "Medical History of the War for Independence," *Macalester College Contributions*, 2nd series (St. Paul, MN: Macalester College, 1892), 242.
14. Estes Howe, "Time Spent as a Surgeon with Gates' Forces during the Saratoga Campaign, 1777–1778." Howe Journals, New York Public Library.
15. James Thacher, *A Military Journal during the American Revolutionary War, from 1775 to 1783* (Boston: Richardson and Lord, 1823), 115.
16. Wilkinson, *Memoirs*, 1:230.
17. Howe, "Time Spent."
18. Wilkinson, *Memoirs*, 1:230.
19. William Scudder, *The Journal of William Scudder* (Ann Arbor: Scholars' Facsimiles, 2005), 13.
20. Captain Benjamin Warren of the Massachusetts 7th noted in his diary that it had "rained hard" on the 26th when "two women" were "killed and scalpt." On the 27th, "Miss McCray was brought up, and buried here." David E. Alexander, "Diary of Captain Benjamin Warren on the Battlefield of Saratoga," *Journal of American History* 3:2 (1909), 205.
21. Jonathan Potts to Thomas Potts, July 28, 1777, *Memorial of Thomas Potts, junior, who Settles in Pennsylvania*, ed. Isabella Potts James (Cambridge: private, 1874), 201.
22. Benedict Arnold to George Washington, July 27, 1777, Washington Papers, Library of Congress. His story is confirmed by the Reverend Enos Hitchcock, "Diary of Rev. Enos Hitchcock, D.D., a Chaplain in the Revolutionary Army," *Publications of the Rhode Island Historical Society* 7 (1899), 122. Washington had overseen Indian scalping during the French and Indian War, when Indians scalped French officers at Jumonville Glen and British soldiers at Monongahela. In his memoirs, Arnold devoted an entire chapter to McCrea, having gathered information from other sources; *My Story: Being the Memoirs of Benedict Arnold: Late Major-General in the Continental Army and Brigadier-General in that of His Britannic Majesty*, ed. Frederic Jesup Stimson (New York: Scribner's, 1917).
23. Barbara Graymont, *The Iroquois in the American Revolution* (Syracuse: Syracuse University Press, 1975), 232.

24. Graymont, *Iroquois in the American Revolution,* 232.
25. Philip Schuyler to George Washington, July 27, 1777, Schuyler Papers, New York Public Library.
26. Julia Livingston Delafield, *Biographies of Francis Lewis and Morgan Lewis* (New York: Randolph & Company, 1877), 85.
27. Jared Sparks, "Journal; Traveling Notes for Historical Research," 1830–31, Houghton Library, Harvard University.
28. Leonard Gansevoort to Peter Gansevoort, Jr., July 28, 1777, *Hero of Fort Schuyler: Selected Revolutionary War Correspondence of Brigadier General Peter Gansevoort, Jr.*, ed. David A. Ranzan and Matthew J. Hollis (Jefferson, NC: McFarland, 2014), 65.
29. Jeduthan Baldwin, *The Revolutionary Journal of Col. Jeduthan Baldwin, 1775–1778*, ed. Thomas Williams Baldwin (Bangor: Du Burians, 1906), 112.
30. *The Diary of the Revolution, a Centennial Volume Embracing the Current Events in our Country's History from 1775 to 1781*, 2 vols., ed. Frank Moore (New York: Evans, 1863), 1:476.
31. National Archives, Revolutionary War Pension Files, Samuel Standish, S.28,899.
32. Epaphras Hoyt, "History of Burgoyne's Invasion," *Proceeding of the New-York Historical Society*, June 1, 1847, 77.
33. Sparks, "Journal."
34. William Digby, *The British Invasion from the North. The Campaigns of Generals Carleton and Burgoyne from Canada, 1776–1777, with the Journal of Lieut. William Digby of the 53d, or Shropshire Regiment of Foot* (Albany: Munsell's, 1887), 235.
35. Julius Friedrich Wasmus, *An Eyewitness Account of the American Revolution and New England Life; The Journal of F. W. Wasmus, German Company Surgeon, 1776–1783*, ed. Mary C. Lyman (Westport, CT: Greenwood, 1990), 66.
36. Wasmus, 99.
37. Quoted in Michael A. McDonnell, *Masters of Empire: Great Lakes Indians and the Making of America* (New York: Hill and Wang), 283.
38. Burgoyne, *State of the Expedition*, appendix 8.
39. See Michael A. McDonnell, "Charles-Michel Mouet de Langlade: Warrior, Soldier, and Intercultural Window on the Sixty Years War," in David C. Skaggs and Larry L. Nelson, *The Sixty Years War for the Great Lakes, 1754–1814* (East Lansing: Michigan State University Press, 2001), 79–103.
40. James Murray Hadden, *Hadden's Journal and Orderly Books: A Journal Kept in Canada and upon Burgoyne's Campaign in 1776 and 1777* (Albany: Munsell's, 1884), 535–36.
41. Thomas Jefferson to John Page, October 31, 1775, Jefferson Papers, New York Public Library.
42. *Letters from America,* 82.
43. Thomas Jefferson to John Page, October 31, 1775, Jefferson Papers, New York Public Library.
44. Koert DuBois Burnham and David Kendall Martin, *La Corne St. Luc—His Flame* (Keeseville, NY: Highlands, 1991), 95.
45. Johann Friedrich Specht, *The Specht Journal: A Military Journal of the Burgoyne Campaign* (Westport, CT: Greenwood, 1995), 57.
46. Burgoyne, *State of the Expedition*, 99.
47. Burgoyne, *State of the Expedition*, 100.
48. *Orderly Book of Lieut. Gen. John Burgoyne*, 51.
49. *Boston Gazette and Country Journal*, August 11, 1777; quoted in Jeremy Engels and Greg Goodale, "Our Battle Cry Will Be: 'Remember Jenny McCrea!' A Précis on the Rhetoric of Revenge." *American Quarterly* 61:1 (March, 2009), 97.

50. Eleazer Williams, *Life of Te-ho-ra-gwa-ne-gen, alias Thomas Williams, A Chief of the Caughnawage Tribe of Indians in Canada* (Albany: Munsell, 1859), 27–30. Edward Barrington de Fonblanque, one of Burgoyne's early biographers, had access to papers that seem to no longer exist today. He said that the Indians that day were under the guidance of Captain John Money of the 9th Regiment of Foot; *Political and Military Episodes in the Latter Half of the Eighteenth Century: Derived from the Life and Correspondence of the Right Hon. John Burgoyne* (London: Macmillan, 1876), 315.
51. Bradford S. Sydney, "Lord Francis Napier's Journal of the Burgoyne Campaign," *Maryland Historical Magazine* 57 (December, 1962), 4:306.
52. Stanley, ed., *For Want of a Horse*, 123.
53. Silliman, *Remarks*, 136.
54. Scudder, *Journal*, 13.
55. National Archives, Revolutionary War Pension Files, Luther Shaw, S.33.509.
56. In later accounts, the officer is called "Lieutenant Palmer." Documents from 1777 do not corroborate his presence, however.
57. Hoyt, "History of Burgoyne's Invasion," 77. Hoyt told Benjamin Silliman that the stories of her being killed near a spring while on horseback were false, that she was instead on foot on a road; Silliman, *Remarks*, 132.
58. William Leete Stone, "The Jane McCrea Tragedy," *The Indian Miscellany*, ed. W. W. Beach (Albany: J. Munsell, 1877), 382.
59. Holden, "Influence," 281–82.
60. Fitch, *Asa Fitch Papers*, 2:14. In another account in Fitch's compendium, the burial spot was "on the N side of the brook that enters the river just above the black house;" 2:52.
61. Fitch, *Asa Fitch Papers*, 2:58.
62. Fitch, *Asa Fitch Papers*, 2:54.
63. Fitch, *Asa Fitch Papers*, 2:69.
64. David R. Starbuck, "Mystery of the Second Body: A Forensic Investigation of Jane McCrea's Final Resting Place," *Plymouth Magazine* (Winter, 2006), n.p. For a fuller explanation see: https://www.youtube.com/watch?v=lJuqhJ3qrC4.
65. Jared Sparks, *The Life and Treason of Benedict Arnold* (Boston: Hilliard, Gray, 1835), 106.
66. Holden, "Influence," 283.
67. David R. Starbuck, *Archeology in the Adirondacks: The Last Frontier* (Hanover: University Press of New England, 2018), 109–21.
68. Starbuck, "Mystery," n.p.
69. David R. Starbuck, *Rangers and Redcoats on the Hudson: Exploring the Past on Rogers Island, The Birthplace of the U.S. Army Rangers* (Hanover: University Press of New England, 2004), 106. See Holden, "Influence," 284. This may be Dr. Samuel T. W. Sanford of Long Island City, the man who invented "Sanford's Liver Invigorator."
70. Starbuck, "Mystery," n.p.
71. For an overview, see Helen MacDonald, *Human Remains: Dissection and Its Histories* (New Haven: Yale University Press, 2006).
72. Jill Lepore, *The Name of War: King Philip's War and the Origin of American Identity* (New York: Knopf, 1999), 174.
73. Teresa Barnett, *Sacred Relics: Pieces of the Past in Nineteenth-Century America* (Chicago: University of Chicago Press, 2013), 30.
74. The fob is in the collection of the New York Academy of Medicine.
75. Barnett, *Sacred Relics*, 35. Benson Lossing reported a collector who went to Revolutionary War battlefields to pull teeth out of the ground for his collection; Lossing, *Pictorial Field Book of the Revolution: Or, Illustrations, by Pen and Pencil, of the History, Biography, Scenery,*

Relics, and Traditions of the War for Independence, 2 vols. (New York: Harper & Brothers, 1851), 2:290.

76. A drawing of one of her ribs is in the Rufus Alexander Grider collection, volume 6, at the New York State Library in Albany.

77. Fitch, *Asa Fitch Papers*, 2:81.

CHAPTER FIVE: THE NATIVE AMERICAN DILEMMA

1. On British strategy, see Bruce Buchan, "Pandours, Partisans, and Petite Guerre: Two Dimensions of Enlightenment Discourse on War," *Intellectual History Review* 23:3 (2013), 329–47.

2. John Burgoyne, "Proclamation," Camp at Bouquet Ferry, June 20, 1777; in Hezekiah Niles, *Principles and Acts of the Revolution in America* (New York: A. S. Barnes, 1876), 178-79.

3. Robert G. Parkinson, *The Common Cause: Creating Race and Nation in the American Revolution* (Chapel Hill: University of North Carolina Press, 2016), 343–44. Technically, the poem is in Hudibrastic verse.

4. Guy Johnson to George Germain, February 15, 1777, in *Documents of the American Revolution*, 13:39.

5. Burgoyne, *Vyner's Motion*, 6–7.

6. George III, "Remarks on the Conduct of the War from Canada," *The Gentleman's Magazine and Historical Chronicle* 99, part 2 (October, 1828), 291.

7. On Indian codes of warfare, see T. J. Linzy, "Military Honour, the British Army and American Indians in the Sixty Years' War," PhD dissertation, King's College, London, 2014.

8. Burgoyne, *State of the Expedition*, appendix 3.

9. Iroquois comes from the French attempt to pronounce the Algonquin word Ireohkwa. For an overview, see Karim M. Tiro, "Ambivalent Allies: Strategy and the Native Americans," in *Strategy in the American War of Independence: A Global Approach*, ed. Donald Stoker, Kenneth J. Hagan, and Michael T. McMaster (New York: Routledge, 2010), 120–40.

10. Caitlin A. Fitz, "'Suspected on Both Sides': Little Abraham, Iroquois Neutrality, and the American Revolution," *Journal of the Early Republic* 28:3 (Fall, 2008), 299–335.

11. The best single volume on the complex relations between Natives and Whites is Colin C. Calloway, *The American Revolution in Indian Country: Crisis and Diversity in Native American Communities* (Cambridge: Cambridge University Press, 1995).

12. Paul Lawrence Stevens wrote an extraordinary 2,496-page doctoral dissertation on "His Majesty's 'Savage' Allies: British Policy and the Northern Indians during the Revolutionary War—The Carleton Years, 1774–1778," State University of New York, Buffalo, 1984. For his discussion of distributed goods, see page 926.

13. Bernard W. Sheehan, "The Famous Hair Buyer General: Henry Hamilton, George Rogers Clark, and the American Indian," *Indiana Magazine of History* 79:1 (March, 1983), 9.

14. Stevens, "His Majesty's," 1018–19.

15. Burgoyne, *State of the Expedition*, appendix 24; Douglas R. Cubbison, *Burgoyne and the Saratoga Campaign: His Papers* (Norman: University of Oklahoma Press, 2012), 200.

16. Holger Hoock, "*Jus in Bello*, Rape, and the British Army in the American Revolutionary War," *Journal of Military Ethics* 14:1 (January 2015), 74–97. For an overview, see Holger Hoock's stunning *Scars of Independence: America's Violent Birth* (New York: Crown, 2017). Also, Armstrong Starkey, *European and Native American Warfare, 1675–1815* (Norman: University of Oklahoma Press, 1998).

17. Burgoyne, *State of the Expedition*, 7.

18. James Kirby Martin, "A Contagion of Violence: The Ideal of *Jus in Bello* Versus the Re-

alities of Fighting on the New York Frontier during the Revolutionary War," *Journal of Military Ethics* 14:1 (January 2015), 57–73.

19. Mark Edward Lender and James Kirby Martin, "Liberty or Death: *Jus in Bello* and Existential Warfare in the American Revolution," *Justifying Revolution: Law, Virtue, and Violence in the American War of Independence*, ed. Glenn A. Moots and Phillip Hamilton (Norman: University of Oklahoma Press, 2018), 147–67.

20. Calloway, *Indian Country*, 122.

21. Quoted in William W. Campbell, *The Border Warfare of New York, During the Revolution, Or, The Annals of Tryon County* (New York: Baker and Scribner, 1849), 84.

22. Joy Bilharz, *Oriskany: A Place of Great Sadness: A Mohawk Valley Battlefield Ethnography* (Boston: National Park Service, 2009), 34.

23. "An Account of the Chief of the Mohock Indians, who lately visited England," *London Magazine* (July, 1776), 339. See Kevin R. Muller, "Palace to Longhouse: Portraits of the Four Indians Kings in a Transatlantic Context," *American Art* 22:3 (Fall, 2008), 26–49.

24. "Mohock Indians," *London Magazine*; Isabel Kelsay, *Joseph Brant: Man of Two Worlds* (Syracuse: Syracuse University Press, 1984), 172; and Esther Chadwick, "Portraiture in Indigenous London: Mohawks at the British Museum in 1776," *American Art* 36:2 (Summer, 2022), 20–25.

25. See Elizabeth Hutchinson, "'The Dress of His Nation:' Romney's Portrait of Joseph Brant," *Winterthur Portfolio* 45:2/3 (Summer/Autumn, 2011), 209–28; and Scott Manning Stevens, "Tomahawk: Materiality and Depictions of the Haudenosaunee," *Early American Literature* 53:2 (2018), 475–511.

26. William M. Beauchamp, "History of the New York Iroquois," *Documents of the Senate of the State of New York: New York State Museum Bulletin* 78 (1905), 354; and William M. Beauchamp, "Metallic Ornaments of the New York Indians," *Documents of the Senate of the State of New York: New York State Museum, Bulletin* 73 (1903), 32.

27. Stevens, "His Majesty's," 1095–96, 2241–47.

28. Stevens, "His Majesty's," 1098.

29. Jeduthan Baldwin, *The Revolutionary Journal of Col. Jeduthan Baldwin, 1775–1778* (Bangor: De Burians, 1906), 60.

30. *Journals of the Continental Congress, 1774–1789*, July 12, 1775, ed. Worthington Chauncey Ford, 34 vols. (Washington: Government Printing Office, 1905), 2:174–75.

31. George Washington to Philip Schuyler, June 20, 1776, Washington Papers, Library of Congress.

32. George Washington to Congress, May 3, 1778, Washington Papers, Library of Congress.

33. Marie Joseph Paul Yves Roch Gilbert du Motier, Marquis de Lafayette, *Memoirs, Correspondence and Manuscripts of General Lafayette*, 3 vols. (New York: Saunders and Otley Ann Street, 1837), 1:42.

34. *Journals of the Continental Congress, 1774–1789*, July 13, 1775, 2:178–83.

35. Joseph Bloomfield, "Journal of Joseph Bloomfield," May 21, 1776, in *Mohawk Country: Early Narratives about a Native People*, ed. Dean R. Snow, Charles T. Gehring, and William A. Starna (Syracuse: Syracuse University Press, 1996), 278.

36. John Norton (Teyoninhokarawen), "Journal of Major John Norton" ed. Carl R. Flinck and James J. Talman, *Publications of the Champlain Society* 72 (Toronto: Champlain Society, 1972), 270. For an overview, see Joseph T. Glatthaar and James Kirby Martin, *Forgotten Allies: The Oneida Indians and the American Revolution* (New York: Hill and Wang, 2007), 104–8. On the logic of Oneida commitment, see David Levinson, "An Explanation of the Oneida-Colonist Alliance in the American Revolution," *Ethnohistory* 23 (Summer, 1976), 265–89.

37. Speech of Congress, August 28, 1775, in Peter Force, *American Archives*, 6 series (Washington, DC: Clarke and Force, 1840), 4th ser., vol. 3:484.
38. Tench Tilghman, *Memoir of Lieut. Col. Tench Tilghman, Secretary and Aid to Washington* (Albany: Munsell, 1876), 92, 94.
39. *Journals of the Continental Congress, 1774–1788*, December 3, 1777, 9:994–96.
40. Caitlin A. Fitz, "Suspected on Both Sides: Little Abraham, Iroquois Neutrality, and the American Revolution," *Journal of the Early Republic* 28:3 (Fall, 2008), 308.
41. Oneida Sachem to Jonathan Trumbull, June 19, 1775, in Force, *American Archives*, 4th ser., vol. 2:1117.
42. "Good Peter's Narrative of Several Transactions Respecting Indian Lands," in Karim M. Tiro, *People of the Standing Stone: The Oneida Nation from the Revolution through the Era of Removal* (Amherst: University of Massachusetts Press, 2011), 47.
43. Quoted in Alan Taylor, *The Divided Ground: Indians, Settlers, and the Borderland of the American Revolution* (New York: Knopf, 2006), 97. Philip Schuyler to the Six Nations, in Force, *American Archives*, 4th ser., 5:772.
44. Philip Schuyler to the President of Congress, August 8, 1776, in Force, *American Archives*, 5th ser., 1:715.
45. Taylor, *Divided Ground*, 97.
46. Burgoyne, *State of the Expedition*, Appendix 6.
47. Burgoyne, *State of the Expedition*, Appendix 6.
48. Digby, *British Invasion*, 121.
49. His *Maid of the Oaks*, a romantic comedy, was performed in 1774. Burgoyne also wrote and directed *The Blockade of Boston* at Faneuil Hall in 1776.
50. Michale O. Logusz discusses the approximate numbers of British in *With Musket and Tomahawk: The Saratoga Campaign and the Wilderness War of 1777* (Philadelphia: Casemate, 2010), 42–43.
51. Logusz, *Musket and Tomahawk*, 68.
52. Arthur St. Clair to Philip Schuyler, June 28, 1777, *Proceedings of a General Court Martial, Held at White Plains, in the State of New-York, by Order of His Excellency General Washington, Commander in Chief of the Army of the United States of America, for the Trial of General St. Clair* (Philadelphia: Hall and Sellers, 1778), 39.
53. The best book on the subject is Michael A. McDonnell, *Masters of Empire: Great Lakes Indians and the Making of America* (New York: Hill and Wang, 2015). The number of Western Indians varies from source to source, from 100 to 400.
54. Specht, *Specht Journal*, 57.
55. *Documents of the American Revolution*, 14:140.
56. Stevens, "His Majesty's," 1136.
57. Burgoyne, *State of the Expedition*, Appendix 7.
58. Simon Jones, "Caldwell and DePeyster: Two Collectors from the King's Regiment on the Great Lakes in the 1770s and 1780s," in *Three Centuries of Woodlands Indian Art: A Collection of Essays*, ed. J. C. H. King and Christian F. Feest (Altenstadt: ZKF Publishers, 2007), 34.
59. Stevens, "His Majesty's," 1025. See McDonnell, *Masters of Empire*, 280–309, for the specific participation of Great Lakes Indians in the Revolution.
60. David A. Armour and Keith R. Widder, *At the Crossroads: Michilmackinac during the American Revolution* (Mackinac Island: State Park Commission, 1978), 67, 215.
61. Specht, *Specht Journal*, 57.
62. "I have Detachment of seventeen different Nations"; Burgoyne to William Howe, August 6, 1777, in Cubbison, *Burgoyne*, 313. Most of the Wyandot recruited by Britain fought

in the Mohawk Valley campaign, yet lore attributed McCrea's death to the Wyandot Panther. Christopher Ward nonetheless wrote, "That the Wyandot Panther killed Jenny McCrae is just as certain as that Hamlet stabbed Polonius"; *The War of the Revolution* (New York: Macmillan, 1952), 898.

63. Unknown author's journal, July 27, 1777, *For Want of a Horse*, 121.

64. *Letters from America*, 82.

65. Burgoyne, *State of the Expedition*, appendix 8.

66. Burgoyne, *Substance of General Burgoyne's Speeches*, 3.

67. John Burgoyne to William Howe, August 6, 1777, in Cubbison, *Burgoyne*, 313.

68. See Thomas S. Abler, "Scalping, Torture, Cannibalism and Rape: An Ethnohistorical Analysis of Conflicting Cultural Values in War," *Anthropoligica* 34:1 (1992), 3–20.

69. Cadwallader Colden, *The History of the Five Indian Nations, Depending on the Province of New-York in America* (New York: Morrell, 1866), 15–16.

70. See Marian Smith, "American Indian Warfare," *Transactions of the New York Academy of Sciences* 13 (June, 1951), 348–65; Daniel K. Richter, "War and Culture: The Iroquois Experience," *William and Mary Quarterly* 40:4 (October, 1983), 528–59. On the European origins of scalping, see Simon Harrison, *Dark Trophies: Hunting and the Enemy Body in Modern War* (Brooklyn: Berghahn, 2012), 39–48; and James Axtell, *The European and the Indian: Essays in the Ethnohistory of Colonial North America* (Oxford: Oxford University Press, 1981), 16–38.

71. Roger Lamb, *An Original and Authentic Journal of Occurrences during the Late American War from its Commencement to the year 1783* (Dublin: Wilkinson and Courtney, 1809), 180.

72. George Henry Loskiel, *History of the Mission of the United Brethren among the Indians in North America* (London: Brethren's Society, 1794), 148–49. See Gabriel Nadeau, "Indian Scalping: Technique in Different Tribes," *Bulletin of the History of Medicine* 10:2 (July, 1941), 174–94. See also James Adair, *The History of the American Indians* (London: Dilly, 1775), 387–88.

73. Thacher, *Military Journal*, 137.

74. Lamb, *Journal*, 181.

75. Lamb, *Journal*, 181; Loskiel, *History of the Mission*, 148–49.

76. Thacher, *Military Journal*, 137.

77. John Long, *John Long's Voyages and Travels in the Years 1768–1788* (Chicago: Donnelley, 1922), 32.

78. Stephen Brumwell, *Redcoats: The British Soldier and the War in the Americas, 1755–1763* (Cambridge: Cambridge University Press, 2002), 162.

79. Eileen Harris, *The Townshend Album* (London: National Portrait Gallery, 1974).

80. "The Manuscripts of Captain H. V. Knox," *Report on Manuscripts in Various Collections* (Dublin: Falconer, 1909), 294.

81. As one example, see "Small Arms in the Canadian Department," http://royalyorkers.ca/documents/b-smallarmsquebec.pdf.

82. See Charles E. Hanson, Jr., "The Scalping Knife," *Museum of the Fur Trade Quarterly*, 23:1 (1987), 8–12; Colin F. Taylor, *Native American Weapons* (Norman: University of Oklahoma Press, 2001), 46; and Harold L. Peterson, *American Knives* (New York: Scribner's, 1958). Even in the 1830s, the painter George Catlin was still able to amass a large collection of scalping knives marked with G.R.; George Catlin, *The Manners, Customs, and Conditions of the North American Indians*, 2 vols. (London: Tilt and Bogue, 1842), 1:236.

83. David Wilson, *Life of Jane McCrea, with an Account of the Burgoyne Expedition in 1853* (New York: Baker, Goodwin, 1853), 80.

84. "Rutherford's Narrative—An Episode in the Pontiac War, 1763—An Unpublished Manuscript by Lieut. Rutherford of the 'Black Watch,'" *Transactions of the Canadian Institute*

3 (1891–92), 231. The ownership of prisoners is also noted in *Henry Hamilton and George Rogers Clark in the American Revolution,* ed. John D. Barnhart (Crawfordsville, IN: Banta, 1951), 151.

85. Loskiel, *History of the Mission*, 148–49.

86. Graymont discusses some of the codes of killing and scalping used by Indians, in *Iroquois*, 232–33.

87. Anburey, *Travels*, 1:371.

88. Burgoyne, *State of the Expedition*, 129.

89. Axtell, *European and the Indian*, 232.

90. Margaret Haig Roosevelt Sewall Ball, "Grim Commerce: Scalps, Bounties, and the Transformation of Trophy-Taking in the Early American Northeast, 1450–1770," Ph.D. dissertation, University of Colorado, 2013, 148. See Henry J. Young, "A Note on Scalp Bounties in Pennsylvania," *Pennsylvania History* 24:3 (July 1957), 207–18; and Mairin Odle, *Under the Skin: Tattoos, Scalps, and the Contested Language of Bodies in Early America* (Philadelphia: University of Pennsylvania Press, 2023), 68–91, 102–4, 120.

91. Benjamin Franklin, *A Narrative of the Late Massacres in Lancaster County, of a Number of Indians, Friends of this Province* (Philadelphia, 1764), 12–27. See Jeremy Engels, "'Equipped for Murder': The Paxton Boys and 'the Spirit of Killing all Indians' in Pennsylvania, 1763–1764," *Rhetoric & Public Affairs* 8:3 (2005), 355–82.

92. Franklin, *Narrative*, 27.

93. This was known as the Yellow Creek Massacre. Gregory Evans Dowd discusses white scalping in *Groundless: Rumors, Legends, and Hoaxes on the Early American Frontier* (Baltimore: Johns Hopkins University Press, 2015), 167–86.

94. Robert W. Venables, "'Faithful Allies of the King:' The Crown's Haudenosaunee Allies in the Revolutionary Struggle for New York," in *The Other Loyalists: The Ordinary People, Royalism, and the Revolution in the Middle Colonies, 1763–1787*, ed. Joseph S. Tiedemann, Eugene R. Fingerhut, and Robert W. Venables (Albany: SUNY Press, 2009), 148.

95. See Ball, "Grim Commerce."

96. Axtell, *European and the Indian,* 218.

97. See Sheehan, "Henry Hamilton," 1–28.

98. Brumwell, *Redcoats*, 164; Thomas Gray to Thomas Wharton, January 23, 1760, in Thomas Gray, *Poems, Letters, and Essays* (London: Dent, 1966), 224.

CHAPTER SIX: CONSEQUENCES

1. William B. Weeden, "Diary of Enos Hitchcock, D.D.; A Chaplain in the Revolutionary Army," *Publications of the Rhode Island Historical Society* 7 (July, 1899), 123. For a dramatic rendering of the Allen and McCrea stories, see Arthur Reid, *Reminiscences of the Revolution, or, Le Loup's Bloody Trail from Salem to Fort Edward* (Utica: Roberts, 1859).

2. Martin W. Walsh, "A War Council for the Drawing Room: Arent Schuyler de Peyster's 'Speech to the Western Indians,'" *Michigan Historical Review* 28:1 (Spring, 2002), 102–3.

3. La Corne Saint-Luc to John Burgoyne, October 23, 1778, in Hadden, *Hadden's Journal*, 529–32.

4. "We had about 50 Savages (all that remained of near 500 who crossed the Lake with us), the rest having deserted under various pretences till Msr. Luke Le Corn's departure, when the defection became almost general," in Hadden, *Hadden's Journal*, 153.

5. Burgoyne, *State of the Expedition*, 130.

6. See Jonathan Gregory Rossie, *The Politics of Command in the American Revolution* (Syracuse: Syracuse University Press, 1975), 134–54.

7. Burgoyne, *State of the Expedition*, appendix 14.

8. Max M. Mintz, *Generals of Saratoga: John Burgoyne and Horatio Gates* (New Haven: Yale University Press, 1992), 180.
9. Andrew Jackson O'Shaughnessy, *The Men Who Lost America: British Leadership, the American Revolution, and the Fate of the Empire* (New Haven: Yale University Press, 2013), 158.
10. Scudder, *Journal*, 13.
11. Burns, "Massacre or Muster?," 133–44.
12. The numbers are discussed in Mintz, *Saratoga*, 183; and Logusz, *Musket and Tomahawk*, 295, 306. Quote from Thacher, *Military Journal*, 96–97.
13. For the role of the Oneida, see Glatthaar and Martin, *Forgotten Allies*, 149–93.
14. Stevens, "His Majesty's," 1408.
15. *Encampment of the Convention Army*, published by William, Leadenhall Street, London (Prints Division, Library of Congess). See Richard Sampson, *Escape in America: The British Convention Prisoners, 1777–1783* (Chippenham: Picton, 1995).
16. Henry Laurens to John Burnet, July 24, 1778, *Letters of Delegates to Congress, 1774–1789*, 25 vols. (Washington: Library of Congress, 1976–2000), 10: 345.
17. Danske Dandridge, *American Prisoners of the Revolution* (Charlottesville: Mitchie, 1911), 126. See Robert P. Watson, *The Ghost Ship of Brooklyn: An Untold Story of the American Revolution* (New York: DaCapo, 2017).
18. Sampson, *Escape in America*, 184.
19. Paul David Nelson, *General Horatio Gates, A Biography* (Baton Rouge: Louisiana State University Press, 1976), 153.
20. Benjamin Franklin to David Hartley, October 14, 1777, Franklin Papers, Library of Congress.
21. Benjamin Franklin to David Hartley, February 2, 1780, in *The Life of Benjamin Franklin, Written by Himself*, 3 vols. (Cambridge: Cambridge University Press, 2011), 2:499.
22. Hilliard d'Auberteuil to Benjamin Franklin, May 25, 1782, Franklin Papers, American Philosophical Society.
23. "Franklin and Lafayette's List of Prints to Illustrate British Cruelties," May 1779, Library of Congress.
24. Samuel Cooper to Benjamin Franklin, September 8, 1780, in *The Papers of Benjamin Franklin*, 43 vols. (New Haven: Yale University Press, 1997), 33:262.
25. See Parkinson, *Common Cause*, 400–407. Parkinson notes the example of seventeenth-century Dutch propaganda books that condemned the invading French for their atrocities.
26. Benjamin Franklin, "Journal of the Peace Negotiations," May 9, 1782, Library of Congress.
27. *Memoirs of the Life and Writings of Benjamin Franklin*, ed. William Temple Franklin, 2 vols. (London: Colburn, 1818), 1:338–40. See Carla J. Mulford, *Benjamin Franklin and the Ends of Empire* (New York: Oxford University Press, 2015), 295–300.
28. Robert L. O'Connell, *Revolutionary: George Washington at War* (New York: Random House, 2019), 218–19.
29. Governor Blacksnake, *Chainbreaker: The Revolutionary War Memoirs of Governor Blacksnake*, ed. Thomas S. Abler (Lincoln: University of Nebraska Press, 2005), 128.
30. See Jeffrey Ostler's magisterial *Surviving Genocide: Native Nations and the United States from the American Revolution to Bleeding Kansas* (New Haven: Yale University Press, 2019).
31. John Sullivan and Frederick Cook, *Journals of the Military Expedition of Major General John Sullivan against the Six Nations of Indians in 1779* (Albany: Knapp, Peck & Thomson, 1887), 122, 225–26.
32. Quoted in Calloway, *Indian Country*, 124–25.
33. Quoted in Graymont, *Iroquois*, 190.

34. George Washington to John Sullivan, May 31, 1779, Washington Papers, Massachusetts Historical Society.
35. John N. Hubbard, *Sketches of Border Adventures in the Life and Times of Major Moses Van Campen* (Bath, NY: Underhill, 1842), 177.
36. George Washington to Lafayette, September 30, 1779, Washington Papers, Library of Congress.
37. Page Smith made the analogy in *A New Age Now Begins: A People's History of the American Revolution*, 2 vols. (New York: McGraw-Hill, 1976), 2:1172.
38. Cornplanter to George Washington, December 1, 1790, Washington Papers, Library of Congress.
39. The best book on the subject is Alan Taylor's *Divided Ground*.
40. Francis Paul Prucha, *American Indian Treaties: The History of a Political Anomaly* (Berkeley: University of California Press, 1994), 46.
41. *Journals of the American Congress*, December 3, 1777, 34 vols. (Washington: Government Printing Office, 1907), 9:996.
42. Graymont, *Iroquois*, 242.
43. Nathan Fiske, "An Historical Account of the Settlement of Brookfield, in the County of Worcester, and its Distresses during the Indian Wars, 1775," *Collections of the Massachusetts Historical Society, for the Year 1792* (Boston: Munroe & Francis, 1792), 267.
44. For the fate of the Iroquois, see J. David Lehman, "The End of the Iroquois Mystique: The Oneida Land Cession Treaties of the 1780s," *William and Mary Quarterly* 47:4 (October, 1990), 523–47.
45. W. DeLoss Love, *Samson Occum and the Christian Indians of New England* (Boston: Pilgrim, 1899), 276.
46. *The Journal of Samuel Kirkland: 18th-Century Missionary to the Iroquois, Government Agent, Father of Hamilton College*, ed. Walter Pilkington (Clinton, NY: Hamilton College, 1980), 171.
47. For the diplomatic history, see Douglas M. George-Kanentiio, *Iroquois on Fire: A Voice from the Mohawk Nation* (Westport: Praeger, 2006).
48. William Leete Stone, *Life of Joseph Brant (Theyendanegea)*, 2 vols (Albany: Munsell, 1865), 126.
49. Burgoyne, *State of the Expedition*, 86.
50. Fryer, *King's Men*, 194; Fraser, *Skulking*, 54–55. The Articles of Convention had a provision that considered every member of the British campaign "of whatever country" to be "British subjects." See *Articles of Convention*, October 20, 1777, in Cubbison, *Burgoyne*, 337.
51. Logusz, *Musket and Tomahawk*, 303; Burgoyne, *State of the Expedition*, 87; Sampson, *Escape in America*, 48. John Burgoyne to George Germain, October 20, 1777, in Burgoyne, *State of the Expedition*, appendix 14. See Corbett, *No Turning Point*, 247–51.
52. Stevens, "His Majesty's," 1438–40, 2336–38; Baldwin, *Revolutionary Journal*, 124; Hadden, *Hadden's Journal*, 480.
53. Stevens, "His Majesty's," 1440.
54. William Heath, *Memoirs of Major-General William Heath* (New York: Abbatt, 1901), 126.
55. Mercy Otis Warren, *History of the Rise, Progress and Termination of the American Revolution, Interspersed with Biographical, Political and Moral Observations*, 3 vols. (Boston: Larkin, 1805), 2:45–46. The most colorful description of the Convention Army's time in Cambridge is in Samuel Adams Drake, *Historic Mansions and Highways around Boston* (Boston: Little Brown, 1899), 157–68.
56. Gerald Howson, *Burgoyne of Saratoga; A Biography* (New York: Times Books, 1979), 246; Sampson, *Escape in America*, 55–81.

57. Heath, *Memoirs*, 139.
58. Sampson, *Escape in America*, 94.
59. Sampson, *Escape in America*, 89–100.
60. *Proceedings of a General Court-Martial, Held at Cambridge, on Tuesday the Twentieth of January; and Continued by Several Adjournments to Wednesday the 25th of February, 1778: upon the Trial of Colonel David Henley* (Boston: Gill, 1778), 81.

CHAPTER SEVEN: A GREAT NOISE IN BRITAIN AND AMERICA

1. The chapter title is a quotation from Lamb, *Journal*, 145.
2. Philip Schuyler to Congress, December 14, 1775. This is beautifully discussed by Parkinson, *Common Cause*, 180–84.
3. Samuel Adams to John Adams, December 22, 1775, Adams Papers Digital Edition, Massachusetts Historical Society.
4. John Adams to James Warren, June 7, 1775, Adams Papers Digital Edition, Massachusetts Historical Society.
5. John Adams to Abigail Adams, April 14, 1776, Adams Papers Digital Edition, Massachusetts Historical Society.
6. James Duane to Robert Livingston, June 7, 1775, *Letters of Delegates to Congress, 1774–1789*, 26 vols., ed. Paul H. Smith (Washington: Library of Congress,1976–2000), 1:454.
7. Moore, *Diary of the American Revolution*, 1:80. Parkinson discusses this newspaper item and many others in *Common Cause*, 92.
8. Henry Laurens to William Brisbane, August 14, 1777, *The Papers of Henry Laurens*, ed. David R. Chesnutt and C. James Taylor, 16 vols. (Columbia: University of South Carolina Press, 1988), 11:456.
9. Richard Henry Lee to Landon Carter, August 19, 1777, *Letters of Delegates to Congress, 1774–1789*, ed. Paul H. Smith et al., 26 vols. (Washington: Library of Congress, 1976–2000), 7:513.
10. Benjamin Silliman printed the letter of "Dr. S. Reynolds," in *Remarks*, 135.
11. For a list of newspaper citations, see Parkinson, *The Common Cause*, 345–46.
12. Native Americans were not, technically, mercenaries, who by definition are under contract. Instead, they were auxiliaries, not bound by documents.
13. Parkinson, *Common Cause*, 341.
14. Parkinson, *Common Cause*, 341.
15. *Pennsylvania Packet*, August 13, 1777.
16. *Independent Chronicle*, Boston, August 14, 1778.
17. *Independent Chronicle and Universal Advertiser*, August 14, 1777; quoted in Engels and Goodale, "Our Battle Cry," 99.
18. Parkinson, *Common Cause*, 342.
19. Parkinson, *Common Cause*, 342–43.
20. Parkinson, *Common Cause*, 346.
21. William Livingston, "Burgoyne's Proclamation," in Stone, *Ballads and Poems*, 7–15.
22. David Ramsay, *History of the American Revolution*, 2 vols. (Philadelphia: Aitken, 1789), 1:213.
23. Parkinson, *Common Cause*, 346.
24. Ramsay, *History of the American Revolution*, 2:37.
25. See Alden Vaughn, *Transatlantic Encounters: American Indians in Britain, 1500–1776* (Cambridge: Cambridge University Press, 2006); and Troy O. Bickham, *Savages within the Empire: Representations of American Indians in Eighteenth-Century Britain* (Oxford: Clarendon, 2006).

26. Bickham, *Savages*, 252.
27. *Gentleman's Magazine* (September 1775), 446.
28. *Weekly Magazine*, 43 (March 3, 1779); *The Annual Register, or a View of the History, Politics, and Literature for the Year* (London: Dodsley, 1778), 156.
29. *Gazette and New Daily Advertiser* (September 10, 1777), 2.
30. For example, see transcriptions and comments in: *General Evening Post* (November 26, 1777); *London Chronicle* (November 26, 1777); *London Evening Post* (November 26, 1777); *General Advertiser and Morning Intelligencer* (November 27, 1777); *Gazette and New Daily Advertiser* (November 27, 1777); *Adams's Weekly Courant* (December 23, 1777).
31. Lamb, *Journal*, 158.
32. *London Gazette* (November 26, 1777); *Derby Mercury* (November 28, 1777).
33. *Public Advertiser* (November 19, 1777).
34. *The Annual Register . . . for the Year 1777*, 156.
35. *Ipswich Journal* (January 3, 1778), quoted in Bickham, *Savages*, 255.
36. *St. James's Chronicle, or the British Evening Post* (February 21, 1778).
37. Edward Raymond Turner, "The King's Closet in the Eighteenth Century," *American Historical Review* 45 (July, 1940), 761–76.
38. It is not known if the print was published in a journal. It was for sale at Williams's shop on 39 Fleet Street; see Joan D. Dolmetsch, *Rebellion and Reconciliation: Satirical Prints on the Revolution at Williamsburg* (Williamsburg: Colonial Williamsburg, 1976), 93–94.
39. *Monthly Review, or Literary Journal* 60 (January-June, 1779), 372.
40. Ahab Salem [James Murray], *The New Maid of the Oaks, A Tragedy, Lately Acted near Saratoga* (London: printed by the author, 1778).
41. See Steve Ferenzi, "Proxy Blowback in the Revolutionary War? The Curious Story of Jane McCrae and the Battle of Saratoga," *Modern War Institute at West Point Journal* (July 18, 2016), https://mwi.usma.edu/jane-mccrae-battle-saratoga/. *Blowback* is a word invented by the Central Intelligence Agency; see Chalmers Johnson, *Blowback: The Costs and Consequence of American Empire* (New York: Holt, 2001); and Andrew Mumford, *Proxy Warfare: War and Conflict in the Modern World* (Cambridge: Polity, 2013).
42. Gerald Brown, *The American Secretary; The Colonial Policy of Lord George Germain* (Ann Arbor: University of Michigan Press, 1963), 61–62.
43. *London Evening Post* (January 28, 1779).
44. William Pitt, *The Speeches of the Right Honourable the Earl of Chatham in the Houses of Lords and Commons: With a Biographical Memoir and Introductions and Explanatory Notes to the Speeches* (London: Aylott & Jones, 1848), 150–56.
45. John Adolphus, *The History of England from the Accession of King George the Third to the Conclusion of Peace in the Year One Thousand and Seven Hundred and Eighty-Three*, 3 vols. (London: Cabel and Davies, 1810), 3:3–12.
46. *General Evening Post*, December 4, 1777. In reply to the Whig cry, one Tory legislator quipped, "when the suffering of the Americans, their wives and children, are attended with exclamations and tears, I smile the mock tragedy." Burke and his crew merely "*affect* an amazing humanity. . . . The truth is, they are hurt that Indians are employed not for their friends, but against them; had they scalped English instead of rebels, we should have had no lamentations"; *Series of Letters of the First Earl of Malmesbury, His Family and Friends, from 1745 to 1820*, 2 vols. (London: Bentley, 1870), 1:397.
47. See Troy Bickham, "American Indians and the Eighteenth-Century British Press," in Tim Fulford and Kevin Hutchings, eds., *Native American and Anglo-American Culture, 1750–1850* (Cambridge: Cambridge University Press, 2013), 68–70.

48. *The Speeches of the Right Honourable Charles James Fox in the House of Commons*, 6 vols. (London: Longman, Hurst, 1815), 1:99.
49. *Parliamentary History of England from the Earliest Period to the Year 1803*, 36 vols. (London: Hansard, 1806–20), 19:1198–99.
50. Nick Bunker, *An Empire on the Edge: How Britain Came to Fight America* (New York: Knopf, 2014), 129.
51. John Wilkes, *The Speeches of Mr. Wilkes in the House of Commons* (London, 1786), 179.
52. *Speeches of Mr. Wilkes*, 187.
53. *Speeches of Mr. Wilkes*, 187–88.
54. *Speeches of Mr. Wilkes*, 229.
55. *Speeches of Mr. Wilkes*, 228.
56. *Speeches of Mr. Wilkes*, 269.
57. *Speeches of Mr. Wilkes*, 271.
58. *Speeches of Mr. Wilkes*, 271–72.
59. *Speeches of Mr. Wilkes*, 272.
60. *Speeches of Mr. Wilkes*, 226, 228, 278; also *Public Advertiser* (March 9, 1778).
61. George Otto Trevelyan, *George the Third and Charles Fox*, 2 vols. (New York: Longmans, Green, 1921), 1:210.
62. Harry T. Dickinson, "Burke and the American Crisis," in *The Cambridge Companion to Edmund Burke*, ed. David Dwan and Christopher J. Insole (Cambridge: Cambridge University Press, 2012), 156–67.
63. Burgoyne, *Proclamation*, 178.
64. *The Parliamentary Register; Or, History of The Proceedings and Debates of The House of Commons Containing an Account of the Most Interesting Speeches and Motions; Accurate Copies of the Most Remarkable Bills, Letters and Papers; of the Most Material Evidence, Petitions, &c. Laid Before and Offered to the House, During the Second Session of the Fourteenth Parliament of Great Britain* (London: J. Almon, 1778), 350.
65. N. William Wraxall, *The Historical Memoirs of My Own Times*, 2 vols. (London: Cadell and Davies, 1815), 2:36. Edmund Burke, *The Writings and Speeches of Edmund Burke*, 9 vols., ed. Warren M. Elofsen and John A. Woods (New York: Oxford University Press, 1981–2015), 3:282.
66. Edmund Burke, *An Impartial History of the War in America Between Great Britain and Her Colonies, from Its Commencement to the End of the Year 1779* (London: Faulder and Milliken, 1780), 466.
67. Burke, *Writings and Speeches*, 3:363.
68. Horace Walpole, *The Last Journals of Horace Walpole during the Reign of George III*, 2 vols., ed. Archibald Stewart (London: J. Lane, 1910), 2:104.
69. Burke, *Writings and Speeches*, 3:361.
70. Walpole, *Last Journals*, 2:105.
71. *Public Advertiser* (February 7, 1778).
72. Walpole, *Last Journals*, 2:105.
73. Walpole, *Last Journals*, 2:105. By far the best essays on Burke in this period are Luke Gibbons, "'Subtilized into Savages': Edmund Burke, Progress, and Primitivism," *South Atlantic Quarterly* 100 (Winter 2001), 83–109; and Robert W. Jones, *Literature, Gender and Politics in Britain during the War for America, 1770–1785* (Cambridge: Cambridge University Press, 2011), 49–118.
74. William Burke and Edmund Burke, *An Account of the European Settlements in America*, 2 vols. (London: Dodsley, 1758), 1:194.

75. On the subject of race in Parliament, see Daniel I. O'Neill, *Edmund Burke and the Conservative Logic of Empire* (Berkeley: University of California Press, 2016), 63–75.
76. Burke, *Writings and Speeches*, 3:365.
77. *Parliamentary Register*, 349.
78. *Parliamentary Register*, 87.

CHAPTER EIGHT: THE SCAPEGOAT

1. C. C. P. Lawson, "The 16th Light Dragoons, 1759," *Journal of the Society for Army Historical Research* 28:115 (Autumn, 1950), 95–96.
2. See Andrew Trees, *The Founding Fathers and the Politics of Character* (Princeton: Princeton University Press, 2004), 255; Jeffrey Richards, *Theater Enough: American Culture and the Metaphor of the World Stage, 1607–1789* (Durham: Duke University Press, 1991), 226–29.
3. For Burgoyne's fetes, see Alistair Rowan, "Lord Derby's Reconstruction of the Oaks," *Burlington Magazine* (October 1985), 678–87.
4. See George Athan Billias, *George Washington's Opponents: British Generals and Admirals in the American Revolution* (New York: Morrow, 1969), 142–92. He was dubbed "Gentleman Johnny" in a later biography.
5. On Burgoyne, the theater, and the war, see Daniel O'Quinn, *Entertaining Crisis in the Atlantic Imperium, 1770–1790* (Baltimore: Johns Hopkins University Press, 2011), 43–89. Thomas Hickey's painting of Frances Abington as Lady Bab is in the British Museum.
6. *Parliamentary History*, 17:1271. Richards, *Theater Enough*, 226–29.
7. Howson, *Burgoyne*, 83.
8. Paul David Nelson, *Francis Rawdon-Hastings, Marquess of Hastings: Soldier, Peer of the Realm, Governor of India* (Teaneck: Fairleigh Dickinson University Press, 2005), 32.
9. Benjamin Blydenberg Wisner, *The History of the Old South Church in Boston* (Boston: Crocker and Brewster, 1830), 30–35; and Hamilton Andrews Hill, *History of the Old South Church, Boston, 1669–1884*, 2 vols. (Boston: Houghton Mifflin, 1889), 2:175–80.
10. Abigail Adams to John Adams, July 25, 1775, Adams Papers, Digital Edition, Massachusetts Historical Society.
11. Quoted in Billias, *Washington's Opponents*, 156.
12. John Adams to Abigail Adams, June 26, 1776, Adams Papers, Digital Edition, Massachusetts Historical Society.
13. Justin H. Smith, *Our Struggle for the Fourteenth Colony: Canada and the American Revolution*, 2 vols. (New York: Putnam, 1907), 2: 410.
14. O'Shaughnessy, *Men who Lost America*, 146.
15. Sampson, *Escape in America*, 4–6.
16. Fonblanque, *Political and Military Episodes*, 316–17.
17. Wraxall, *Historical Memoirs*, 2:51.
18. *Parliamentary History*, 19:1174.
19. *Speeches of Mr. Wilkes*, 265.
20. Burgoyne, *State of the Expedition*, 1.
21. Burgoyne, *State of the Expedition*, vii.
22. Burgoyne, *Vyner's Motion*, 5.
23. Burgoyne's accusations were printed in newspapers, such as *Gentleman's Magazine, and Historical Chronicle* (June 1778), 250.
24. Burgoyne, *Vyner's Motion*, 6–8.
25. Burgoyne, *Vyner's Motion*, 41–42.
26. For an interesting analysis of Burke's involvement in *State of the Expedition*, see Robert W. Jones, *Literature, Gender, and Politics in Britain during the War for America, 1770–1785*

(Cambridge: Cambridge University Press, 2011), 84–117. The author groups the writing style under the heading "sentimental heroism." For the Tory response to Burgoyne's pamphlet, see *Remarks on General Burgoyne's State of the Expedition from Canada* (London: G. Wilkie, 1780).

27. Burgoyne, *State of the Expedition*, 42–50.
28. Burgoyne, *State of the Expedition*, 99–100.
29. Burgoyne, *State of the Expedition*, 130.
30. See Burke's letters in Hadden, *Hadden's Journal*, 410–15.
31. On Burgoyne's knowledge of Howe's actions, see Billias, *Washington's Opponents*, 172–73.
32. William Howe to John Burgoyne, July 17, 1777, in *State of the Expedition*, appendix 10.
33. O'Shaughnessy, *Men Who Lost America*, 152.
34. Burgoyne, *State of the Expedition*, 2 and appendix 3.
35. Burgoyne, *State of the Expedition*, appendix 9.
36. Burgoyne, *State of the Expedition*, appendix 4.
37. Burgoyne, *State of the Expedition*, 95 and appendix 9.
38. Burgoyne, *State of the Expedition*, 3.
39. Burgoyne, *State of the Expedition*, appendix 4.
40. Burgoyne, *State of the Expedition*, appendix 4.
41. Burgoyne, *State of the Expedition*, appendix 9.
42. Burgoyne, *State of the Expedition*, 3.
43. Burgoyne, *State of the Expedition*, 90.
44. *Parliamentary Register*, 38.
45. Wraxall, *Memoirs*, 2:49.
46. O'Shaughnessy, *Men Who Lost America*, 165.
47. Fonblanque, *Political and Military Episodes*, 259.
48. Diary of John Quincy Adams, July 14, 1786, Adams Papers Digital Edition, Massachusetts Historical Society.

CHAPTER NINE: THE TABLES TURNED

1. Nathan Hale was a militiaman when he was hanged by the British in New York in 1776. Hale was a true spy, infiltrating, gathering, and passing information across enemy lines, and thus an illegal combatant unprotected by the rules of war. André was a major in the British regulars. He would not have been guilty of spying if he had not changed from his regimentals into civilian clothes.
2. Moore, *Diary of the American Revolution*, 2:329.
3. Winthrop Sargent, *The Life of Major John André: Adjutant-General of the British Army in America* (New York: D. Appleton, 1871), 446.
4. Sargent, *André*, 447.
5. Sargent, *André*, 397. See Judith L. Van Buskirk, *Generous Enemies: Patriots and Loyalists in Revolutionary New York* (Philadelphia: University of Pennsylvania Press, 2004), 93–100.
6. *André's Journal: An Authentic Record of the Movements and Engagements of the British Army in America from June 1777 to November 1778 as Recorded from Day to Day by Major John André*, ed. Henry Cabot Lodge, 2 vols. (Boston: Bibliophile Society, 1903), 1:xiv.
7. Thacher, *Military Journal*, 228.
8. Joel Barlow to Ruth Baldwin, October 2, 1780, in *Life and Letters of Joel Barlow, LL.D., Poet, Statesman, Philosopher, with Extracts from his Works and Hitherto Unpublished Poems*, ed. Charles Burr Todd (New York: Putnam's, 1886), 35.

9. Benjamin Talmadge to Samuel B. Webb, September 30, 1780, in *Reminiscences of General Samuel B. Webb of the Revolutionary Army* (New York: Globe, 1882).
10. *André's Journal*, 1:xiii.
11. *The Fate of Major André: A Letter from Alexander Hamilton to John Laurens* (New York: Heartman, 1916), 17.
12. *Fate of Major André*, 18.
13. *André's Journal*, 1:1.
14. For a summary, see O'Quinn, *Entertaining Crisis*, 145–85.
15. Sarah Knott, *Sensibility and the American Revolution* (Williamsburg: Omohundro Institute, 2009), 154–84.
16. For a comprehensive discussion see Andrew Burstein, *Sentimental Democracy: The Evolution of America's Romantic Self-Image* (New York: Hill and Wang, 2000).
17. Adam Smith, *The Theory of Moral Sentiments* (New York: Oxford University Press, 1976), 122, 137, 152.
18. *The Twilight of British Rule in Revolutionary America: The New York Letter Book of General James Robertson, 1780–1783*, ed. Milton M. Klein and Ronald W. Howard (Cooperstown: New York State Historical Association, 1983), 159.
19. Holger Hoock, *Empires of the Imagination: Politics, War, and the Arts in the British World, 1750–1850* (London: Profile, 2010), 63.
20. *Westminster Magazine* (November, 1780), 603; *Gentleman's Magazine* (December, 1780).
21. *London Gazette* (November 15, 1780). *Universal Magazine of Knowledge and Pleasure* (November, 1780), 261–62.
22. Martin Myrone, *Bodybuilding: Reforming Masculinities in British Art, 1750–1810* (New Haven: Yale University Press, 2005), 203.
23. Anna Seward, *Monody on Major André* (Boston: W. Spotwood and C. P. Wayne, 1798), 20. See Robert D. Arner, "The Death of Major André: Some Eighteenth-Century Views," *Early American Literature* 11 (Spring, 1976), 52–67. See Larry J. Reynolds, "Patriots and Criminals, Criminals and Patriots: Representations of the Case of Major André," *South Central Review* 9 (Spring, 1992), 57–84.
24. Seward, *Monody.*
25. Sargent, *André*, 453–54.
26. *Twilight of British Rule*, 157.
27. Benedict Arnold to George Washington, October 1, 1780, Washington Papers, Library of Congress.
28. Edward Barnard, *The New, Comprehensive History of England, from the Earliest Period of Authentic Information to the Middle of the Year 1783* (London: Alexander Hogg, 1783).
29. See Stanley Weintraub, *Iron Tears: Rebellion in America, 1775–1783* (New York: Simon and Schuster, 2005), 245–64.
30. See Margaret K. Reid, *Cultural Secrets as Narrative Form: Storytelling in Nineteenth-Century America* (Columbus: Ohio State University Press, 2004), 16–35.
31. Sargent, *André*, 441.
32. Sargent, *André*, 446.
33. Sargent, *André*, 29. For excellent insights, see Elisa Tamarkin, *Anglophilia: Deference, Devotion, and Antebellum America* (Chicago: University of Chicago Press, 2008), 140.
34. For André, Westminster, masculinity, and the American war, see Myrone, *Bodybuilding*, 201–26. André's remains, like McCrea's, became sacred. According to firsthand accounts, in spite of protests from emotionally attached Americans who, surprisingly, insisted on retaining André's body, workmen were sent in August of 1821 to his gravesite to dig. "At the depth of three feet, the spade stuck the coffin-lid, and the perfect skeleton was soon exposed

to view." Not only did they discover bones, there were also "a few locks of the once beautiful hair." On that day, "ladies sent garlands to decorate the bier" and "many of the children wept"; see Sargent, *André*, 459–60. The bones were placed in a mahogany sarcophagus and transported to London where they were reinterred at Westminster Abbey.

35. Bruce A. Rosenberg, *The Neutral Ground: The André Affair and the Background of Cooper's "The Spy"* (Westport: Greenwood, 1994). The best book on the connections between André and McCrea is Reid, *Cultural Secrets*, 1–68.

36. A watercolor of the powder horn can be found in Rufus A. Grider and Alexander J. Wall, "Powder Horns, Their History and Use," *New-York Historical Society Quarterly Bulletin* 15 (April, 1931), 19.

37. Delia Bacon, *The Bride of Fort Edward: Founded on an Incident of the American Revolution* (New York: S. Coleman, 1839).

38. See Caleb Crain, *American Sympathy: Men, Friendship, and Literature in the New Nation* (New Haven: Yale University Press, 2001), 2–15.

39. John Quincy Adams to Elizabeth Cranch, April 18, 1784, Adams Papers Digital Edition, Massachusetts Historical Society.

40. Thomas Digges to John Adams, November 22, 1780, *Papers of John Adams*, 20 vols., ed. Gregg L. Lint and Richard Alan Ryerson (Cambridge: Harvard University Press, 1996), 10:365–66.

41. John Trumbull, *Autobiography, Reminiscences, and Letters of John Trumbull, 1756–1841* (New York: Wiley and Putnam, 1841), 59.

42. The newspaper version of the evidence is in *London Magazine, or, Gentleman's Monthly Intelligencer* (November, 1780), 529–31.

43. Trumbull, *Autobiography*, 69. Ironically, Trumbull designed the mahogany casket that would carry André's remains back to England; see Theodore Sizer, "The Perfect Pendant: Major André and Colonel Trumbull," *New-York Journal of American History* 65 (2003), 42–46.

44. Trumbull, *Autobiography*, 316.

45. Abigail Adams to John Thaxter, May 23, 1781, Boston Public Library.

46. Sir Joshua Reynolds, *Discourses on Art* (London: Collier Macmillan, 1966), 47.

47. John Trumbull to Jonathan Trumbull, Jr., November 15, 1784, Trumbull Papers, Yale University. See Paul Staiti, *Of Arms and Artists: The American Revolution Through Painters' Eyes* (New York: Bloomsbury, 2016).

48. Trumbull's decision to test out McCrea as a subject may have been triggered while working on the paintings of Warren and Montgomery in London. A London theater buff, he could see that the 1786 newspapers were full of praise for Burgoyne's new play, *The Heiress*, a comedy igniting audiences at the Drury Lane. To Trumbull, however, he was still the British general bombing Bunker Hill in 1775 and mounting a devastating assault from Canada and into New York in 1777. Notices of Burgoyne's comedy may have rekindled the tragedy of Jane McCrea, enough so as to add her to Trumbull's list of painting projects.

49. See Irma Jaffe, "Fordham University's Trumbull Drawings; Mistaken Identities in *The Declaration of Independence* and Other Discoveries," *American Art Journal* 3:1 (Spring, 1971), 21–24.

CHAPTER TEN: IN FRANCE

1. Durand Echeverria, *Mirage in the West: A History of the French Image of American Society to 1815* (Princeton: Princeton University Press, 1969), 39. For how the French viewed America, see Durand Echeverria, *The French Image of America; A Chronological and Subject Bibliography of French Books Printed before 1816 Relating to the British North American Colonies and the United States* (Metuchen: Scarecrow, 1994).

2. Echeverria, *Mirage in the West*, 127.
3. McCrea's story could easily be adapted to fit French agendas. For example, see "Janey M. Crea, jeune femme, tuée de sang-froid," *Courier de l'Europe* (October 14, 1777).
4. Thomas Anburey, *Voyages dans les Parties Intérieures de l'Amérique*, 2 vols. (Paris: Chez Briand, 1790), 1:310–15.
5. Michel René Hilliard d'Auberteuil, *Essais Historiques et Politiques sur les Anglo-Américains*, 2 vols. (Brussels, 1781–1782), 2:206.
6. Hilliard, *Essais Historiques*, 2:282–83. See the biographical essay by Eric LaGuardia in Hilliard, *Miss McCrea: A Novel of the American Revolution* (Gainesville: Scholars' Facsimiles, 1958), 9. French edition: *Mis Mac Rea: Roman Historique* (Paris: n.p., 1784). For Hilliard, see Carine Lounissi, "French Writers on the American Revolution in the Early 1780s: A Republican Moment?" in *Beyond 1776: Globalizing the Cultures of the American Revolution*, ed. Maria O'Malley and Denys Van Rehen (Charlottesville: University of Virginia Press, 2019), 74–104.
7. Hilliard d'Auberteuil to Benjamin Franklin, May 25, 1782, Franklin Papers, American Philosophical Society.
8. Hilliard, *Miss McCrea*, 28–29.
9. Hilliard, *Miss McCrea*, 32.
10. Hilliard, *Miss McCrea*, 16. See John R. Flanagan, "An Early Novel of the American Revolution," *New York History* 32:3 (July 1951), 316–22; and Ian Haywood, *Bloody Romanticism: Spectacular Violence and the Politics of Representation, 1776–1832* (New York: Palgrave Macmillan, 2006), 158–80.
11. Hilliard, *Miss McCrea*, 58.
12. Hilliard, *Miss McCrea*, 58.
13. This argument is worked out by Blake Grindon in "Hilliard d'Auberteuil's *Mis Mac Rea:* A Story of the American Revolution in the French Atlantic," *William and Mary Quarterly*, 3rd ser., 79, no. 4 (October, 2022), 563–94.
14. Hilliard d'Auberteuil to Benjamin Franklin, July 11, 1784, Franklin Papers, American Philosophical Society. Thomas Jefferson to Hilliard d'Auberteuil, February 20, 1786, Jefferson Papers, Library of Congress.
15. By far the best source of information on Vanderlyn is William Oedel, "John Vanderlyn: French Neoclassicism and the Search for American Art," Ph.D. dissertation, University of Delaware, 1981. The best introduction to Vanderlyn, Aaron Burr, and politics is Katherine Woltz, "Aaron Burr and His Protégé John Vanderlyn in Paris, 1810–1811," in *Aaron Burr in Exile: A Pariah in Paris, 1810–1811*, ed. Jane Merrill and John Endicott (Jefferson, NC: McFarland, 2016), 194–226.
16. William Dunlap, *A History of the Rise and Progress of the Arts of Design in the United States*, 3 vols. (Boston: Goodspeed, 1918), 2:157.
17. Aaron Burr to Thomas Morris, September 18, 1801, in *The Private Journal of Aaron Burr, reprinted in full from the original manuscript in the library of Mr. William K. Bixby, of St. Louis, Mo.* (Rochester: Genesee Press, 1903), 418.
18. Still unsurpassed is Samuel Y. Edgerton, Jr., "The Murder of Jane McCrea: The Tragedy of an American *Tableau d'Histoire*," *Art Bulletin* 47:4 (December, 1965), 481–92. See William H. Truettner, "Picturing the Murder of Jane McCrea: A Critical Moment in Transatlantic Romanticism," in *Transatlantic Romanticism*, ed. Andrew Hemingway and Alan Wallach (Amherst: University of Massachusetts Press, 2015), 229–58. For the triangular relationship between Barlow, Fulton, and Vanderlyn, see Carrie Rebora, "Robert Fulton's Art Collection," *American Art Journal* 22:3 (Autumn, 1990), 40–63.

19. Dated March 10, 1798, quoted in Oedel, "Vanderlyn," 90.
20. Katie Hornstein, *Picturing War in France, 1792–1856* (New Haven: Yale University Press, 2018), 26.
21. For example, Philippe-Auguste Hennequin, *The Battle of the Pyramids, July 21, 1798*, 1806, Musée National des Châteaux de Versailles et de Trianon. See Thomas Crow, *Emulation: Making Artists for Revolutionary France* (New Haven: Yale University Press, 1995).
22. Joel Barlow, *The Columbiad, A Poem* (London: R. Phillips, 1809), 179. For a rich discussion of the poem, see Stephen Blakemore, *Joel Barlow's Columbiad: A Bicentennial Reading* (Knoxville: University of Tennessee Press, 2007).
23. Barlow, *Columbiad*, 198.
24. Barlow, *Columbiad*, 205.
25. Barlow, *Columbiad*, 207–8.
26. Barlow, *Columbiad*, 205.
27. Barlow, *Columbiad*, 391.
28. Quoted in Oedel, "Vanderlyn," 221.
29. Oedel offers convincing sources in "Vanderlyn," 233–38.
30. See Oedel, "Vanderlyn," 231. The Borghese Gladiator was touted in the French academy by Jean-Galbert Salvage. In the same year that Vanderlyn painted *McCrea*, he was being hailed by leading French artists for his detailed anatomical analysis of the sculpture; see Mechthild Fend, *Fleshing out Surfaces: Skin in French Art and Medicine, 1650–1850* (Manchester: Manchester University Press, 2017), 207–16.
31. Vanderlyn's reference to Niobe's daughter was timely because her father was king of Phrygia, and in post-Revolutionary France those who embraced liberty wore a soft, conical "Phrygian" cap.
32. Quoted in Amelia F. Rauser, *The Age of Undress: Art, Fashion, and the Classical Ideal in the 1790s* (New Haven: Yale University Press, 2020), 7. See Anne Higonnet, *Liberty, Equality, Fashion: The Women Who Styled the French Revolution* (New York: W. W. Norton, 2024).
33. See Fend, *Fleshing out Surfaces*, 143–235. In Paris, artists learned about race from Jean-Joseph Sue, a surgeon who lectured on anatomy at the Louvre and elsewhere; see his *Essais sur la Physiognomie des Corps Vivants Considérée depuis l'Homme jusqu'à la Plante* (Paris, 1797).
34. See Anne Lafont, "How Skin Color Became a Racial Marker: Art Historical Perspectives on Race," *Eighteenth-Century Studies* 51:1 (Fall, 2017), 89–113.
35. This was Lessing's "pregnant moment"; see H. B. Nisbet, *Gotthold Ephraim Lessing: His Life, Works, and Thought* (Oxford: Oxford University Press, 2013), 321; and Cecilia Sjoholm, "Lessing's Laocoon: Aesthetics, Affects and Embodiment," *Nordic Journal of Aesthetics* 46 (2013), 18–33.
36. Besides Burke, it is important to consider Lessing's belief in the affective value of the visual; Gotthold Ephraim Lessing, *Laocoon: or, the Limits of Poetry and Painting*, trans. William Ross (London: Ridgeway, 1836), 3.
37. Oedel, "Vanderlyn," 221.
38. Oedel, "Vanderlyn," 223.
39. I thank Ben Elwes Fine Art for bringing to my attention Smirke's oil sketch of the subject.
40. Original letters between Vanderlyn and Barlow can be found in Kathleen Pritchard, "John Vanderlyn and the Massacre of Jane McCrea," *Art Quarterly* 12:4 (1949), 361–66.
41. Quoted in Edwin G. Burrows and Mike Wallace, *Gotham: A History of New York to 1898* (New York: Oxford University Press, 2000), 538.
42. Nathaniel Hawthorne, "Friday, July 13th, 1838," *Passages from the American Note-Books* (Boston: Houghton: Mifflin, 1903), 141.

43. Patricia Cline Cohen, *The Murder of Helen Jewett: The Life and Death of a Prostitute in Nineteenth-Century New York* (New York: Knopf, 1998), 108–11. She speculates that New York businessman John R. Livingston, a client at the brothel, may have acquired the Vanderlyn during the declining days of the American Academy. Also see Wendy Jean Katz, *Humbug! The Politics of Art Criticism in New York's Penny Press* (New York: Fordham University Press, 2020), 25–57.
44. *New York Herald* (April 11, April 12, April 13, April 14, 1836). See William E. Huntzicker, "Sex, Sin, and Sensation: Two Major Crime Stories in Antebellum New York," in *Sensationalism: Murder, Mayhem, Mudslinging, Scandals, and Disasters in 19th Century Reporting*, ed. David B. Sachsman and David W. Bulla (New Brunswick: Transaction, 2013), 201–22.
45. Halttunen, "The Pornography of Violence," 60–90.
46. Kenneth C. Lindsay reproduces the 1839 copy in *The Works of John Vanderlyn: From Tammany to the Capitol* (Binghamton: State University of New York, 1970), 87, 142.
47. Burrows and Wallace, *Gotham*, 448.
48. For Bennett, see James L. Crouthamel, "James Gordon Bennett, the *New York Herald*, and the Development of Newspaper Sensationalism." *New York History* 54:3 (July, 1973), 294–316.

CHAPTER ELEVEN: TOURISTS

1. Already by 1913, Holden, the official historian of the state of New York, had compiled a 288-item bibliography of her death; "Influence," 300–310.
2. François-Jean, Marquis de Chastellux, *Travels in North-America in the Years 1780–81–82* (New York, 1828), 175.
3. Chastellux, *Travels*, 190–91.
4. Henrietta Liston Papers, National Library of Scotland.
5. Silliman, *Remarks*, 131.
6. A brief biography of Fitch appeared in *Scientific American* (November 16, 1879), 116–20. Fitch's notebooks are in the New York Genealogical and Biographical Society. The published compilation of those notebooks is in Fitch, *Asa Fitch Papers*.
7. Fitch, *Asa Fitch Papers*, 53.
8. Fitch, *Asa Fitch Papers*, 82.
9. Fitch, *Asa Fitch Papers*, 82.
10. Asa Fitch, "Who Killed Jane McCrea?" in Robert O. Bascom, *The Fort Edward Book* (Fort Edward, NY: James D. Keating, 1903), 61–73. This is, without question, the most lucid and intelligent valuation of all the stories told about Jane McCrea.
11. Fitch, *Asa Fitch Papers*, 33.
12. Fitch, *Asa Fitch Papers*, 33.
13. Fitch, *Asa Fitch Papers*, 64.
14. See Elizabeth Loftus, "The Malleability of Human Memory," *American Scientist* 67:3 (May-June, 1979), 312–20.
15. Fitch, *Asa Fitch Papers*, 86–87.
16. Fitch, *Asa Fitch Papers*, 87.
17. Wilson, *Life of Jane McCrea*, ix–x. Arthur Reid, a journalist, based his pamphlet on Wilson's work, with its own elaborations; *Reminiscences of the Revolution*.
18. Wilson, *Life of Jane McCrea*, 16, 19, 66, 82, 84.
19. Wilson, *Life of Jane McCrea*, 95.
20. Wilson, *Life of Jane McCrea*, 107–12.
21. William Leete Stone, *The Campaign of Lieut. Gen. John Burgoyne* (Albany: Munsell, 1877), 302–13. Stone's account is very similar to the one provided by Judge William Hay;

see Lasselle, "Remembering Jane McCrea," 76–80. Hay added the results of his own investigation, namely that David Jones had never sent for McCrea.
22. Fitch, *Asa Fitch Papers*, 67.
23. Fitch, *Asa Fitch Papers*, 83.
24. Fitch, *Asa Fitch Papers*, 84.
25. Fitch, *Asa Fitch Papers*, 84.
26. Fitch, *Asa Fitch Papers*, 84.
27. For Lossing, see Harold E. Mahan, *Benson J. Lossing and Historical Writing in the United States, 1830–1890* (Westport: Greenwood Press, 1996), 2.
28. Lossing, *Pictorial Field-Book*, 1:89.
29. Lossing, *Pictorial Field-Book*, 1:95.
30. Lossing, *Pictorial Field-Book*, 1:97.
31. Lossing, *Pictorial Field-Book*, 1:100.
32. Lossing, *Pictorial Field-Book*, 1:101.
33. The cane is on loan to the Bennington Museum in Vermont.
34. Harvey and Burdick took out a full-page ad in Wilson's *Life of Jane McCrea*, 156.
35. Holden, "Influence," 280.
36. William Wirt to William Pope, August 29, 1821, in John Pendleton Kennedy, *Memoirs of the Life of William Wirt, Attorney General of the United States*, 2 vols. (New York: G. P. Putnam, 1972), 2:141.
37. By far the best book on the topic of relics and mementoes is Barnett, *Sacred Relics*.
38. See Sally A. Heath, "Native Americans on Stage," *Native American Playwright's Newsletter* 11 (Summer, 1996), 3.
39. *American & Commercial Daily Advertiser* (July 3, 1815).
40. James S. Moy, "John B. Ricketts' Circus, 1793–1800," Ph.D. dissertation, University of Illinois, 1977, 8.
41. See Ellen G. Miles, "John Bill Ricketts," in Carrie Rebora Barratt and Ellen G. Miles, *Gilbert Stuart* (New Haven: Yale University Press, 2005), 210–12.
42. Moy, "Ricketts' Circus," 63.
43. Moy, "Ricketts' Circus," 121; also, the *Aurora and General Advertiser* (January 23, 1799).
44. Michael D'Alessandro, "Storms! Shipwrecks! Massacres! Playbill Puffery and Other Visual Collisions in Nineteenth Century America," *American Art* 33:1 (Fall, 2019), 94–113.
45. Susan Stabile, "Still(ed) Lives," *Early American Literature*, 45:2 (Summer, 2010), 371–395.
46. George Clinton Densmore Odell, *Annals of the New York Stage*, 15 vols. (New York: Columbia University Press, 1928), 4:514.
47. Playbill of the Chestnut Street Theatre, February 7, 1842, Library Company, Philadelphia, quoted in Karl M. Kippola, *Acts of Manhood: The Performance of Masculinity on the American Stage, 1828–1865* (New York: Palgrave Macmillan, 2012), 175.
48. Louis C. Jones, "Crazy Bill had a Down Look," *American Heritage* 6:5 (August, 1955), 6–12; Erkki Huhtamo, *Illusions in Motion: Media Archaeology of the Moving Panorama and Related Spectacles* (Cambridge: MIT Press, 2013), 385.
49. For example, *New York Herald* (January 15, 1842).
50. Newspaper advertisement for the Boston Museum; *The Barre* [Vermont] *Patriot* (September 15, 1850); *The Pittsfield* [Massachusetts] *Sun* (October 24, 1850).
51. Claire McGlinchee, *The First Decade of the Boston Museum* (Boston: B. Humphries, 1940), 29, 34.
52. McGlinchee, *First Decade*, 38; the original playbill is in the Harvard Theater Collection, MS509, Houghton Library.

53. James H. Head provided scenarios, complete with compositions and music, for ninety-nine tableaux; see *Home Pastimes: Or Tableaux Vivants* (Boston: J. E. Tilton, 1860).
54. See Robert M. Lewis, "Tableaux Vivants: Parlor Theatricals in Victorian America," *Revue Français d'études Américaines* 36 (April, 1988), 280–91.
55. Head, *Home Pastimes*, 78–79.
56. Nathaniel Deering, "Tableau Vivant 'Down East,'" *The Knickerbocker: Or, New-York Monthly Magazine* 13 (March, 1839), 189–97.
57. James Warner Barber, *Historical Scenes in the United States or, A Selection of Important and Interesting Events in the History of the United States: illustrated by numerous engravings* (New Haven: Monson, 1827), 78.
58. James Warner Barber, *Incidents in American History: being a Selection of the Most Important and Interesting Events which have Transpired since the Discovery of America, to the Present Time*, 3rd ed. (New York: Philbrick, 1856). James Warner Barber, *Historical Collections of the State of New York: Being a General Collection of the Most Interesting Facts, Biographical Sketches, Varied Descriptions, &c. Relating to the Past and Present: with Geographical Descriptions of the Counties, Cities, and Principal Villages throughout the State* (New York: Clark, Austin & Co., 1851), 353. Also similar to Vanderlyn's picture was a story and accompanying print in *The Pictorial National Library: A Monthly Miscellany of the Useful and Entertaining in Science, Art, and Literature* 2 (March, 1849), 129.
59. William Dunlap, *A History of New York, for Schools*, 2 vols. (New York: Collins, Keese, 1837), 1:183. For Christian content, see also Robert Sears, a publisher of illustrated reference books, who included a similar image of McCrea in *The Pictorial History of the American Revolution: with a Sketch of the Early History of the Country, the Constitution of the United States, and a Chronological Index* (New York: R. Sears, 1848), 253.
60. That print found its way into the German-language *Der Lecha Patriot* (June 28, 1854), 3. Also, see Nicola Monachesi, from Tolentino in the Marche region, who made a name in Philadelphia with giant murals at the Merchant's Exchange and the churches of Saint Augustine and Saint John the Evangelist. During an East Coast tour of his "true copies" of old master paintings, as well as some original works, he included his easel painting of *The Massacre of Miss Jane M'Crea*. That picture has not survived, though in a descriptive pamphlet, Monachesi said he chose to base the design on Samuel Standish's recollections that were published in 1835 by Harvard historian Jared Sparks. In that version, McCrea was first shot in the chest, and then scalped by a chief who "tossed it in the face of a young warrior," and "uttered a yell of savage exultation." Cited in Jared Sparks, *The Life and Treason of Benedict Arnold* (Boston: Hilliard, 1835), 103.
61. Benson Lossing, *Our Country: A Household History for All Readers, From the Discovery of America to the Present Time*, 3 vols. (New York: H. J. Johnson, 1877–1880), 2:928.
62. Late in the eighteenth century, Joel Barlow, of all people, wrote a few sentences about her in an updated version of David Hume's magisterial *History of England*. In the 1780s, John Andrews wrote a four-volume history of the war, in which he claimed Burgoyne had used all "care and precaution" to tamp down the "barbarous disposition" of his auxiliaries, but the "usual cruelties" nonetheless occurred. "A young lady, the daughter of Mr. Macrea, a zealous Royalist, being on her way to the British army, where she was to have been married to an officer," was captured by Indians, who, "without regard to her youth and beauty, murdered her with many circumstances of barbarity." Such actions, Andrews added, "must disgrace the best cause," and served "to render the Royal party extremely odious."
63. John Cassell, *Cassell's Illustrated History of England*, 9 vols., new and revised ed. (London: Cassell, Petter & Galpin, n.d.), 5:187.

CHAPTER TWELVE: REVOLUTIONARY PATHOS

1. Mason Locke Weems, A *History of the Life and Death, Virtues and Exploits of General George Washington: Faithfully Taken from Authentic Documents*, 3rd ed. (Philadelphia: Bioren, 1800), 18.

2. Even a century after Weems, John Fiske, philosopher and famous interpreter of the work of Charles Darwin, continued to burnish McCrea's "lamentable story," which he said "was told at every village fireside, and no detail of horror or pathos was forgotten." In Fiske's telling, McCrea was "a watchword" among "stout and resolute farmers" who flocked to the Saratoga theater. John Fiske, *The American Revolution*, 2 vols. (Boston: Houghton Mifflin, 1880), 1: 280.

3. Mercy Otis Warren, *History of the Rise, Progress, and Termination of the American Revolution*, 3 vols (Boston: E. Larkin, 1805), 2:27.

4. Emma Willard, *History of the United States, or, Republic of America* (Philadelphia: A. S. Barnes, 1842), 199–200.

5. See Gary B. Nash, *The Unknown American Revolution: The Unruly Birth of Democracy and the Struggle to Create America* (New York: Viking, 2005), 379; he points out that the number of Indian women killed by white hands far exceeded the number of white women killed by Indians.

6. Wheeler Case, "The Tragical Death of Miss Jane McCrea, who was Scalped and Inhumanely Butchered by a Scouting Party of Burgoyne's Army, on his Way towards Albany," in *Poems Occasioned by Several Circumstances and Occurrences, in the Present Grand Struggle of America for Liberty* (New Haven: Thomas and Samuel Green, 1778), 18–19.

7. The exodus involved General Schuyler's wife, Catherine, as she too was "hurrying along the highway to Albany." Amid the exodus, Bleecker said she encountered a "crowd of panic-stricken people," who talked "of the tragic death of Jane McCrea as a warning to her of the great dangers of being overtaken by the enemy." See Cuyler Reynolds, *Albany Chronicles: A History of the City Arranged Chronologically, from the Earliest Settlement to the Present Time* (Albany: J. B. Lyon, 1906), 300. Bleecker's own flight became a double tragedy when her mother and infant daughter, Abella, died before reaching the safety of Red Hook; see Sharon M. Harris, *Executing Race: Early American Women's Narratives of Race, Society, and the Law* (Columbus: Ohio State University Press, 2005), 87.

8. *The Posthumous Works of Ann Eliza Bleecker, in Prose and Verse* (New York: Swords, 1793), 358–67.

9. Philip Freneau, "America Independent, and Her Everlasting Deliverance from British Tyranny and Oppression," *The Poems of Philip Freneau: Poet of the American Revolution*, 2 vols. (Princeton: Princeton University Library, 1902), 271–83.

10. Lydia Sigourney, *Sketch of Connecticut, Forty Years Since* (Hartford: Cooke and Sons, 1824), 126.

11. Sigourney, *Sketch*, 128.

12. Sigourney, *Sketch*, 129.

13. Sigourney, *Sketch*, 133.

14. George Lippard, "The Bridal Eve," in *Washington and His Generals, or, Legends of the Revolution* (Philadelphia: T. B. Peterson, 1847), 172–76.

15. James Fenimore Cooper, *The Last of the Mohicans: a Narrative of 1757*, 2 vols. (Philadelphia: H. C. Carey & I. Lea, 1826), 1:165.

16. Cooper was consistently interested in paintings and painters and was close friends with them. Haywood, *Bloody Romanticism*, 172.

17. Haywood, *Bloody Romanticism*, 170.

18. Cooper, *Last of the Mohicans*, 2: 265, 266.
19. See Ellwood Parry, *The Art of Thomas Cole: Ambition and Imagination* (Newark: University of Delaware Press, 1989), 48–49.
20. Further illustrations of Cora facing death were similar, even in the 1828 French edition of Cooper's *Mohicans*. Antoine Johannot, known in France as the "king of illustration" for having brought to life the words of Alexandre Dumas, George Sand, and Molière, produced a picture of Cora's last seconds for the frontispiece of the French translation of Cooper's novel; James Fenimore Cooper, *Le dernier des Mohicans: histoire de 1757* (Paris: Charles Gosselin, 1826). There, she is down on one knee, again with Vanderlyn's concept in mind; see Théophile Gautier's article in *La Presse* (June 16, 1845), for more.

CHAPTER THIRTEEN: POLITICS

1. Anthony F. C. Wallace, *Jefferson and the Indians: The Tragic Fate of the First Americans* (Cambridge: Harvard University Press, 1999), 11.
2. No less than seventy-three nineteenth-century memoirs and novels detailed Indian predations against women; see Jane Tompkins, *Sensational Design: The Cultural Work of American Fiction* (New York: Oxford University Press, 1985), 110–12.
3. On this concept, see Michael Zuckerman, "The Fabrication of Identity in Early America," *William and Mary Quarterly* 34:2 (April, 1977), 201.
4. Andrew Jackson to Thomas Jefferson, April 20, 1808, in *Correspondence of Andrew Jackson*, ed. John Spencer Bassett and David Maydole Matteson, 7 vols. (Washington: Carnegie Institution, 1926–1935), 1:186.
5. Thomas Jefferson to John Adams, June 11, 1812, in *The Writings of Thomas Jefferson*, ed. H. A. Washington (New York: Derby and Jackson, 1859), 62.
6. Parkinson, *Common Cause*, 658.
7. The finest book on removal is Claudio Saunt, *Unworthy Republic: The Dispossession of Native Americans and the Road to Indian Territory* (New York: Norton, 2020).
8. See Roxanne Dunbar-Ortiz, *An Indigenous Peoples' History of the United States* (Boston: Beacon, 2014), 277.
9. *Register of Debates of Congress, 18th Congress* (Washington: Gales and Seaton, 1825), 639–45.
10. William Clark to Lewis Cass, June 8, 1832, in Ellen M. Whitney, *The Black Hawk War, 1831–1832* (Springfield: Illinois State Historical Library, 1973), 283.
11. See, for example, *An Authentic Narrative of the Seminole War; its Cause, Rise and Progress, and a Minute Detail of the Horrid Massacres of the Whites, by the Indians and Negroes, in Florida, in the Months of December, January and February* (Providence: D. F. Blanchard, 1836).
12. Barry Alan Joyce, *The First U. S. History Textbooks: Constructing and Disseminating the American Tale in the Nineteenth Century* (New York: Rowman and Littlefield, 2015), 205–18, 284.
13. John Mack Faragher, *Daniel Boone* (New York: Holt, 1993), 130–40.
14. Reprinted in Trevor B. McCrisken, "Exceptionalism: Manifest Destiny" in *Encyclopedia of American Foreign Policy*, 3 vols. (New York: Charles Scribner's Sons, 2002), 2:68.
15. Francis Parkman, *The Conspiracy of Pontiac and the Indian War after the Conquest of Canada* (Boston: Little, Brown, 1913), 9.
16. See Kathryn Zabelle Derounian-Stodola and James Arthur Levernier, *The Indian Captivity Narrative, 1550–1900* (New York: Twayne, 1993). The titles of books capture the breathtaking conjunction of racism, entertainment, and female exploitation, such as *Indian Atrocities! Affect and Thrilling Anecdotes Respecting the Hardships and Suffering of Our Brave and Venerable Forefathers in their Bloody and Heartrending Skirmishes and Contests with the Ferocious Savages* (Boston: A. J. Wright's Steam Press, 1846).

17. Mary Barber, *The True Narrative of the Five Years' Suffering & Perilous Adventures* (Philadelphia: Barclay & Co, 1873).
18. See the superlative article by Nicole Fabricand-Person, "From the Wild West to the Far East; The Imagining of America in a Nineteenth-Century Japanese Woodblock Print," *Record of the Art Museum, Princeton University* 68 (2009), 16–37.

CHAPTER FOURTEEN: LEGEND

1. Charles Schreyvogel painted a large picture on the same subject in 1907, based on conversations with Buffalo Bill; the picture is in the Buffalo Bill Center of the West, Cody, Wyoming.
2. The film can be screened at: https://codyarchive.org/multimedia/wfc.vid00002.html.
3. Gregory A. Borchard, Stephen Bates, and Lawrence J. Mullen, "Publishing Violence as Art and News: Sensational Prints and Pictures in the 19th-Century Press," in *Sensationalism: Murder, Mayhem, Mudslinging, Scandals, and Disasters in 19th-Century Reporting*, ed. David B. Sachsman and David W. Bulla (New Brunswick: Transaction, 2013), 53–74.
4. John P. Harty, Jr., *Cinematic Challenge: Filming Colonial America*, 2 vols. (Minneapolis: Langdon Street, 2016), 1:124.
5. *Time* 50 (October 27, 1947), 99.
6. Greene, "Two U.S. Capitol Statues," 34.
7. Margaret Wallace, "An Epic Tale of the Revolution," *New York Times Book Review* (November 19, 1933), 8.
8. Graham Greene, "Fiction," *Spectator* 151 (December 15, 1933), 910.
9. Kenneth Roberts, *Rabble in Arms: A Chronicle of Arundel and the Burgoyne Invasion* (Garden City: Doubleday, 1933), 714–15.
10. Roberts, *Rabble in Arms*, 16.
11. Roberts, *Rabble in Arms*, 725–26.
12. Roberts, *Rabble in Arms*, 728.
13. Roberts, *Rabble in Arms*, 740.
14. Roberts, *Rabble in Arms*, 742.
15. Roberts, *Rabble in Arms*, 749–50.
16. Roberts, *Rabble in Arms*, 754–55.
17. Pauline Meier writes about the lasting potency of the Founding in *American Scripture: Making the Declaration of Independence* (New York: Vintage, 1998). Jill Lepore put it this way: "When in doubt, in American politics, left, right or center, deploy the Founding Fathers"; *Whites of Their Eyes: The Tea Party's Revolution and the Battle over American History* (Princeton University Press, 2011), 14.
18. Rebecca Bedell elegantly discusses emotionality in *Moved to Tears; Rethinking the Art of the Sentimental in the United States* (Princeton: Princeton University Press, 2018).
19. Jerry Barlow's sad instrumental for Celtic guitar, "Ode to Jane McCrea," is featured on a 2006 album, *Bring Down the Storm*; Videos of the music can be found at https://itunes.apple.com/us/artist/jerry-barlow/id403709710 and https://www.youtube.com/watch?v=GpppZoeTfE8. Bobby Bradford and Maywood Kate recorded a poignant duet, "Murder of Jane McCrea." Videos of the music can be found at https:// statueofliberty.bandcamp.com/track/the-murder-of-jane-mccrea and https://www.youtube.com/watch?v=M1eVpk5GGvI. Ballads about McCrea were common in the nineteenth century; see Stone, *Ballads and Poems*, 129–207.
20. Interview with Noryan Baker, June 29, 2021. He used an image of Annie Oakley for the woman in the upper register of the picture. A portfolio of his work can be found at Iron & Gold Tattoo in Spokane https://www.ironandgoldtattoo.com/noryan-baker.

CHAPTER FIFTEEN: NECESSARY FICTIONS

1. *The Works of Jonathan Swift*, ed. Thomas Roscoe, 2 vols. (London: Bohn, 1843), 1:300.
2. See Michael Kammen, *From Liberty to Prosperity: Reflections upon the Role of Revolutionary Iconography in National Tradition* (Worcester: American Antiquarian Society, 1977).
3. On the subject of the eclipse of British culture in America, see Michael D. Hattem, *Past and Prologue: Politics and Memory in the American Revolution* (New Haven: Yale University Press, 2020); and Staiti, *Of Arms and Artists.*
4. Parkinson, *Thirteen Clocks: How Race United the Colonies and Made the Declaration of Independence* (Chapel Hill: University of North Carolina Press, 2021), 36–67, 164–85.
5. Eran Shalev, *Rome Reborn on Western Shores: Historical Imagination and the Creation of the American Republic* (Charlottesville: University of Virginia Press, 2009), 99.
6. Sarah Purcell, *Sealed with Blood; War, Sacrifice, and Memory in Revolutionary America* (Philadelphia: University of Pennsylvania Press, 2002), 92–132; David Waldstreicher, *In the Midst of Perpetual Fetes: The Making of American Nationalism, 1776–1820* (Chapel Hill: Omohundro Institute and University of North Carolina Press, 1997); Alfred Young, *The Shoemaker and the Tea Party: Memory and the American Revolution* (Boston: Beacon, 1999), 94, 108, 140; Michael Kammen, *A Season of Youth: The American Revolution and the Historical Imagination* (New York: Knopf, 1978); and Parkinson, *Common Cause*, 642.
7. See Katharine Erhard, "Rape, Republicanism, and Representation: Founding the Nation in Early American Women's Drama and Selected Visual Representations," *American Studies* 50:3 (2005), 507–34.
8. Holden, "Influence," 294.
9. Richard Snowden, *The History of the American Revolution in Scripture Style* (Frederick, MD: Mattias Bartgis, 1823).
10. Engels and Goodale, "Our Battle Cry," 97.
11. Brian Burns corrects the record, "Massacre or Muster?" 133–44. Washington Irving, creator of charming American mythologies, wrote in his five-volume *Life of George Washington* that "the murder of Miss McCrea resounded throughout the land." Overnight, "Armies sprang up from . . . the blood of this unfortunate girl"; *The Life of George Washington*, 5 vols. (New York: G. P. Putnam, 1859), 3:134.
12. Dionysius of Halicarnassus, *The Roman Antiquities of Dionysius of Halicarnassus* (London: Booksellers of London, 1758), 269.
13. See Sonya Lawson Parrish's excellent essay, "A New, American Lucretia: Jane McCrea and the Formation of an American Republic," *Pennsylvania Literary Journal* 1:2 (Winter, 2009), 30–47.
14. John Adams to Benjamin Rush, December 4, 1805, Adams Papers, National Archives.
15. Titus Livius, *The History of Rome; Books 1–5* (Indianapolis: Hackett, 2006), 81.
16. Cassius Dio, *Dio's Roman History*, trans. Earnest Cary, 9 vols. (New York: Macmillan, 1914), 1:89.
17. See Norman Bryson, "Two Narratives of Rape in the Visual Arts: Lucretia and the Sabine Women," in Sylvana Tomaselli and Roy Porter, *Rape: An Historical and Social Enquiry* (Oxford: Blackwell, 1989), 152–173; Melissa M. Matthes, *The Rape of Lucretia and the Founding of Republics: Reading in Livy, Machiavelli, and Rousseau* (University Park: Pennsylvania State University Press, 2007); and Ernest Renan, "Qu'est-ce qu'une nation?," *Oeuvres Complètes de Ernest Renan*, ed. H. Psichari, 10 vols. (Paris: Calmann-Lévy, 1947), 1:887–906.
18. Thomas Paine, *Common Sense* (Dedham, MA: Mann and Bryant, 1844), 29.

ACKNOWLEDGMENTS

WHEN I was an undergraduate, I was in the odd habit of leafing through back issues of *The Art Bulletin* for my own education and entertainment. I skipped too many articles to admit to, but I stopped to read an intriguing essay by Samuel Edgerton, a notable scholar of the Italian Renaissance who had made a brief excursion into American art and culture. His topic was Jane McCrea. Edgerton's excellent essay has stuck with me, and you might think of this book as a long-simmering contemplation of his fine original work.

I have had the luxury of four stellar readers. Joseph Ellis disappeared for a few days with the manuscript, not only to review my reading of American history, but also to comment on the overall tone and structure of the book. Over numerous conversations over many years, he saved me from a few blunders, clarified the essence of what I was trying to say, and, as always, urged me on. Donald Weber, a specialist in American literature and an astute prose stylist, poured over every sentence and paragraph. Carrie Rebora Barratt, with whom I collaborated on the John Singleton Copley exhibition at the Metropolitan Museum of Art, trained her curatorial eye on my discussion of the artworks and adeptly used her sharp pencil on the prose style. Monika Schmitter, to whom the book is dedicated, read, re-read, and re-read again with honesty and affection.

One of the pleasures found in researching and writing a book comes in the form of conversations between old friends and new acquaintances. My thanks to Tim Barringer, Bettina Bergmann, Chris Bryant, Rachel Elwes, George Gibson, Barbara Heisler, Terry Karl, Matthew Keagle, Kieran O'-Keefe, Philippe Schmitter, Eric Schnitzer, David Starbuck, and Wendy Watson. Comments at a BSECS conference in Oxford were especially helpful.

Michael Davis and Ronald Davidoff listened to me chatter for hours about the project while cycling through the Connecticut River Valley. The late Joe Cutshall-King was my consistently lively, generous, and informed correspondent. Darwin Michener-Rutledge prospected for the photographs you see in the book.

Though there were a few skeptical looks from the Italian librarians, I worked for weeks in the Marciana Library and the Correr Library in Venice. The Caffe Chioggia made the espressos that kept me going.

I am indebted to my colleague William Oedel for his groundbreaking work on John Vanderlyn. Let me also single out Robert Parkinson for his masterful and exhaustive study on print culture during the Revolution.

My intrepid agent, Roger Williams, has hacked his way through the forests and bushes of publishing with a combination of charm, persistence, and persuasiveness. My publisher, Bruce H. Franklin, believed in the project and has enthusiastically brought it into being. Noreen O'Connor-Abel studied every word I wrote, found some new ones, and expelled the bad ones.

Clearly, Jane McCrea's death still carries clout. When a friend with a birthday gift on his mind ordered a customized coffee mug with Vanderlyn's 1804 painting on it, he was informed it conflicted with the company's "content guidelines." The order was cancelled. That speaks to the lasting power of an event that took place in the eighteenth century, which is not so distant after all.

INDEX